80°   60°   78

GREENLAND

SMITH SD.

JONES SD.

Melville B.   76

BAFFIN

DEVON

LANCASTER SD.

BAY

74°N

Route
laid down in
Franklin's Instructions

Uppernavik

BAFFIN

DAVIS

72

LAND

MELVILLE
PEN.

Fury & Hecla STR.

Disco I.

Whalefish Is.

Egedesminde

ARCTIC
CIRCLE

STRAIT

80°   60°

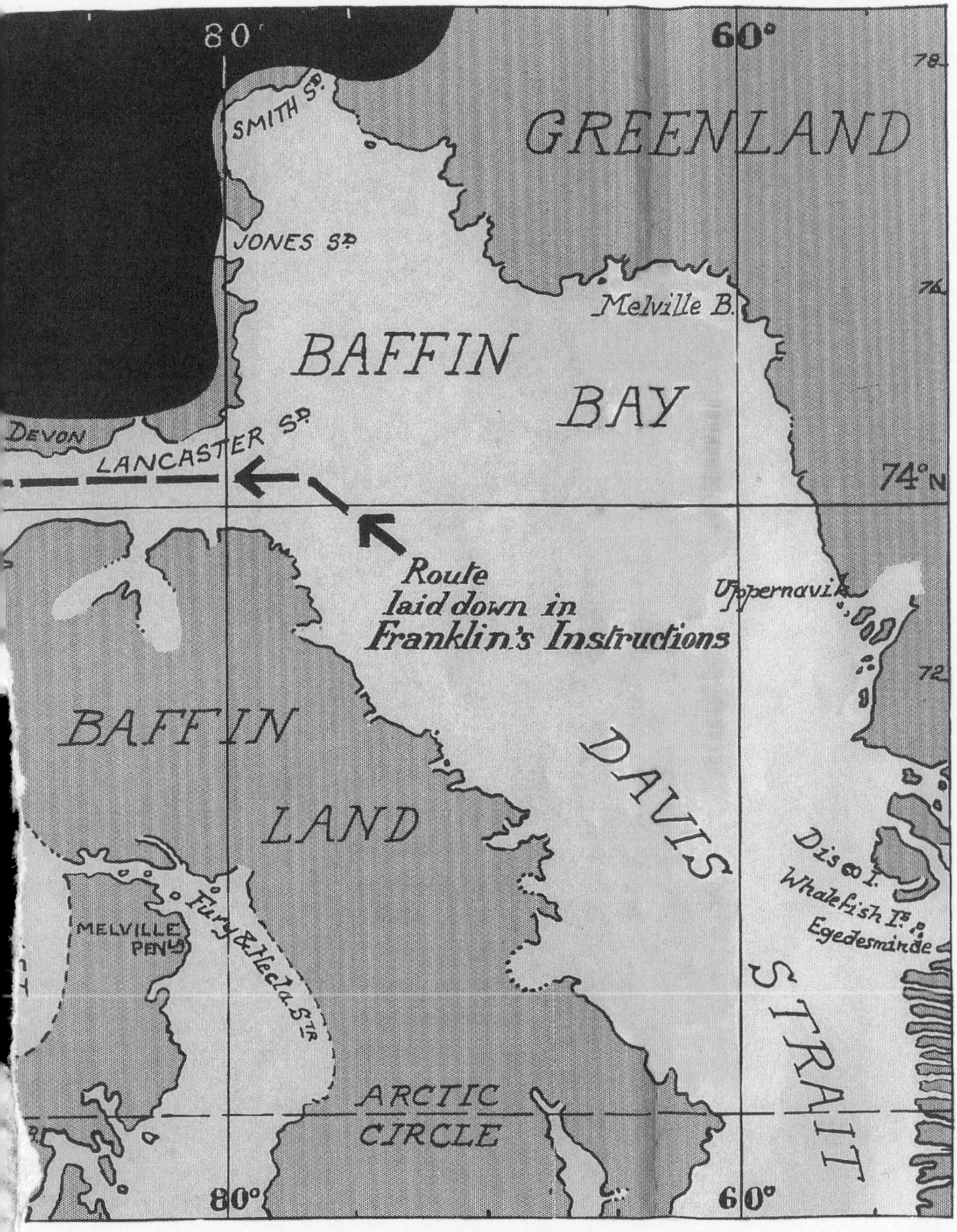

1845, WHEN THE FRANKLIN EXPEDITION SAILED

Seasons Greetings 2005

From Vertex One Asset Management Inc.

Ken McGoogan

FATAL PASSAGE

The Untold Story of John Rae,
the Arctic Adventurer Who Discovered the Fate of Franklin

HarperCollins*Publishers*Ltd

The financial assistance of the Alberta Foundation for the Arts
is gratefully acknowledged.

Canadian Cataloguing in Publication Data

McGoogan, Kenneth
Fatal passage : the untold story of John Rae, the Arctic
adventurer who discovered the fate of Franklin

"A Phyllis Bruce book".
Includes bibliographical references and index.
ISBN 0 00 200054 7

1. Rae, John, 1813–1893.
2. Arctic regions – Discovery and exploration –
   British.
3. Northwest, Canadian – Discovery and exploration –
   British.
4. Franklin, John, Sir, 1786–1847.
5. Northwest Passage – Discovery and exploration –
   British.
6. Explorers – Scotland – Biography.
I. Title.

FC3961.1.R33M33 2001   917.1904′1′092   C00-932345-7
G635.R5M33 2001

01 02 03 04 WEB 4 3 2

Printed and bound in Canada
Set in Monotype Janson
Jacket design: Alan Jones

CONTENTS

PART ONE

THE TRUTH OF DISCOVERY

A WILD LIFE
IN RUPERT'S LAND

In June 1833, in the rugged Orkney Islands of northern Scotland, a restless, energetic young ship's doctor stood on the deck of a weather-beaten fur-trading vessel as it sailed out of Stromness harbour. Watching the trawlers, pilot boats, and white-sailed pleasure craft of his youth recede into the distance, John Rae—a wiry, broad-shouldered man of middle height—exulted in the salty breeze. At last he was bound for Rupert's Land, the vast wilderness empire ruled by the Hudson's Bay Company.

Two of his older brothers had already sailed with the HBC and finally his own turn had come. Since boyhood, Rae had dreamed of exploring North America—the lakes and rushing rivers, the forests filled with dangerous animals. His father, who managed tenant farmers for a Scottish nobleman, also served as an agent for the HBC, recruiting Orkneymen and sending them west. Those men, and others who preceded them from these rolling, windswept islands, had kept the British fur trade thriving since early in the eighteenth century. Hundreds of them had sailed to Rupert's Land, and now they made up three-quarters of the staff in the territory. Over time, they had earned a reputation as loyal, hard-working employees—sober, obedient, and capable of enduring unusual cold, hunger, and hardship.

Two months earlier, the nineteen-year-old Rae had graduated from medical school in Edinburgh. For four winters, he had attended Edinburgh University, which had the reputation, in London, of being a hotbed of radical dissent. Having discovered that by transferring to the Royal College of Surgeons he could receive his diploma without waiting until he was twenty, Rae had promptly made the switch.

The four winters he spent in Edinburgh, a bustling city of 160,000, he later described as uneventful: "steady plodding through the various courses of study considered at that time requisite before going up for a surgeon's diploma." The young man visited London at least once, but apart from snowball fights between students and town lads, Rae would find little to remember from his Edinburgh years. In April, 1833, after passing an extensive oral examination, he had qualified as a licentiate of the Royal College of Surgeons.

Then adventure beckoned. Rae was young, after all, and this was the age of exploration. Since 1816, when the end of the Napoleonic Wars had created a lasting peace, British explorers had been roaming the globe, filling in blanks on the charts and atlases of the day, bent on discovering not only the Northwest Passage but also, in the heart of darkest Africa, Timbuktoo and the mouth of the River Niger. Instead of becoming a small-town doctor in Orkney, or even beginning a practice in Edinburgh, Rae would join the Hudson's Bay Company as a ship's surgeon—at least for a season, to see whether he liked it.

All his life, he had watched the Company supply ships, two or three each year, that visited Stromness as their final port of call before crossing the Atlantic. They came to stock up on fresh vegetables and to draw water from Login's Well in the heart of town, just as they had since the seventeenth century. Rae had grown up hearing a cannon signal the arrival of each supply ship and relishing the excitement at the docks as sailors streamed out of the vessels to enjoy their final leave before crossing the ocean.

Since 1819, Rae's father had been the HBC's chief representative in Orkney. He recruited tradesmen, clerks, and tenant farmers for the trading posts of Rupert's Land, offering them twice the wage an agricultural labourer could earn at home in Orkney. John Rae, Sr., had previously secured clerical postings for two of Rae's older brothers, William in 1827 and Richard in 1830. And it was he who received the letter appointing his son "Jock" surgeon to the *Prince of Wales*.

In June 1833, the three-masted vessel entered the choppy grey waters of Hoy Sound and swung to starboard, and John Rae stood enjoying the stiff breeze and the spray of salt air. As he watched Stromness recede into the distance to the music of creaking masts, cracking halyards, and snapping sails, the young man never once imagined that fourteen years would elapse before he would again see these shores.

Legendary sailors had departed from Stromness before him—Henry Hudson, James Cook, Edward Parry. Twelve years from now, one of the most famous of them all would stand on a deck not unlike this one, on H M S *Erebus*, and gaze out at this same rocky coastline as he sailed to seek the Northwest Passage. But John Rae couldn't know that. Nor could he know that Sir John Franklin's departure would reverberate through the Ocean of Time like an earthquake, generating a tidal wave of catastrophe that would change his own life forever.

Rae was fascinated by sailing vessels of all kinds, and he had thoroughly investigated this sixty-year-old, four-hundred-ton barque, which was one of two supply ships—the other was the *Prince Rupert*—

The Prince Rupert *as it would have appeared to John Rae during his first voyage to Hudson Bay on the* Prince of Wales

making its annual voyage to Hudson Bay. Its foremost and mainmast sails were square-rigged, its mizzenmast sails fore-and-aft rigged, and it carried a full complement of lifeboats. The broad-beamed ship had rounded sides built of solid oak five to seven feet thick, and its bow had been reinforced with iron bars against the pack ice.

Bound for Moose Factory, the second largest of all HBC ports, the *Prince of Wales* was packed to the gunwhales with provisions and trade goods—everything from nails, muskets, flints, saws, and sealing wax to beads, fish hooks, knives, kettles, and axe heads. Great quantities of food had been carefully stored, including salt beef and pork, cheese, flour, oatmeal, peas, biscuits, malt, vinegar, raisins, butter, lemons, and spices, along with a notable supply of alcohol—cases of wine, rum, and French brandy for the chief factor at Moose Factory and, for the majority of men, kegs of "English brandy," really cheap London gin coloured with molasses. As a medical man who understood the need for fresh meat, Rae also noted with approval in his journal that the ship carried "several coops filled with a variety of poultry for the cabin mess; in the long-boat half a dozen sheep; and there was a pen of five young pigs forward."

Besides this miscellaneous cargo, the ship carried several passengers in the cabins aft and another thirty-five or forty in "the 'tween decks forward." Those in cabins, including Rae, enjoyed civilized meals with the captain and his officers (fresh trout and poultry, followed by the finest French wines). The steerage passengers, who ate mainly salt beef and pork, included thirty-one men from Orkney, the largest number in a decade to leave those northern islands.

Crowded into a stinking, unventilated space not more than five feet high, these men slept in hammocks and rough wooden berths that lined the walls, their baggage piled around them. From the outset, Rae worried about these conditions. Some of the men suffered seasickness, rendering their normally fetid quarters more wretched still. Worse, shortly after leaving Orkney, typhoid fever broke out among the steerage passengers and many became seriously ill. For two weeks, the anxious, inexperienced doctor spent most of his time, day and night, below decks, ministering to the sick. Later, with characteristic understatement, he wrote, "Fortunately, they were all a strong and healthy lot of young fellows and recovered very rapidly."

When he wasn't tending the sick, the nimble, irrepressible Rae explored the rigging. He badgered sailors and officers to teach him the name and use of every rope, block, and stick on the ship and to train him to tie various knots and splices—knowledge he would later put to good use.

Early in July, after crossing the North Atlantic and passing south of Greenland, the *Prince of Wales* entered Hudson Strait. Here, south of Baffin Island in the only entrance to Hudson Bay, Rae encountered Arctic seas. He saw his first icebergs and marvelled at their grandeur, their "beauty and purity, vastness and variety." Often larger even than the ships, with miniature cataracts flowing from their peaks, they sparkled white and green in the sunlight. Some boasted so many columns, arches, and spires that they resembled glorious cathedrals. Rae felt that he would never tire of standing on deck while the ship threaded its way through the serpentine canals that opened among them. But then the canals narrowed and disappeared, the pack ice grew

Voyagers entering Hudson Strait for the first time
were invariably impressed by icebergs

thicker and finally halted all progress, and the young doctor found his pleasure in observation waning while the *Prince of Wales* sat for days in the same spot.

For two weeks, a mile and a half apart, the HBC ships remained beset. The ice was so thick and firm that passengers, among them two English ladies, walked back and forth to visit, enjoying the novelty and welcoming the chance to stretch their legs on something other than a deck. The enterprising Rae climbed the mainmast of the *Prince of Wales* and declared that he could not find a single pool of open water. When at last the ice broke up thanks to a rising wind, dozens of Inuit arrived at the ships in kayaks, proclaiming friendship even from a distance: "*Chimo! Chimo!* Friends!" Rae judged these Baffin Islanders to be harmless and good-natured, though noisy. They traded seal oil and walrus-tusk ivory for knives, files, axe heads, needles, beads, and hoop iron—all items brought for this purpose.

After finally navigating Hudson Strait and entering the Bay, the two ships separated, each making for a different HBC fort, or "Factory," so named to indicate the presence of a chief agent or factor. The *Prince Rupert* crossed the Bay to York Factory, the largest and most important of the HBC's fur-trading posts, while the *Prince of Wales*, with John Rae aboard, sailed 870 miles south to James Bay and Moose Factory, which was located on an island in the Moose River. The ship arrived on September 7, 1833, roughly two weeks late, and put in at Ship's Hole, an anchorage seven miles out from the fort, passable only at high tide.

This late arrival meant a rush even more desperate than usual. Small boats ferried back and forth, night and day, unloading cargo and stowing furs for the return voyage, now threatened by the onset of winter. On shore, Rae encountered HBC officers sporting vests, jackets, and even three-piece suits. The Company's rough-and-ready labourers looked better adapted to the rugged environment. Rae admired the panache of the French-speaking *voyageurs* decked out in calf-high moccasins, hooded frock coats, tall hats, and colourful sashes, and he secretly envied the deerskin outfits of the natives who served the fur trade using rivers as highways to transport a kind of gold from the animal-rich wilderness around the Bay.

When he saw an opportunity, Rae stepped forward to lend a hand. The chief factor at Moose Factory, John George MacTavish, noticed the young man's energy and wide-eyed enthusiasm and invited him to remain at the post as a doctor. Tempted, Rae nevertheless demurred: his friends and family expected him home, especially his mother. MacTavish also presented the young doctor with an Indian birchbark canoe for performing some notable medical service. Rae had little opportunity to test this intriguing craft, however; on September 24, just seventeen days after arriving, he boarded the *Prince of Wales* and sailed for home.

At the entrance to Hudson Strait between Southampton Island and Point Wolstoneholme, the ship encountered a sailor's Arctic nightmare: a barrier of pack ice. For several days, the *Prince Rupert* had been exploring the ice edge without finding any opening. Now, John Rae stood on deck watching as the captains of the two sturdy-hulled ships tried repeatedly to breach the ice wall to no avail. Finally, bitterly disappointed—not least because they would forego their bonuses for making a single-season passage—the captains turned their ships around.

York Factory was overburdened and under-supplied, so the *Prince Rupert* made for the more northerly Churchill, 350 miles west across the Bay. That small outpost would not be able to sustain more than a single crew of unexpected visitors, however, so the *Prince of Wales*, with two feet of ice on her foredeck and a great deal more clinging to her bows, made for Charlton Island at the bottom of the Bay, 800 miles away. As the old ship beat south driven by fierce gales, Rae observed that "every rope of our standing rigging was so thickly coated with ice as to be two or three times its natural size. The sea washing over our forecastle was frozen there to the depth of two feet, which together with the ice clinging to our bows set us down two or three feet by the head, and made the ship for a time most difficult to steer."

Charlton Island, an inhospitable depot seventy miles north of Moose Factory, remained accessible (unlike Moose Factory itself) despite the lateness of the season and the encroaching ice. The *Prince of Wales* had wintered there as recently as 1830–31, but the post had since been abandoned. Rae and his thirty-or-so fellow voyagers found the ground covered in deep snow, the woods almost empty of animals. After exploring the dreary scattering of tumbledown log-and-frame houses, most without windows and roofs, the new arrivals erected an immense tent using sails and spars from the ship and trees from the surrounding forests. Here they stored the ship's cargo of furs, mainly beaver and muskrat, but also bear, lynx, marten, mink, fisher, otter, wolf, wolverine, and various kinds of fox (silver, cross, red, and white).

After beaching the ship, the men set to work repairing the ramshackle houses, using clay to plaster the seams—though already temperatures were so low that the mud froze and cracked. The captain sent a lifeboat to Moose Factory with news that the ship's crew was wintering over and with two paying passengers who had been returning to England. The boat came back carrying salted geese, blankets, warm clothing, and moosehide for moccasins, and the men settled unhappily into their cramped quarters.

John Rae met the change of plans with equanimity, even pleasure. "Personally, I enjoyed the situation immensely," he would write, citing the novelty of the experience and the idea of having abundant fine, dry snow on which to go snowshoeing, though initially he was skeptical of this footwear. The lure of hunting unfamiliar game also enticed him, and he started with geese and wild duck. This adventuring he found "extremely attractive, a feeling which was not altogether shared by the older portion of our party."

During the cold, hard winter that ensued, the young doctor would have ample opportunity to discover how well equipped he was to cope with the exotic ferocity of Rupert's Land: his outdoorsy youth in Orkney had prepared him to flourish in just such an environment, to overcome challenges that could kill men who were less well suited— and on this occasion, flourish he would.

The rocky, wind-swept islands of Orkney lie, as poet and native son George Mackay Brown would have it, "like sleeping whales . . . beside an ocean of time." Dotted with Neolithic remains dating back over 5,500 years—including stone houses complete with shelving units and linked by covered passages—these seventy-four islands present an atmosphere of palpable antiquity. The roughly 20,500 people here, unique in the British Isles, are strongly connected to Norway and France by history (through a Norse conquest over 1,000 years ago) and heritage (through the families of the *yarls,* or earls). This singular history, according to Peter St. John, the current earl of Orkney, "has produced a rational, independent citizenry that is egalitarian in outlook and perfectly at home abroad."

Located off the north coast of Scotland, which annexed the islands in 1472, Orkney lies almost directly east of the southern tip of Greenland and the entrance to Davis Strait. This meant that early voyagers, lacking the instrumentation to calculate longitude, could simply sail due west from Stromness. The Vikings had discovered the great natural harbour there during the first millennium. Whalers, sealers, explorers, fur traders—Stromness eventually served them all. Late in the sixteenth century, while seeking the Northwest Passage, the buccaneering explorer Martin Frobisher put in many times at Stromness; early in the seventeenth century, Henry Hudson watered at Login's Well before embarking on his final, tragic voyage. By 1816, Stromness was supplying fresh water to more than thirty-four whalers a year.

Early in the eighteenth century, fur-trading ships from the Hudson's Bay Company, already in the habit of stopping for water and food, began recruiting Orcadians to serve in the fur-trade posts of Rupert's Land. These new employees proved to be not only hardy, industrious, and egalitarian, but also remarkably adept as fishermen and boatmen. Between 1772 and 1800, while it was gradually taking greater control of its empire, the HBC expanded its labour force from 180 to just under 600, fully three-quarters of whom were Orcadian. The first HBC surveyor, an Englishman named Philip Turnor, described Orcadians as "a set of the best men I ever saw together, as they are obliging, hardy, good canoe men." Most could also read and write, while other Scots and English boys often could not, and so they made excellent keepers of journals and records. The Orcadians also impressed the Cree and the Chipewyan, whose languages they often mastered and with whom they freely intermarried.

Stromness (population 2,200), which perches on Hamnavoe or "Haven Bay" and overlooks the natural harbour of Scapa Flow, can today be reached with relative ease. Visitors can travel north from Edinburgh by train or road to the tiny port of Scrabster and there catch an ultra-modern ferry. The *St. Ola*, for example, accommodates 500 passengers and 180 vehicles and can make its way to Stromness even through heavy seas in two and a half hours. Or, visitors can fly into the bustling Orkney capital of Kirkwall (population 7,500), less than fifteen miles away, and reach Stromness over a winding two-lane highway.

For John Rae, growing up here early in the nineteenth century, travelling was more difficult. Even in 1830, when he was seventeen, the only way to journey between Orkney and the Scottish mainland was by sailing packet. During the stormy winter months, these small vessels would be forced to take a roundabout route and would often require several weeks to make the voyage. The only alternative was to risk one's life crossing the treacherous Pentland Firth in the tiny, open boat that carried the mails.

Far more accessible than it once was, the Stromness that Rae knew

The Hall of Clestrain, where Rae was born, today shows the ravages of time

remains everywhere in evidence in today's cosy, salty-aired warren of stone buildings and narrow, winding, flagstone streets. From many vantage points in town, a contemporary visitor can see Rae's boyhood home, the Hall of Clestrain, two and a half miles across the Bay of Ireland. Originally a laird's dwelling, this impressive stone mansion, now in considerable disrepair, stands alone on a hill looking out over rolling fields and rough waters.

John Rae was born on September 30, 1813, in this dwelling, as the sixth child (there would be three more) and fourth son of John Rae, Sr., a "ferrylouper," or newcomer, who had arrived from Lanarkshire, south of Glasgow. A driving, self-made man whose gravestone would identify him as "esquire of Wyre Island," Rae's father served as a factor, or land agent, to Sir William Honeyman, Lord Armadale, one of the most powerful men in northern Scotland.

In Orkney, where most families eked out a living on the land, the gentrified Raes were sufficiently prominent that in 1814, while researching his novel *The Pirate*, Sir Walter Scott came calling in a lighthouse yacht. Eventually, he modelled two characters, Brenda and Minna, after Rae's two older sisters. "I was very young at the time," Rae wrote later, "but the 'great unknown' took early lunch and got 'mounts' to ride over to the Stones of Stennis [an ancient archaeological site] and the cathedral in Kirkwall, about fourteen miles distant."

In his diary, after admiring the well-cultivated farm and the excellent breed of horses that the factor was breeding ("strong, hardy Galloways, fit for labour or hacks"), Scott mentioned that Rae's father was responsible for 300 tenant farmers, the vast majority of whom lived in small, windowless, dirt-floored dwellings built of stone and turf. The menfolk fished and hunted whales, seals, birds, and small game, grew barley and potatoes, and kept cattle and sheep, yet they still battled frequent food shortages.

From birth, then, the explorer-to-be was set apart. But young Rae showed no signs of feeling superior, revelling instead in the same pursuits as the sons of tenant farmers. A solitary youth who thrived on physical challenge, Rae enjoyed fishing, hiking, riding, shooting, rock scrambling, cliff climbing, and boating in rough waters. He hunted birds on the water and in swamps, seals that turned up on the nearby rocks, and, most exciting and rarest of all, the occasional whale that strayed into Hoy Sound.

John Rae, Sr., provided his sons with two excellent boats on condition that they maintain them in pristine shape. One was small, light, and handy for fishing and served as a tender to the other, an eighteen-foot yawl called the *Brenda*. Rigged with a jib, foresail, mainsail, and mizzen or jigger, she was both fast and safe. As the fourth oldest brother, Rae started sailing at the jib sheet and worked his way aft. The *Brenda* could be hard to handle in the sudden squalls that are so frequent in Orkney, but Rae found that when he took her out alone in bad weather, the boat worked beautifully under the reefed foresail and small rigger aft.

Rae and his brothers were wildly proud of the *Brenda*, which could outrun almost anything her own size. To take the boat neatly through high tides in half a gale of wind "gave us I fancy about the same amount of pleasure as a good rider mounted on a favourite horse feels in crossing a difficult country with a lot of bad jumps over water, wall and fence." Rae sailed through snow, sleet, and gale-force winds. He thought nothing of enduring wet and cold all day and never dreamed of donning a waterproof coat.

The Rae brothers not only raced against town boys from Stromness, but also competed with men sailing pilot boats, which were longer and built for speed. "There was tremendous rivalry between us boys and these brave and experienced boatmen; we had no chance with them in fine weather . . . but whenever it blew hard and the sea was especially rough we never lost an opportunity of racing; and generally went ahead much to the chagrin of our big opponents and to the gratification of the boys."

Before Rae reached his teens, his father gave him an old flintlock that he could hardly lift. The boy made holes at carefully chosen points in the stone wall that circled the farm, and, using these apertures as gunrests, began hunting heron, curlews, wild ducks, golden plover, and other small game. He found an excellent grouse moor within a five-minute run of the house. After school hours and during holidays, he would scamper off with his musket and dog, a pointer named Carlo, returning later to add two or three brace of grouse to the family larder. By the age of fifteen, Rae had become an excellent hunter, rock climber, and hiker. He often swung home across the moors carrying a hefty load of game on his back and waving proudly to anyone he met.

Later the youth would beam when the family sat down at the great, long, wooden table to eat a dinner that he had provided. His father, stern and preoccupied, would say grace, and then his mother, refined and gracious, would watch carefully from the opposite end of the table to see that the smallest children, scattered among the hungry teenagers and young adults, received their fair share of food.

As the credulous sixth child in a high-spirited family, Rae had to endure more than the usual amount of teasing—though often his mother would leap to his defence: "I have mentioned sensitiveness and credulity as two of my many weak points, the latter, I think, being extensive, because I could not imagine or understand any one telling an untruth, more especially for no other apparent reason than the raising of a laugh. I was therefore constantly being hoaxed...."

John Rae, like his siblings, received a private education. A resident governess gave way to a succession of live-in tutors, one of whom kept pet eagles, which demanded a steady supply of small birds for food—birds the boy was happy to provide. Later Rae would regret never having had the advantage of attending a grammar school and of studying among other young people, but he contrived to learn enough that at age sixteen, avid to escape into the wider world, he travelled south to Edinburgh to begin training as a doctor.

Nineteenth-century sailors who visited the shores of Hudson Bay, from the captains to the lowliest cabin boys, felt superior to those who lived ashore and detested having to do so themselves. In the autumn of 1833, experienced hands also knew that winter at Charlton Island would bring short days, freezing cold, howling gales, and fierce blizzards.

On Charlton Island, Rae hunted ptarmigan, geese, and wild duck

Above all, they feared scurvy, long the scourge of maritime expeditions. Caused by a lack of vitamin C, the disease was not yet understood, though its symptoms were all too familiar: loose teeth, blackened gums, stiff joints, internal bleeding, and, if not treated, an extremely painful death.

As the winter dragged on into 1834, most of the marooned men spent their time sheltering in the drafty cabins, wrapped in furs and huddled around large, iron, wood-burning stoves. Without fresh fruits and vegetables, they survived on biscuits and salt meat. Rae used his hunting skills to supply what fresh game he could, but ptarmigan, geese, and wild duck remained scarce until spring. Before long, the thirty men ran out of lemon juice, and half of them began showing symptoms of scurvy.

Rae drew on his medical training to comfort the men and combat the baffling disease as best he could. Decades before its discovery, he deduced the existence of vitamin C. Later he reported, "I consider scurvy a blood disease caused by the lack of something that it gets from vegetables and that when you have no vegetables or no bread there is something that the system wants which is in very small quantities in animal food and therefore you have to eat a very great deal more than you want to get at the quantity from meat."

Rae tried making spruce beer, a concoction well-known to HBC men—and mentioned in James Lind's classic medical text *A Treatise of the Scurvy*, published in 1753—by boiling spruce branches and adding sugar. He did not find this effective, however, probably because boiling destroyed the vitamin C contained in the young spruce shoots.

Four or five of the sick men ended up in terrible shape, barely able to crawl about, their limbs swollen and discoloured, their gums dark purple and bleeding, their teeth so loose they could be removed by hand: "In fact, one fine humorous fellow named Letham missed two of his [teeth] one morning and could only account for their disappearance by asserting that, 'By Jove, I must have swallowed 'em, sir,' with a grin at the thought of making such a use of his own best grinders."

Over forty years later, giving evidence before an Admiralty committee investigating scurvy, Rae would paint a grim picture of how two men, the captain and the first mate, died that winter:

The only case that was exceptional was that of the captain, but he had, I think, something wrong with his lungs; so far as I can remember he had oedematous swelling of his legs. I do not think his mouth was affected but clearly it was scurvy combined with some other disease that he died of. The chief mate died also in the most fearful state that I ever saw. His skin was perfectly black, his mouth black, his saliva was as dark as ink and the odour from him was so horrible that there was no person could come near him but myself. . . . These two men I believe had taken more spirits than were good for them, and consequently it was no wonder they were more affected than the other men.

While most of the healthy men, fearing contagion, refused to approach their sick comrades, the unflinching Rae manifested not only an iron constitution, but also, for an untried doctor, singular dedication and resolve. In his unpublished memoir, he noted that poor Mr. Terry, the first mate, died after lingering "in a terrible state—his mouth and tongue were black; his saliva as black as night, his limbs all purple, and latterly terribly wasted. The effluvia from his body was so offensive that no one could lift him out of or into bed except myself, who was then a young lad of twenty, not particularly squeamish."

Realizing that some readers might find such a description harrowing, Rae added that the graphic details were chiefly intended for medical or surgical brethren, should any of them happen to look at his narrative. Alluding to the cheap "English brandy" distributed to most HBC men, he added that he did not know in 1834, as he later learned by experience, that alcohol in any form was injurious in a cold climate: "I abstained at that time from drinking my allowance of grog (my associates invariably drank all theirs) not because I thought it distasteful or hurtful, but because I had an idea it might be more useful to others . . . as liniments or stimulants." Rae himself remained perfectly healthy throughout the winter, with the exception of a toothache that bothered him mainly at night.

Early in the spring, as the weather warmed, Rae made soup from the tender sprouts of the vetch, or wild pea. Out snowshoeing near the woods one afternoon, typically alone and searching for these sprouts, he noticed some red-stained snow and thought he had discovered blood. Looking more closely, he realized that he had crushed some cranberries underfoot. The resourceful doctor began gathering them to feed to his scurvy patients, while "those who could hobbled to the cranberry ground." Scurvy responds well to treatment, and soon most of the sick men had recovered. Had the ground on their arrival not been so deeply covered in snow, Rae might have found the cranberries early enough to prevent much suffering and perhaps even to save the two men who died.

In mid-June 1834, undaunted by the misery of the long winter—the captain and the first mate lay buried in humble graves marked by wooden crosses—Rae unpacked the birchbark canoe he had received the previous autumn from Chief Factor MacTavish. As the ice cleared along the shoreline, he led two companions in a four-day, ninety-mile journey around Charlton Island. For a young man used to boats, travelling by canoe was both exciting and challenging. By the end of the trip, Rae had progressed from novice to journeyman and intended to become a master.

In mid-July, the men hauled the *Prince of Wales* off the beach and restowed the Company's furs. Toward the end of the month, just as a forest fire broke out, they sailed south for Moose Factory. There Rae learned that during the winter, the chief factor had used the overland express to Montreal—men travelling mostly on snowshoes—to send letters to his family in Orkney, advising them that he wished to hire and retain the young doctor. The responses, Rae wrote, "left me at perfect liberty of choice." MacTavish had also communicated with Sir

George Simpson, the HBC governor, who had responded by proposing for Rae a five-year contract as clerk and surgeon.

MacTavish reported to Simpson that Rae would agree to remain for only two years exclusively as a surgeon and "cannot be prevailed upon to become a counting-house clerk." MacTavish added, "He is a very attentive and pleasant young man, hardy and well-adapted to the country; however, he only wishes to feel his way and may in time take a notion of remaining." Rae would indeed take such a notion. He would spend the next ten years at Moose Factory, assuming a variety of duties and responsibilities and mastering the intricacies of the fur trade.

On August 12, 1834, however, when from shore he watched the *Prince of Wales* sail for Orkney without him, carrying letters and tokens for his family, especially for his mother, John Rae knew only that he felt fiercely attracted to "the wild sort of life to be found in the Hudson's Bay Company service." At the first major crossroads of his life, he had struck off down the less trodden path, embarking on a singular journey that would make him arguably the greatest Arctic explorer of the century.

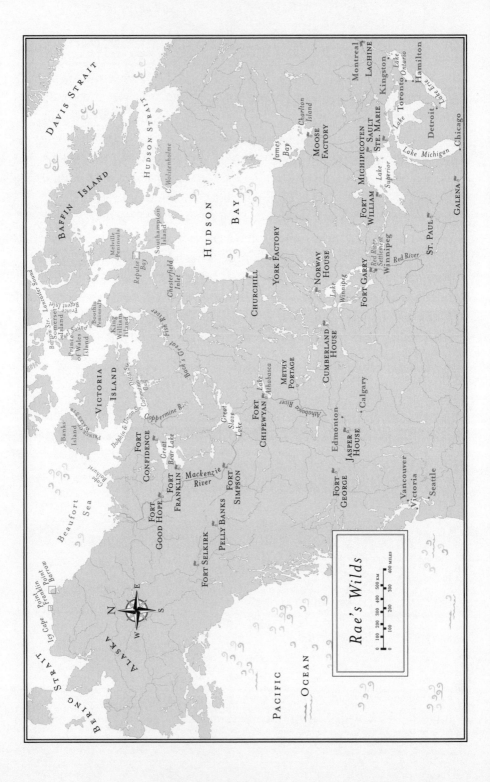

Rae's Wilds

2

MOOSE FACTORY DOCTOR

$\mathbb{N}$othing had prepared John Rae for Christmas at Moose Factory—not his adventurous youth in Orkney, not his studious four winters in Edinburgh, and certainly not his miserable first Christmas in Rupert's Land, when on Charlton Island he had been hard pressed to rouse the stranded sailors, some of whom were already showing signs of scurvy, to any thought of celebration.

At Moose Factory, as at the larger settlement of York Factory to the north, Christmas Day signalled the beginning of a week of festivities—a bacchanalia, in fact. From then until New Year's Day, the entire community, some 180 people including the "homeguard Indians" who lived in the vicinity, would indulge in every conceivable excess, overeating, overdrinking, and revelling in what disgruntled clergymen had, not infrequently, denounced as villainy and downright debauchery.

That first Christmas at Moose Factory, John Rae rose early, as always. With a few of his closest friends, among them a Swampy Cree man named George Rivers, he donned snowshoes, trekked into the forest, and spent the day hunting wild duck, rabbit, and ptarmigan (a partridge-like Arctic grouse), bent on adding a grace note to a festive table. However full his game bag, Rae would have made certain to arrive back at the so-called fort by late afternoon.

At five o'clock, as a Company surgeon and one of twenty-six "officers" based at Moose Factory—among them clerks and accountants of various grades, one or two chief traders, and the chief factor himself—Rae made his way to a building next door to the "fort," or

Celebrating Christmas in Bachelor's Hall

complex, in which he lived, pausing only to participate enthusiastically in a snowball fight. He climbed the rough stairs to the dining hall
above the provision store and found the place so warm and merrily
decorated as to be almost unrecognizable. Where usually the hall was
deliberately left cold to discourage hunters and trappers from malin-
gering, now a great fire blazed in the hearth. Streamers and wreaths
hung from the walls, and a ceiling-high Christmas tree stood in one
corner, sparkling with colourful handmade ornaments.

Several tables had been placed end-to-end and covered with white
linen tablecloths. Graced with platters of wild goose and roast beef, of
ptarmigan and duck and Arctic char, and of caribou and moose meat
traded with the natives, the tables glowed invitingly. One sideboard
was piled high with plum puddings and cranberry tarts, while on
another, surrounded by tumblers and glasses, stood many bottles of
wine and several decanters of port, French brandy, and even Madeira.

The HBC officers, men mostly in their twenties and early thirties, settled themselves around the long table with much pushing and shoving. Chief Factor John George MacTavish insisted that Rae, both as surgeon and as one of his own favourites, sit near the head of the table. MacTavish offered up a heartfelt grace, and the men dug into Christmas dinner with gusto.

The wine flowed freely and the diners grew increasingly merry. Amid the clinking of glasses, they traded jibes and shouted jokes, and then, one after another, they rose to their feet to say a few words. The men fell painfully silent when a senior clerk proposed a toast to absent loved ones, all those present becoming suddenly aware of their isolation and loneliness, of the forested wilderness extending around them for hundreds of miles. But then a young man jumped to his feet and cried, "To the ladies!" This prompted an enthusiastic chorus of "The ladies!" and restored the festive mood.

Rae, who had turned twenty-one in September, enjoyed all this enormously, though as a serious young medical man he suspected that alcohol did more harm than good and confined himself to sipping a single glass of wine and sampling the Madeira. After two hours at the table, and with many of the men having become convinced of their invincibility, one enthusiastic reveller stood up and cried, "To Bachelor's Hall!" Chief Factor MacTavish, himself more red-faced than usual, nodded his assent, and the entire company poured out of the hall and down the stairs into the freezing cold night.

Rae marched with his companions along a broad, well-worn path whose snowbanks stood three feet high, past the workshops of blacksmith and tinsmith, carpenter and boat builder, and he marvelled anew at the way the night air made white clouds of everybody's breath. He glanced up at the canopy of stars high above, picked out Ursa Major, Cygnus, and Orion the Hunter (his favourite), and remembered learning to identify those same constellations in the skies above Stromness.

From up ahead came the sound of someone tuning a fiddle. A dozen dogs had begun to bark at their approach and, by the side of the path, Rae noticed several dog sleighs, or carioles: hunters and trappers had journeyed here from fifty miles around. Rae followed his friends into Bachelor's Hall, where most of the single labourers lived. Again he hardly recognized the place: tallow candles had been placed in tin sconces around the walls, and the largest Christmas tree he had ever seen took up one corner of the hall.

Never had John Rae seen the Hall so crowded: Orcadian labourers and apprentice clerks in white shirts, vests, and jackets (their Sunday best) joked and tussled with French Canadian *voyageurs* in their most colourful sashes and Cree men in deerskin jackets and trousers. The "homeguard Indians" had arrived *en famille*: the oldest men and women, obviously grandparents, sat on benches along the walls, many dandling babies that could not have been six months old. As Rae and the other HBC officers streamed into the hall, native women of all ages, most wearing calico gowns and ornamented moccasins and blouses with great balloon sleeves, threw off their blanket shawls and hurried to greet the new arrivals with warm hugs and kisses—a favourite tradition.

One of the fiddlers launched into a Scottish reel, and two more joined in. A top-hatted *voyageur* began clacking spoons, and two Cree men picked up the rhythm on drums. Before he knew what was happening, Rae found himself being led onto the dance floor by a tawny-skinned woman he had noticed working around the fort. As he began jigging and whirling around the hall, following her lead, Rae must have realized on some level that this was it, the wild sort of life he had been seeking—the transformative magic of Rupert's Land.

Granted to the Hudson's Bay Company in 1670 by King Charles II and named after its first governor, Charles's cousin Prince Rupert, this vast wilderness of lakes and rivers, vaguely defined as including all lands that drained into Hudson Bay, covered 1.5 million square miles—almost forty per cent of what is now Canada, plus parts of Minnesota and North Dakota. Extending from Labrador to the Rocky Mountains, the HBC's territory eventually encompassed some of the largest lakes in North America—Winnipeg, Athabasca, Great Slave, and Great Bear—and a myriad mighty rivers—Churchill, Nelson, Hayes, Back, and Coppermine.

The territory included what is now northern Quebec, most of Ontario, all of Manitoba and Saskatchewan, and great swatches of Alberta and the Northwest Territories—all lands that had been occupied for centuries by native North Americans. Notable among them were the Cree, who peopled the northern woods and coastal lowlands around Hudson Bay, their related allies, the Ojibwa, and their friends, the Assiniboine. Among the native peoples, too, were traditional enemies of the Cree: the Chipewyan and Inuit (Eskimo) to the north, the Dakota and Blackfoot to the south and west.

During its first two decades, while profits soared because of a Europe-wide fashion craze for beaver hats, the Hudson's Bay Company established several fur-trading posts in Cree country around the shores of James and Hudson bays, Moose Factory and York Factory among them. A competing colonial power, France, seized these coastal forts and controlled them from 1686 until 1713, when the HBC regained them under the Treaty of Utrecht.

Despite the British conquest of New France in 1759, fur-trading competition resumed. The HBC reacted by building an inland network of trading posts. From 1774, when the fur-trade explorer Samuel Hearne established Cumberland House (in what is now Saskatchewan), the Company built dozens of outposts along rivers and in the forested wilderness, among them Norway House and Rocky Mountain

Moose Factory in 1854: little had changed from when John Rae lived there

House, and such "forts" as McLeod, Chipewyan, Smith, Resolution, Garry, and Edmonton.

For four decades starting in the 1780s, the HBC engaged in a ferocious rivalry with the upstart North West Company, headquartered in Montreal. But in 1821, a dozen years before John Rae arrived, the HBC absorbed its competitor and extended its monopoly to include present-day Oregon, Washington, Idaho, and British Columbia and parts of Montana and Wyoming.

Everywhere in this wilderness empire, living conditions were primitive. Moose Factory, one of the oldest posts, was celebrated in some circles and deplored in others as the wildest of the fur-trade forts, the "most corrupted"—which meant the one that had most nearly "gone Indian." Established in 1673 when the Company of Adventurers was only three years old but already mindful of French competition, Moose Fort (as it was originally called) developed on a heavily wooded island, six miles in circumference and twelve miles from the mouth of the Moose River at the bottom of James Bay. This put it fourteen days' journey from Lake Superior, thirty from Montreal, using traditional canoe routes.

Nevertheless, in 1686, the French, with an army of only one hundred including Algonquin allies, surprised, seized, and destroyed the fort. In the 1720s, the HBC rebuilt the post only to see it ravaged by fire on Christmas Day, 1735—the direct result, according to Chief Factor Richard Staunton, of drunkenness and debauchery, vice and ignorance, and a "monsterous degree of wickedness both amongst the English and Indians," who had brought their women into the fort.

In 1810, the HBC made Moose Factory the headquarters of its southern department, as York Factory was that of the northern. Here, the governing council would meet annually. By 1834, when John Rae became its surgeon, Moose Factory had long since become a "company town," in Peter C. Newman's felicitous phrase, with almost the entire population of 180 dependent on the HBC for their livelihood.

Contemplating the varieties of service available with the Company, Rae identified three "styles of life"—a quiet, peaceful one among the orderly natives of the wooded inland country (northern Ontario and Manitoba); a more adventurous one in the prairie districts

(Saskatchewan and Alberta), where large, threatening native bands often compelled the Company to shut fort gates, lock doors, and post sentinels at night; and a varied but secure one at coastal depots such as Moose Factory, which Rae regarded as "the best place east of the Rocky Mountains, [though] in this I may be misled by partiality as it was a very happy home to me for ten years."

Having grown up in Orkney, a rugged island world that lies at a latitude hundreds of miles farther north than James Bay, Rae adapted more readily than most Europeans to the primitive living conditions. Moose Factory was made up of a wooden "fort" and a variety of outbuildings. The fort consisted of four two-storey wings arranged in a large square. As surgeon, Rae lived in the south wing and for five years shared a second-floor suite with the accountant Alexander Simpson, brother of the explorer Thomas Simpson. They occupied a large hall with an iron stove, two bedrooms, and a comfortable sitting room.

Rae practised medicine in the east wing, which housed his surgery, a trading post, and an area for issuing provisions. The west wing contained the accountant's office, the general office, and a couple of all-purpose rooms; the north, a general store. An adjacent building contained, on its upper floor, a dining hall (the location of the Christmas dinner), a large storage room, and several bedchambers for visitors from the interior; a provision store occupied its lower level.

The enthusiastic doctor became a favourite of Chief Factor MacTavish, who lived with his family in a large two-storey house overlooking the river about one hundred yards from the fort. Rae enjoyed visiting this comfortable home, which had a verandah, a small library, and a large dining room. Here, he realized that the life of a chief factor, or "bourgeois," might not be a bad one—though already, inspired by letters that Thomas Simpson wrote to his brother, Rae had begun to dream of exploration.

Almost every day, Rae took the time to shoulder his musket and go for a hike. If he headed upriver to hunt in the forest beyond the chief factor's house, he passed several well-kept cottages that housed married officers and their families. A couple of years after he arrived at Moose Factory, a Wesleyan clergyman built a neat little church beyond these cottages, and there Rae faithfully attended Sunday services.

When Rae walked downriver, he passed various workshops and then Bachelor's Hall, waving to any men who happened to be outdoors working on canoes or boats or cleaning their guns. He would stride on beyond the cottages of the various smiths and overlookers, most of whom lived with their families, and survey the warehouses that dotted the riverbank, filled with goods brought from England and furs that would eventually be shipped overseas.

Toward the end of the island, Rae would pass another six or eight cottages for men with families before striking into a thick forest whose trees were sufficiently large and numerous that, later in the century, Moose Factory would give rise to a lumber mill that produced masts, spars, and battens for the London market. In winter, when he could cross the frozen Moose River to the mainland on snowshoes, Rae would fearlessly plunge into a sparsely settled wilderness that extended for thousands of miles, where rivers provided the only means of long-distance travel and where dangerous animals lurked, including wolves, cougars, and grizzly bears.

The governor of the HBC, the notoriously tight-fisted Sir George Simpson, had originally offered Rae a five-year contract at one hundred pounds per year, "feeling satisfied, from the report I had of your character, and from what I know of your family [Rae's brothers], that you would do honour to my recommendation . . . in the double capacity of Clerk and surgeon." When he signed on, Rae had politely stipulated that he would serve only as a doctor, and for two years not five. He found himself with too little to do, however, so he volunteered to assume general duties on condition that these would never interfere with his attendance on the sick. Soon he was supervising the packing and distribution of provisions for the inland posts, some of them over one hundred miles away.

Rae also oversaw the packing and preparation of furs for shipping to England. This involved making the furs into rectangular parcels weighing from eighty-four to ninety pounds each, compressing these "packs" with wedges or screw devices. In the interior of each pack were three hundred to six hundred small, fine skins, like those of muskrats, martens, and otters, while the outside included the skins of bears, wolves, and caribou or reindeer. Men bound each pack with stout thongs of hide called pack-cords. At far-flung trading posts in times of starvation, these cords would become the first substitute for food: prolonged boiling lent them a jelly-like consistency, and the leather—untanned, untreated, not denatured—retained some food value.

While doing this supervisory work, Rae noticed that the most muscular natives took great pride in how much they could carry, some arriving with up to 950 pounds on their backs. The competitive young doctor and a rather scrawny chap, a storeman named James Gaston,

The Trading Store hummed with activity for weeks at a time

had developed a technique of neatly hoisting great kegs of shot onto shelves that ran along the wall two feet above the floor. The mischievous Rae decided to put this technique to use.

He took to leading muscular visitors into the shot room, where he and Gaston had scattered several three-hundred-pound kegs on the floor. Casually, he would ask the native men to hoist these awkward kegs into place. Finding them unable to do so, he would express mild surprise and then, without showing any particular effort, flip and hoist the kegs. On one occasion, Gaston added a couple of bags weighing fifty-six pounds and worked the same trick. As for the visitors, "their surprise and chagrin were excessive."

As the only doctor in the vicinity, Rae tended not only HBC employees, but also natives and Métis for hundreds of miles around—and for free, travelling whenever and wherever duty called. During his ten years at Moose Factory, he treated some serious illness but saw no epidemics and very few deaths. The native peoples, he found, suffered mostly from rheumatism and diseases of the chest. Rae also treated countless axe wounds acquired while splitting wood and many injuries caused by explosions of gunpowder and "carelessness in the using of guns, requiring occasional amputation." This would be a grim business indeed, with alcohol serving as the only anaesthetic. The victim's most stoic friends and relations would hold down the howling unfortunate while Rae worked away with a saw.

John Rae thrived in Rupert's Land, partly because of his constitution and partly because of his abilities as an outdoorsman and as a doctor, but mainly because of his unique attitude. His egalitarian outlook toward native peoples and his avid willingness to learn from them enabled him to develop his skills while more conventional men languished in ignorance. "It was at this place," he would write of Moose Factory, crediting its native peoples, "that I learned all the different methods of hunting, fishing, sledge-hauling, snowshoe walking and camping out . . . in winter, summer, spring and autumn that were afterwards so useful to me in my Arctic explorations."

As Edinburgh museum curator Dale Idiens notes in a book-length tribute called *No Ordinary Journey*, Rae's attitude emerged out of his "natural admiration for those who excelled, as he did, in hunting, shooting, fishing and sailing." In Rupert's Land, Rae preferred the company of Cree and Inuit hunting partners and Scots "half-breeds" to that of the supercilious members of the white establishment. Rae himself took pains to clarify his terminology:

In using the term "half-breed" I mean any of those who have Indian blood in their veins, in a greater or lesser degree, nor is this meant in the least as a term of reproach, for they are a very fine race, active, good-looking, intelligent.... I especially refer to the English and Scotch half-breeds, with whom I am best acquainted, and who for travelling ... and for shooting and fishing companions I would prefer to any man I know.

From his early twenties on, Rae recognized people as people, regardless of their race, an attitude far ahead of that of his times. Indeed, he took pride in adapting to harsh conditions by "going native." In winter, he wore a coat of light-cut, close-grained mole or beaver skin with a strip of fur round the cuff; this fur fitted comfortably into large mitts similarly bordered, an arrangement that kept out both cold and snow. In freezing weather, Rae would add rabbit fur or feathers inside the mitts and a cap made of the skin of a young seal called a "white-coat." Such a cap he found durable, cheap, the right colour for winter shooting, and warm enough in any weather. (In 1862, Rae would don just such an outfit, indifferent to tribal markings, to pose for a memorable portrait by William Armstrong.)

Idiens also notes that in everything Rae wrote—his one published book, *Narrative of an Expedition to the Shores of the Arctic Sea*, his post-humously published *Arctic Correspondence*, and his massive, unpublished memoir—he recorded, to a degree unmatched by any contemporary, the names not only of his companions, whether Orcadian, Scottish, French Canadian, First Nations, or Inuit, but also of those native people he merely encountered. In his expedition narrative, Rae would name fourteen Inuit, or "Eskimos," individually, and in his autobiographical memoir, he refers by name to nineteen native North Americans.

Rae also took pains to acknowledge native women. Many of them, he observed admiringly, could manage a canoe, set fishing nets, angle for trout through holes cut in the ice, set snares to catch hares, and shoot ptarmigan and geese, often winning the annual prize for bringing down the first goose of spring. Of the Inuit women farther north, Rae observed that they were especially adept at hunting seals: they could wriggle across the ice in emulation of the seals and so entice them to leave their ice holes and approach hunters—though on occasion, lacking spears or hunting companions, the women would have to use a small club to kill a seal by striking it on the nose.

Rae marvelled at the abilities of Cree women as seamstresses and at the craft and workmanship they displayed in creating and decorating clothes and moccasins. His collection of memorabilia, now at the Scottish National Museum in Edinburgh, includes several beautifully ornamented items—a belt, a pair of garters, two bags, and a gun cover, all made of moose or caribou hide and decorated with intricate porcupine quillwork, moosehair, or embroidered silk. Rae even designed patterns for bead and silkwork and induced a Cree woman to produce an especially delightful "octopus bag" embroidered with Scottish thistles—perfect for carrying small trinkets.

During his years at Moose Factory, Rae almost certainly enjoyed intimate relations with several native woman and probably experienced at least one meaningful relationship, though not a "country marriage," with a slightly older woman, a relationship that developed his open-minded egalitarianism, fostered in his native Orkney, into a generosity of spirit that fiercely repudiated any prejudice directed against native peoples.

If at Moose Factory Rae had avoided all liaisons with native women, resisting all blandishments and invitations, he would have been a singular young fellow indeed—almost freakish. Sir George Simpson himself, governor of the HBC, at least twice married native women *à la façon du pays*. In 1821, Simpson wrote to the Company's London committee, "Connubial alliances are the best security we can have of the good will of the natives. I have therefore recommended the Gentlemen to form connections with the principal Families immediately on their arrival, which is no difficult matter, as the offer of their Wives and Daughters is the first token of their friendship and hospitality."

Such alliances, as Peter C. Newman has noted, provided HBC men with a crash course in wilderness survival, the women teaching them how to snare rabbits, prepare raw furs for market, or chew tough moosehide into moccasin leather. Sylvia Van Kirk shows in *Many Tender Ties*, a notable study of women in fur-trade society, that "country marriages" advanced trade relations and placed the Indian wife in the role of cultural liaison between the fur traders and her kin. The norm for sexual relationships was not the casual, promiscuous encounter—though of course these happened—but rather the development of an emotionally committed union.

Simpson's advice, admonitions, and personal example notwithstanding, the Hudson's Bay Company turned a blind eye in practice but officially discouraged cross-cultural relationships. As a result, written documentation is scarce. Even so, writing to Sir George from Moose Factory when at last he was about to depart, John Rae would observe that, "having hourly expected some days past to see the signal of the ship's arrival at our commodore's mast head, I deferred writing until the eleventh hour, but as I intend starting tomorrow as proposed, it is now necessary to scribble all my epistles, having many adieus (some of them *TENDER ONES*) to make." And four years later, writing from much farther north, Rae would confess to Simpson that he had lately been thinking of seeking a wife in Great Britain: "However pleasant, charming and useful the native ladies are in some respects, I do not at all fancy buckling myself for life to one of them."

All that said, much of Rae's progress and development as a North American survival expert came as a result of his close friendship with George Rivers, a Cree hunchback with whom he went on countless hunting trips. Originally a tall, well-built, powerful young fellow, Rivers had suffered an accident to the spine that caused him to be so bent over that his actual height did not exceed five feet three inches. Together, in the forests around Moose Factory, the two men hunted caribou or reindeer, animals that provided the Cree not only with a staple food, but also with hide that, once tanned, they fashioned into jackets, trousers, and skirts.

Rivers introduced Rae to native techniques of hunting and trapping, showing him how to cache meat under heavy stones to protect it from predators, and how to clean, skin, and butcher large game, securing the blood in a bag made by turning the stomach inside out. He also taught Rae to remove the gullet of a carcass, explaining that if this were not done, the meat would quickly become so tainted as to be unfit to eat.

Rivers proved to be a fearless canoeist, an admirable shot, and an excellent cook. Rae observed that "when Rivers was with me we lived most luxuriously, as he brought his admirable cooking qualities to the marsh, and the ducks, geese or godwits when either boiled or fried by him were very different articles of diet from the same food when cooked by myself." The young doctor repaid Rivers for his tutelage by satisfying his great ambition of acquiring a double-barrelled shotgun: he ordered his friend a powerful one from England, with which Rivers made wonderfully challenging shots.

When hunting large animals such as moose or caribou, Rae learned that he could save himself the hard labour of hauling or carrying game by taking along a young native or half-breed. But when Rivers or another experienced hunter couldn't come, he usually preferred going alone and handling his own rough work. He adopted this position after trying to train an inexperienced young man, who no doubt wished he had never met the intrepid doctor.

This trip started off well as Rae and the youth camped out on a low, flat island at the mouth of a wide river. During the night, however, a gale blew up and began to steamroll waves over the island. Working in pitch blackness with the current roaring around him, Rae righted the canoe and bundled supplies into it. But now what? If he paddled directly for shore, the canoe would almost certainly capsize. He remembered that about a mile down river and a hundred yards from shore, there lay another flat island, one with a clump of willows on it six or seven feet high. That clump of trees represented their only chance of safety.

Rae pushed off as the tide rose, making for this willow haven. The darkness was so thick that the men could not see the bow of their own canoe. By watching the way the rising water splashed white against the rocky shoreline, Rae remained on course. For half an hour, with the current racing, Rae paddled vigorously toward where he hoped the island might be, unable to see even the willows: "I have had few more pleasurable sensations than when I felt . . . the bow of the canoe scrape against some branches."

Rae plunged into the water and shoved the canoe as far as possible into the willows, but now the rain turned to snow. While the storm raged through the night and the river roared past not fifteen yards away, the two men huddled in the canoe. Rae's companion, "not being so habituated as myself to this work, shook so with cold that the tremor was communicated to our canoe, and his teeth chattered so as to be quite audible." The river rose higher and higher until only a foot and a half of willows remained above water, but then it began to fall, and when day dawned, Rae discovered he could walk about on parts of the island, which now lay covered in several inches of snow.

Rae made his shivering companion "as snug as I could, by adding my blanket to his, and covering him up in the oil cloth, whilst I went to shoot, wading about in snow and deep water. The snow geese were eager to feed on the first bit of ground left bare by the ebb tide, and came very near to us in their flight." The snow was still coming down so thick and fast that Rae could see only fifteen or twenty yards, but he quickly shot a few birds, gathered the game, and returned to the canoe.

The craft was so covered with snow that he almost missed it, and he had to call his young friend before he could see him huddled up in the oilcloth, as directed. After checking around, Rae found a piece of driftwood tangled in the willows. He cut this into pieces and started a fire, then put the kettle and frying pan to work and produced a hot breakfast of tea and fried duck and bacon that went a long way toward restoring his companion.

Rae's ability to endure cold was extraordinary: "All this time I may mention that I was very wet, having no waterproof coat on, but I had no impression of being particularly uncomfortable. It came on so bitterly cold that for fear of injury to my companion, I paddled some nine miles against a strong current, my friend being quite helpless, and although my wet clothes and moccasins froze hard, I suffered no bad effect." Rae never suggested as much, but on this occasion, he probably saved his young companion's life.

If as an outdoorsman John Rae had few peers, as a snowshoe walker he had none. Robert Campbell, who in the winter of 1852–53 would establish a distance record of three thousand miles on snowshoes, put it succinctly: Rae "was the best and ablest snowshoe walker not only in the Hudson Bay Territory, but also of the age."

Having been introduced to snowshoes on Charlton Island in 1833–34, Rae soon began designing his own, commissioning Cree women to make the deerskin netting, called "babiche." Later he would write at length about snowshoe technology. As a travelling doctor, Rae frequently used snowshoes to make long-distance house calls. On one occasion he walked twenty-four miles between 9 p.m. and 3 a.m., rested briefly, then retraced his steps.

What happened was this: late in the evening of the day that the "winter express"—two vigorous young men on snowshoes—left Moose Factory carrying mail, Rae realized he had forgotten to send a letter containing important medical advice. He knew the mail carriers would bed down roughly twenty-four miles south along the Hudson Bay coast. And so, at around nine o'clock, Rae donned snowshoes and, hauling a small sledge with a tent and emergency supplies, set out to overtake the express. The night was clear and fine but moonless, so he had some trouble keeping to the track that the carriers had made, especially in places where the snow was packed too hard to reveal traces.

Nonetheless, Rae tramped along under a star-filled sky. At three o'clock in the morning he reached the campsite and found the two mailmen, who famously wasted no time, rising to begin breakfast. He greeted them casually and thoroughly enjoyed their expressions of astonishment. After breakfast, Rae started for home. He had brought his musket, of course, and shot willow grouse along the way, bagging fourteen brace, or pairs, which he hauled along on his sledge.

On this occasion, Rae walked over fifty miles. Yet even that accomplishment pales in comparison with a trip he made after visiting a patient in Fort Albany, just over one hundred miles northwest of Moose Factory. Rae made that return trek in less than forty-eight hours, walking thirty miles the first day and seventy-five the next. On the second day, carrying fifteen pounds of emergency provisions, including a blanket, a kettle, an axe, and food, he left a would-be travelling companion far behind. Even with a couple of stops to make tea, he reached the fort in eighteen and one-half hours. Rae arrived at Moose Factory at about 9:30 p.m. in fine shape. The next morning, he rose at his usual hour for that time of year, half past six, with no ache, pain, or blister of any kind. This he relished reporting to his colleagues, who must have found him insufferable. Later the indefatigable doctor would learn the value of stoic understatement. He would casually observe, for example, that "a long day's march on snowshoes is about the finest exercise a man can take."

John Rae had been actively waiting for days. When the firing of guns in the distance announced the imminent arrival of Sir George Simpson on his periodic tour of inspection, Rae dropped his pen, snapped his record book shut, and, with a growing throng of excited people, hurried down to the docks to welcome the governor of the HBC. Minutes before the canoes hove into sight, Rae could hear the *voyageurs* singing. At last, two magnificent canoes appeared in the distance, each manned by eight of the best paddlers in North America. Long before most others, the eagle-eyed Rae spotted the flamboyant Simpson, decked out in his trademark top hat, seated proudly in the leading canoe, his arms folded across his chest, effortlessly orchestrating the entire spectacle.

Since arriving at Moose Factory, Rae had witnessed Simpson's grand entrance four times (1836, '37, '39, '43), though never with such anticipation. He felt almost certain that the governor, a fiercely competitive fellow Scot, would arrive equally eager. Sure enough, after climbing onto the dock and greeting the chief factor, the recently knighted governor turned to Rae and extended his hand: "Ah, Doctor Rae! Are you ready, then?"

"You know I am, Sir."

Climbing the hill with Simpson and a few others toward the chief factor's residence, Rae showed no signs of excitement. Yet he could hardly contain himself. The previous summer, over dinner, the fiftyish governor had regaled the officers of Moose Factory with a story of how, on Lake Winnipeg, he and his elite canoeists, most of them

Governor Simpson, top-hatted, travelled with the best paddlers in North America

Iroquois able to maintain a pace of sixty strokes per minute, had outrun a small boat whose crew had presumed to challenge him. Simpson concluded, chuckling, that given a decent canoe, his men could outrace a small boat any time, anywhere.

John Rae, now in his late twenties, had cleared his throat and begged to differ. Clearly, the men on Lake Winnipeg had been amateurs. A well-designed boat, handled by a well-trained crew of Orkneymen, could certainly outrun even the fastest canoe. And so the wager had been born: during the next few months, Rae would construct a boat and train a crew. The next summer, Rae and Simpson would test their opinions on the water.

That winter, drawing on his Orkney expertise and aided by a Métis carpenter, Rae designed and built a six-oared vessel, which he named the *Brenda* after the superb boat of his boyhood. He chose and trained a crew to sail this craft in any weather, urging the men through weeks of practice.

Three days after Simpson arrived, Race Day dawned. The whole population of Moose Factory gathered at the docks, trappers and officers alike laying wagers, many of them betting that the paddle would defeat the oar. Simpson's famously accomplished guide, Bernard, took charge of the governor's most magnificent canoe, while Rae's trained Orkneymen settled into the *Brenda*. The course was simple: a six-mile run around the island. At the firing of a gun, both crews dug in hard, and the two vessels leapt forward. Within moments, both craft had disappeared around a bend.

The spectators dispersed and, for a while, went about their affairs. Everyone returned within half an hour, however, determined not to miss the close of the race. At last, in the distance, a single craft hove into view. Rae recognized it instantly but waited for the others to see for themselves. To the astonishment of many—and the confused chagrin of Sir George—the *Brenda* arrived far ahead of the canoe.

John Rae took pains not to gloat.

By this time, the early 1840s, Arctic exploration had attained the status of a national obsession in England, with the elusive Northwest Passage serving as its Holy Grail. The HBC's charter included a stipulation that the Company should seek this Passage, and British merchants, dreaming of the wealth such a waterway might bring, had begun to criticize the HBC for accomplishing nothing in this regard.

As a result, the Company's London head office had begun to pressure its overseas governor to resume overland exploration and specifically to complete the survey of the northern coast of North America, an action that would probably entail discovering a navigable Passage. In 1839, two HBC men—William Dease and Thomas Simpson, the governor's nephew—had been forced by bad weather to abandon this project uncompleted, and then Simpson, the driving force behind the two-man team, had died under mysterious circumstances.

Anxious to silence his critics, Sir George had begun to look for someone to complete the Arctic survey. Having heard of Rae's snowshoeing exploits and seen what he could do with a boat, he realized that he had found the right man. After swearing Rae to secrecy, Sir George invited him to prepare a detailed plan to map the northern coast. The governor then invited the junior HBC officer, in an action that was unprecedented, to visit him later that year at his home in Lachine, on the outskirts of Montreal.

Before leaving Moose Factory, Sir George granted the young man permission to visit friends and relations in Upper Canada, where two of Rae's brothers, Richard and Thomas (the former two years older, the latter four years younger), had established a drygoods business in Hamilton. As a pretext for bringing Rae to Lachine, Simpson asked him to carry letters and reports from the inland fur-trading posts.

On September 28, 1843, two days before his thirtieth birthday, when he had lived in Rupert's Land for almost exactly ten years, John Rae left Moose Factory by canoe, accompanied by three natives and a visiting HBC man. The party paddled up the Abitibi River to Lake Abitibi, then portaged to Lake Temiskaming. Here Rae parted company with the other HBC man and canoed down the Ottawa River, running most of its wild and beautiful rapids like the expert canoeist he had become.

From Bytown (now Ottawa), Rae travelled south by horse-drawn coach, rattling through Susanna Moodie country along winding, rutted roads. This was his first visit to Upper Canada, and Rae discovered in the rolling, wooded countryside sprinkled with farming communities a land far more settled and civilized than the rugged territory he had begun almost to call home: this land was reminiscent of northern Scotland.

Toronto, which Rae encountered toward the end of his journey, impressed him as being larger, more substantial, and far more alive than the Orkney capital of Kirkwall, which before he discovered Edinburgh had been the grandest place he knew. Busy with steamboats, bold with gaslit mainstreets, and boasting even sewers, Toronto was a thriving urban centre of more than ten thousand people. Rae sojourned in nearby Hamilton, where he regaled his brothers with his northern adventures and received news of his family; he remained especially anxious about his now-widowed mother, to whom he regularly sent money and, occasionally, such delicacies as buffalo tongues. Then he returned to Toronto and travelled east by steamboat, reaching Kingston on December 15 and Lachine shortly thereafter.

In Lachine, long the heart of the Montreal-based fur trade, Sir George Simpson had built a stone mansion graced with impressive front-entrance columns. From the second floor, he could look out at the St. Lawrence River and watch the loading and unloading of furs at a main storage depot. Rae spent the Christmas of 1843 in Simpson's mansion, elaborating his plan to complete the Arctic survey and, quite possibly, discover the Northwest Passage. Where Simpson had offered him a schooner, Rae proposed a more efficient plan involving two boats, and he eventually carried the day.

The thirty-year-old doctor also visited Montreal, a bustling city four times the size of Toronto, and a centre in which, for the past decade, citizens of British origin had constituted a majority. Here Scottish fur-trade merchants such as Simon McTavish, James McGill, and the Frobisher brothers (Benjamin, Joseph, and Thomas) had created, along Sherbrooke Street and up the slope of Mount Royal, a concentration of magnificent mansions, the so-called Square Mile, that would have done even Edinburgh proud.

Early in 1844, after a season of wining and dining, Rae departed for Moose Factory, travelling mostly by snowshoe. Later, describing the return trip, he made it sound clearly preparatory: "The snow was unusually deep and soft for the greater part of the distance of about 700 miles, and the walking and sledge hauling very bad, our snowshoes sinking fully twelve or fifteen inches. I hauled a sledge or carried a load all the way, not of necessity but to try what kind of work it was, this being my first comparatively long journey."

Early the following May, Sir George sent an official letter putting Rae in charge of Rupert's River District in place of the veteran Robert Cowie, who had fallen ill. Cowie felt well enough to write, "If Mr. Rae takes charge of the District, a little lecture in economy will not be lost on him. I have no doubt that he would be very popular with Indians as well as the officers and servants, but am aware that he is over liberal in all payments to Indians on his private account and might be disposed to go a little beyond the mark in Company dealings."

Indeed, he might.

Rae would never take charge of Rupert's River District, however, because along with the official letter detailing the promotion, Sir George sent a private missive telling Rae to meet him at Moose Factory in mid-July. He wished to discuss another matter.

"An idea has entered my mind," he wrote, as if the two had never broached the subject, "that you are one of the fittest men in the country to conduct an Expedition for the purpose of completing the Survey of the Northern Coast that remains untraced. . . . As regards the management of the people & endurance of toil, I think you are better adapted for this work than most of the gentn. with whom I am acquainted in the country, & with a little practice in taking observations, which might very soon be acquired, I think you would be quite equal to the scientific part of the duty."

3

APPRENTICE EXPLORER

The challenge, as John Rae understood only too well, was to solve the geographical mystery of the Northwest Passage. The blanks in the map were so extensive that the late Thomas Simpson had imagined he could fill them in by descending the Back River to the Arctic coast, from where he would travel eastward, possibly all the way to Hudson Bay. Rae wisely resolved to reverse this approach. Using two small boats, he would sail north up the coast of Hudson Bay and then sledge westward across Boothia Felix, so named by analogy with Arabia Felix of ancient Roman cartography and also to honour Felix Booth, a British patron of Arctic exploration. If Boothia Felix proved to be an island, as most experts expected, Rae would not only complete the survey of North America's Arctic coastline, but would also discover the Northwest Passage, establishing a link between navigable waterways extending from the Atlantic and from the Pacific.

Sir George Simpson in 1857

Later, although his own fingerprints are all over this plan, Rae credited Sir George Simpson with having devised it—certainly the only way he would have been allowed to implement it. Sir George, a ruthless, tyrannical potentate known as the Little Emperor, had long been acting with one eye on posterity. Born a bastard in 1792 and raised by his aunt and his grandfather, a Presbyterian minister, in Inverness in northern Scotland, Simpson had already contrived to eradicate so much of the historical record that even his biographers know little about his youth and early manhood.

In his written orders, Sir George took pains to make Rae's expeditionary plan sound like his own, warning, for example, that the explorer would have to winter among the Inuit while living off the land. Rae, though not the originator of this practice, would become its foremost exemplar and practical exponent. He accepted the formal invitation with alacrity and ever after went along with the governor's fiction: "My life for some years past had been such as was best fitted to prepare me constitutionally to endure such hardships and privations as one is likely to be exposed to during an Arctic summer or winter, whilst my sportsman's experience might possibly be useful in another way in the event of scarcity of food; such I know was Sir George Simpson's idea."

Before he could even begin to act, Rae would face so many challenges that, in retrospect, it looks as if Fate wished to test both his abilities and his resolve. The first problem—a relatively small one—was that he knew nothing about surveying. Simpson ordered him to travel to the HBC fort at Red River Settlement and to spend the winter of 1844–45 acquiring this skill and studying such useful sciences as astronomy, geology, and botany.

On August 20, 1844, full of anticipation, Rae left Moose Factory in a canoe with three Indians and John Corrigal, a muscular, capable Orkneyman who would travel with him widely during the next three years. The men ascended the Moose and Missinaibi rivers. They portaged as necessary, then canoed the Michipicoten River south to Lake Superior and followed the usual fur-trade route west to Red River. When he arrived on October 9, Rae learned to his dismay that his intended instructor had fallen ill.

While waiting for the man to recover, the young doctor explored Red River Settlement, which had grown up around an HBC trading post established in 1822 at the meeting of the Red and Assiniboine rivers (now downtown Winnipeg). Four years later, the worst flooding in living memory almost destroyed the original fort, prompting the construction, twenty miles north, of Lower Fort Garry—this an idea of George Simpson's: he had married his seventeen-year-old cousin, Frances, and wished to keep her far away from the "country wives" and children he had disgracefully abandoned. In 1836, the Company had returned to the original site and built Upper Fort Garry, the fort Louis Riel was to seize in 1870 during the Red River Rebellion.

In 1844, Rae found in Red River a farming community that would not have been out of place in Orkney, although farms had been developed in the style of New France, running back from the rivers in long, narrow strips. Within five years, Red River would have a population of almost 5,400, including 2,500 French and Métis, 1,725 fur-trade officers and servants (mostly Scottish "half-breeds"), and 460 Swampy Cree. Rae enjoyed the diversity of the people and admired the Red River cart they had developed. This cart, which he would one day have occasion to use, could carry 1,000 pounds through mud and marsh and float that same load across a river. It was basically a light box fitted with an axle connecting two enormous spoked wheels. To facilitate repairs, the cart was constructed solely of wood. The wheels were never greased because dust would mix with the lubricant and wear down the axles; as a result, the cart was notorious for its infernal squeaking.

While Rae got to know Red River, his designated mentor grew increasingly ill. The man died in November and Rae resolved that, rather than travel north unprepared, he would delay his expedition and find another surveying instructor. If that meant travelling east, then so be it. The rivers and lakes had frozen over, making canoeing impossible. Rae waited until the heavy snows fell, keeping in shape by snowshoeing back and forth between the upper and lower forts. Then, in January of 1845, accompanied by John Corrigal and two other men, wearing snowshoes and driving a dog team, Rae set out for Sault Ste. Marie, 1,200 miles away.

As the fittest of the party, Rae and Corrigal had to "raise the road," which involved walking ahead and tramping down the snow, without which the dogs would have been unable to travel. Years later, while giving evidence about a proposed railway along the north shore of Lake Superior, Rae would describe the almost impenetrable country that he traversed in the dead of winter as "a continuous series of ridges having deep ravines between them where the streams running out to Lake Superior pass through."

Rae travelled by compass, shooting game as he went, and he must have astonished the occasional group of natives he encountered. "I went to the north about one hundred miles," he would observe, "and found the country there difficult to travel over; we were obliged to leave our dogs and carry our clothes and provisions on our backs." North of Superior, passing Lake Nipigon, the apprentice explorer visited James Anderson, a former Moose Factory clerk now in charge of an HBC post; like Rae, he would later be swept into the Franklin controversy.

On March 3, 1845, after travelling rough for almost two months, Rae reached Sault Ste. Marie. Bisected by the border between Upper Canada and the U.S., this busy town had long been a fur-trading crossroads, with canoeists portaging past the St. Marys River Rapids, which linked Lake Huron with Lake Superior. On weighing himself, Rae couldn't help exclaiming over his superb physical condition, noting that he had actually gained two pounds, to 172, while Corrigal, who had disdained to snowshoe between the two forts, had lost twenty-two. Nevertheless, "We had both become as tough as nails."

From the Sault, roughly two-thirds of the way to Toronto, Rae wrote Sir George asking where he should now go to learn surveying. Communications were rudimentary—no telegraph, no railway, just overland express—and the response, he knew, would take a while.

In the meantime, the would-be explorer spent time socializing on both the Canadian and the U.S. sides of the water. The former consisted of only two or three respectable-looking houses and a motley collection of huts, while the latter was the site of a good-sized village, a well-kept fort, and a garrison of fifty or more men, among them several officers. Sir George eventually sent letters complimenting Rae on his initiative in snowshoeing to the Sault and directing him to continue east to the magnetic observatory in Toronto. There, from a leading astronomer and soldier-surveyor, Captain J.H. Lefroy, Rae learned how to use a sextant and establish locations precisely. Again he visited his brothers in Hamilton and Sir George in Lachine, and his time in Toronto "passed pleasantly enough . . . though I would rather have been in Indian country."

By the end of July 1845, back in Sault Ste. Marie, Rae received the official resolution of the HBC's northern council authorizing his expedition. He was to sail north from Churchill, on Hudson Bay above York Factory, and chart the Arctic coastline from Fury and Hecla Strait, which Edward Parry had discovered from the east in 1822, to the mouth of Castor and Pollux River, where in 1839 Thomas Simpson had arrived from the west and built a cairn. Rae would command two small sailboats and twelve men, just as he had proposed.

Sir George sent Rae an inflatable India rubber boat designed by a young naval lieutenant named Peter Alexander Halkett. The prototype, tested on the Thames near Westminster Bridge, included an umbrella sail that doubled as a heavy cloak and so was called a "cloakboat." Rae would declare that "this useful and light little vessel ought to form part of the equipment of every expedition." Now Simpson advised him that at Red River, where he would collect certain necessary instruments, he would also find India rubber paste to repair this airboat. The sailboats would be built at York Factory. Rae hoped they were not yet begun because he wanted to see them put together. On August 5, as a seven-gun salute resounded over Lake Superior, Rae started paddling west in a canoe.

On September 7, 1845, an HBC clerk named Robert Ballantyne, canoeing southeast on the Winnipeg River, accompanied by natives and carrying furs, was astonished to see a lone canoeist, obviously not a *voyageur* but a remarkably energetic and powerful gentleman, approaching from the other direction. Ballantyne, who would later gain fame as an author of adventure stories, knew that, at this late season, all the canoes that normally traversed these wilds had long since passed this way. The approaching stranger set him and his men to speculating out loud: Who could this be?

The water was too rough for midstream discussion, but the meeting was sufficiently singular that both parties made for a flat rock. At that convenient landing spot, as he would later relate in his book *Hudson Bay, or, Everyday Life in the Wilds of North America* (1850), Ballantyne learned that John Rae was on his way to York Factory, several hundred miles north. There he would fit out an expedition to complete the survey of the Arctic coast and determine beyond doubt "whether or not there is a communication by water between the Atlantic and Pacific oceans round the north of America."

To Ballantyne, who knew him by reputation, the thirty-two-year-old doctor appeared to be just the man for such an expedition: "He was very muscular and active, full of animal spirits, and had a fine intellectual countenance. He was considered, by those who knew him well, to be one of the best snow-shoe walkers in the service, was also an excellent rifle-shot, and could stand an immense amount of fatigue." Even so, the author would remark, "Poor fellow! greatly will he require to exert all his abilities and powers of endurance."

The chance encounter so excited Ballantyne that in his book, he devoted two full pages to it. Unlike previous expeditions, he observed, which involved many men and large quantities of provisions, Rae would proceed with few supplies and a mere handful of men, relying almost entirely on his own gun for food. The men would sail north, secure their boats at an expedient location, and explore the area on foot. They would then spend the long, dreary winter among the Inuit before resuming operations the following spring.

Ballantyne judged Rae to be "of such pushing, energetic character that there is every probability he will endeavour to prosecute his discoveries during winter, if at all practicable." He predicted success, noting that Rae entered upon the adventure "not with the vague and uncertain notions of [George] Back and [Sir John] Franklin, but with a pretty correct apprehension of the probable routine of procedure, and the experience of a great many years spent in the service of the Hudson's Bay Company."

For his part, Rae would observe laconically that he enjoyed "a most agreeable encounter" with Ballantyne. "We exchanged views, his from the wilderness, mine from the civilised world, then with a warm shake of the hand and '*bon voyage*,' we parted on our several ways."

At Red River Settlement, Rae switched from a canoe to a York boat, a flat-bottomed HBC workhorse vessel. The largest of these, forty feet long, could carry 120 bales of furs weighing more than 10,000 pounds. York boats evolved from an Orkney design: pointed bow, sharp-angled stern, large square sail. Rae knew them to be the safest way to cross a treacherous body of water such as Lake Winnipeg, which lay directly ahead. Famous among *voyageurs* for its wicked transformations, this lake can suddenly transform an alluring, mirror-like surface into a tantrum of whitecaps, especially late in the season.

Once he had sailed the length of Lake Winnipeg to Norway House, just off the north end, Rae had overcome two major challenges in a year. First, he had coped with the unexpected death of his proposed

HBC York boats at Norway House

surveying tutor and acquired the expertise he needed; then, as winter closed in, he had single-handedly traversed some of the most rugged country in the world.

Just when he hoped the worst was behind him, however, Rae encountered a third obstacle. Experienced guides and steersmen, who were among the most expert of boat and canoe handlers, were predicting that Rae's party would either starve to death or freeze for lack of fuel in the treeless barrens that lay above the Arctic Circle, that line of latitude, roughly sixty-six and one-half degrees above the equator, which circumscribes the earth's north frigid zone.

Men were afraid to sign on for the expedition. Even John George MacTavish, Rae's old mentor at Moose Factory, was skeptical. While visiting Norway House, MacTavish could not help warning, despite his enormous respect for the younger man's abilities, "Na, na, doctor, take as few men as possible, for nane o ye will be seen back again."

But John Rae would not be deterred. Before leaving Moose Factory, he had hired two men: John Corrigal, his trusted lieutenant, and Richard Turner, the Métis carpenter and boat builder whose work had helped win the race with Sir George Simpson. At Norway House, after much debate and discussion, he engaged five more men who knew him by reputation. Confident that he could hire another three at York Factory, Rae beat his way north up the Nelson River and down the Hayes, arriving during a freezing gale on October 8, 1845. He had intended to proceed still farther north to the outpost of Churchill and to leave from there at spring breakup, but when the gale subsided, ice began forming on the rivers and Rae wisely decided to winter where he was.

For over 150 years, York Factory had served as the Hudson's Bay Company's principal headquarters in Rupert's Land. In the 1820s, when the HBC gained control of the North West Company, Sir George Simpson had moved the head office to Lachine, near Montreal. But York Factory, still the main supply depot for the Company's huge northern department, remained the largest and most profitable of all HBC outposts.

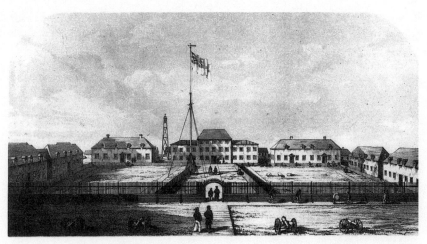

York Factory, 1853: long winters, endless rains, hungry mosquitoes

Strategically located on Hudson Bay on a narrow peninsula between the mouths of the Nelson and Hayes rivers, York Factory had developed around an Old Octagon of workshops and residences built in 1787 after a devastating fire. By the 1820s, as business increased, the population had grown until York Factory began to resemble a village—or, perhaps, a company town. During the following decade, the HBC built a massive two-storey warehouse roughly one hundred feet square, with a storage capacity of 10,000 square feet. By 1845, when John Rae arrived by canoe, the white warehouse dominated a five-acre enclosure that included more than thirty buildings, among them a school, a church, and many houses.

The climate at York Factory inspired no paeans. The settlement lay so near Hudson Bay that it endured dramatic changes of weather. A hot, sunny day would suddenly turn miserably foggy and cold, while the reverse never happened. And there was no possibility of flight or withdrawal: the surrounding countryside consisted of marsh and swamp, so that hikers could not go beyond half a mile without sinking up to their ankles or even their knees. The trees in the area, while diverse (with pines, willows, birches, and poplars), were so stunted that to get firewood, workers would have to travel five miles, slogging back and forth across marshland.

Visitors and residents spoke with one voice. R.M. Ballantyne, who had met Rae on the river, called York Factory "a monstrous blot on a swampy spot, with a partial view of the frozen sea." James Hargrave, who became chief factor in 1844 after serving thirteen years at the outpost, described his long-time home as "nine months of winter varied by three of rain and mosquitoes." His wife, the astute and articulate Letitia Hargrave, initially perceived York Factory as a clump of buildings sitting in "a desolate waste of green swamp grass and small scrub as far as eye could see." Later, thinking no doubt of the disreputable Moose Factory, she qualified that judgement, observing that despite its shortcomings, this was "by far the most respectable place in the territory."

Late in the autumn of 1845, when he arrived at this improbable outpost, John Rae found that Hargrave had already supervised the building of two York boats for his expedition, both twenty-two feet long and seven and a half feet broad. Rae named them the *North Pole* and the *Magnet* and found them to work well and to sail very nearly alike. In his unpublished memoir—although not in his published *Narrative*, which also treats this period—Rae describes how, challenged by an experienced sloop captain "with a by no means poor opinion of his own efficiency as a boatsman" and egged on by Corrigal, he agreed to test the two boats in a race.

Rae gave the captain his choice of boats and beat him soundly. When the sailor complained that the first boat was obviously better made, Rae switched craft and, in a second contest, bested the man again. "After this satisfactory trial," he notes, "by which one or two trifling defects were discovered, the boats were dismantled and housed for the winter."

In his secret heart, Rae, at age thirty-two, must have known that he could not only out-sail, but also out-hike, out-shoot, out-hunt, out-track, out-snowshoe, out-canoe, out-survey, out-smart, and out-survive any man in North America—certainly any European. He had convinced Corrigal. And certainly he impressed Letitia Hargrave, who observed in a letter that he had earned his doctor's diploma unusually early "and has not been home since, nor, he says, opened a medical book for seven years. He is very good-looking and can walk one hundred miles easily in two days."

Rae used the winter of 1845–46 to consolidate plans for his expedition. He built a small observatory in which he took meteorological readings as often as eight times a day, recording temperature, barometric pressure, the force and direction of the wind, and the general state of the weather. There, too, he practiced surveying and taught its rudiments to John Corrigal and Richard Turner. He also tended to Letitia's brother, William, who had cut his foot with an axe. In turn, Letitia taught Rae to make bread, following a recipe that he subsequently used in the Arctic.

Rae and Letitia Hargrave, who was the niece of John George MacTavish, were the same age, Letitia having been born in Edinburgh in 1813. At twenty-seven, she had married James Hargrave, an aloof, self-contained man fifteen years her senior. Hargrave had served with the HBC since 1819. A young doctor based at York Factory, John Sebastian Helmcken, described Hargrave as friendly and affable while on board a sailing ship, but "no sooner did he set foot ashore than he became dignified, cold and distant! Like an admiral, who may be pleasant and urbane ashore, but the moment his foot touches the deck, he is the admiral—discipline prevails, and he may or may not be a tyrant. Hargrave was nevertheless kind in his way, but... he had to go into harness at once."

This same Helmcken described Letitia as "one of those nice ladies one occasionally meets with, kind and affable. Altho' not handsome, she had a decidedly nice face, and a very pleasing expression—with a very good figure." She and Hargrave lived in a well-kept house just outside the fort. Already the mother of two small children, Letitia kept a personal maid (unusual in the wilderness), wore fashionable gowns, and played the piano.

Helmcken described Rae as "an active powerful broad-shouldered man, of medium height—dark and bronzed—full of energy and active as a squirrel, and good-humoured, and natured." The editor of Letitia Hargrave's letters would later observe that the explorer "must have been a welcome addition to York society, as he was a man of great talents and charming personality. It was said of him that he was as much at home at Court or in a London drawing-room as he was in an

Indian tent or an Eskimo snow house. He and the Hargraves found many tastes in common."

In 1840, while passing through Stromness aboard the *Prince Rupert*, James Hargrave had visited the Hall of Clestrain and taken tea with Rae's widowed mother, whom he described as "one of the aristocracy here." Yet now some tension arose between Rae and the chief factor, probably a by-product of the young explorer's close friendship with Letitia. To Sir George Simpson, without elaborating, Rae wrote: "Fortunately, I am under no personal obligation to Mr. Hargrave, he being one of the last persons of my acquaintance from whom I would like to ask a favour. Yet notwithstanding his disagreeable manner, he has a warm and kind heart when his selfishness will permit it."

Later, when Rae was safely far away, he and Hargrave would develop a warm personal relationship. The turning point came in March 1846, when the chief factor travelled on business to Norway House. There he was shocked to learn through the northern grapevine that Rae's older brother William had recently committed suicide in California. William had joined the HBC in 1827 at age eighteen. Five years later, Sir George Simpson described the clerk as a high-spirited and well-conducted young man of tolerably good education. Strong, active and resourceful, known as a mechanical genius who could fix anything, William served at Rainy Lake, Fort Garry, Fort Edmonton, Fort Vancouver, Fort Kootenay, and Stikine.

In 1842, promoted to chief trader, William Rae took charge of HBC operations in California. In San Francisco, according to Simpson, he mismanaged the Company's affairs and embroiled himself in revolutionary politics, then quarrelled with his wife and shot himself to death.

Having known William slightly, James Hargrave wrote John Rae a sensitive, sympathetic letter in which he spoke of the "worth, pure honour and unstained memory" of his brother. This he sent north with a messenger on snowshoes.

During his first year at Moose Factory, John Rae had lost his father, who died at sixty-two in October 1834. Now, on receiving Hargrave's devastating communication, Rae could not help recalling scenes from his Orkney boyhood, remembering countless sunny afternoons when

William had stood like a prince at the helm of the *Brenda*, calling out orders to his younger brothers while the boys raced the boat pilots from Stromness. Yet even in the midst of grieving, Letitia Hargrave tells us, the mechanically adept Rae found time to fix her broken clock.

Toward the end of April, Rae awoke to the honking of wild geese, harbingers of spring, who were returning in growing numbers. A few days later, the ice on the Hayes River began to break up. Rae waited anxiously and tested the ice daily, but Hudson Bay itself didn't clear for a month. Finally, on the afternoon of June 12, 1846, Rae gathered his ten men around him.

He was well-pleased with those he had signed. Six were Scots, four from Orkney, one from Shetland, and one from the northern county of Ross-shire; of the rest, two were French Canadian, one was Métis (Turner the carpenter), and one was Cree (Nibitabo, a renowned hunter). All had considerable experience in the North. Rae told them, "Gentlemen, tomorrow we depart on the adventure of our lives." And he set them to final loading.

The men packed the two boats to the gunwhales. Besides their own minimal luggage, they stowed half a dozen muskets and a three-month supply of pemmican, a nutritious mix of dried buffalo meat and melted fat. As well, they loaded two small sheet-iron stoves (one for each boat), a pair of lamps for burning oil as the Inuit did, several kettles, or "conjurors," with small basins and perforated tin stands for burning alcohol, a fishing net, four small windows (each with two panes of glass), an oiled-canvas canoe, and the inflatable Halkett boat.

The following morning, with all of York Factory at the docks, Rae said his goodbyes. He had long since appointed John Corrigal steersman of the *North Pole* and put the *Magnet* in the charge of George Flett, a veteran sailor who had served with Thomas Simpson and William Dease in the late 1830s. Now, having climbed into the *North Pole*, Rae gave the order to cast off. Chief Factor Hargrave raised and lowered his arm, and the cannons boomed out a seven-gun salute. The assembled throng offered up three rousing cheers as, with ten men and two boats, John Rae sailed north out of York Factory.

In his unpublished memoir, Rae observed that this was the first party of Europeans to sail for the Arctic Sea carrying only three or four months' provisions while intending to remain fifteen months. There would be little or no fuel, and for food, the men would depend largely on hunting. Rae added that he would never have attempted such an expedition with unpractised men, and he noted that those with him were well-equipped to handle the challenges ahead.

Even so, the first night out, Rae lay awake in his tent, assailed by the doubts and fears he had kept at bay during the bustle of preparation:

I could not conceal from myself that many of my brother officers, men of great experience in the Indian country, were of the opinion that we ran much risk of starving; little was known of the resouces of that part of the country to which we were bound; and all agreed that there was little chance of procuring fuel, unless some oil could be obtained from the natives. Yet the novelty of our route, and of our intended mode of operations, had a strong charm for me, and gave me an excitement which I could not otherwise have felt.

For two weeks, Rae beat north against the wind along the coast. On June 27, 1846, he reached Fort Churchill near the mouth of the Churchill River, yet another turbulent highway to the interior. Early in the eighteenth century, the HBC had built a small post at this river mouth to trade with the Dene, who were reluctant to visit York Factory because of the preponderance of their traditional enemies, the Cree. Around 1730, the Company decided to construct a massive stone fortress at this spot overlooking Hudson Bay as a final redoubt in case of another war with France.

After forty-one years, the HBC finally completed Prince of Wales Fort, an imposing, quadrangular structure three hundred feet square with bastions at each of its corners. The walls were twenty feet high and six feet thick and included forty embrasures for guns of different calibres, among them eighteen- and twenty-four- pounders. In 1782, surprised by a small French army, Samuel Hearne surrendered the fortress without firing a shot. With only thirty-nine men and facing more than one hundred interlopers, he decided to fight another day. The French razed Fort Prince of Wales almost to the ground. The following year, when the English regained the territory, Hearne returned, took one look at the devastated site, and built a trading post a couple of miles up the Churchill River. This, optimistically, he named Fort Churchill.

By 1846, the HBC had many posts farther inland. Fort Churchill had devolved into a scattering of buildings on a couple of acres of land, an outpost where perhaps four hundred people regularly traded. There it was that, early in July, Rae received still more official instructions from Sir George Simpson, sent weeks before by overland express. After calling for observations on topography, meteorology, botany, geology, zoology, and the ethnography of the Inuit, the governor advised Rae to return after wintering according to his discretion, either reversing his original route or making his way up the Great Fish River.

Simpson concluded on a rather grand note: "Let me assure you that we look confidently to you for the solution of what may be deemed the final problem in the geography of the northern hemisphere. The eyes of all who take an interest in the subject are fixed on the Hudson's Bay Company; from us the world expects the final settlement of the question that has occupied the attention of our country for two hundred years." The Northwest Passage—as if Rae could have forgotten.

At Fort Churchill, Rae rounded out his expedition party by adding two Inuit hunters: an experienced interpreter named Ouligbuck and one of his sons, William Ouligbuck, Jr., whose native name was Mar-ko. The senior Ouligbuck had served with Sir John Franklin in 1825–27 and with Dease and Simpson in 1836. Young Mar-ko was still to be tested.

On July 5, 1846, at about eleven o'clock in the morning, John Rae and his men climbed back into their two boats. They were all in high spirits: the sun was shining and the breeze was light. As they sailed northwest, the men spotted white whales playing, sometimes coming within a few yards of the boats. The party made good headway, but late the next afternoon, a stiff breeze blew up and turned into a gale-force wind.

The next three weeks brought changeable weather and, sporadically, dangerous rolling floes of melting ice. Rae sailed onward along

Dr. John Rae at Repulse Bay, 1846, painting by Charles Comfort

the coast of Hudson Bay, exploring inlets and surveying the rocky shore for any opening to the Arctic Sea. He collected specimens of birds and other fauna and flora and, to conserve pemmican, shot game and caught fish. On July 24, approaching the Arctic Circle, Rae rounded Cape Hope and felt the temperature plunge dramatically. Running all night into Repulse Bay—so named because of its treeless, forbidding aspect—the explorer could not shake the feeling that something ominous had entered the landscape.

The next afternoon, however, entering a cove at the head of the rocky bay, Rae spotted four Inuit men on shore and felt a great surge of relief: their presence meant that animals would be found nearby. He and his men could hunt successfully. They could trade for fuel and cooking oil and perhaps even for sled dogs. Rae lost no time in putting ashore. Taking the younger Ouligbuck as interpreter, he approached the local men, calling out "*Teyma*," which means "peace." Fearful at first, the Inuit men, two middle-aged and two younger, soon relaxed and stood chatting.

"They were good-looking," Rae would write, "of low stature, and much more cleanly than those in Hudson's Straits. Their dresses were made of deer skin, of the form so often described, the coat having a long tail somewhat resembling that of an English dress coat. Their legs were encased in waterproof boots made of seal-skin, and they all wore mittens, which they seldom took off their hands."

In his *Arctic Narrative*, Rae identifies the two mature men as Oo-too-ou-ni-ak (who had a formidable beard and whiskers) and Kir-ik-too-oo, adding, "We were soon after joined by a fine young fellow with ruddy cheeks and sparkling black eyes, having an expression of exceeding good humour in his laughing countenance. Our new friend wore round his head a narrow leather band of deer-skin ornamented with foxes' teeth, and appeared to be somewhat of a dandy in his own estimation."

Talking with these and other local Inuit people, Rae learned that a great sea lay forty miles to the north-northwest through barren country dotted with lakes and rivers. He decided that instead of sailing north along the east coast of Melville Peninsula and so approaching Fury and Hecla Strait as Edward Parry had done, he would make first for the mouth of the Castor and Pollux River. This meant hauling and sailing at least one of the boats across what is now called Rae Isthmus.

Edward Parry named Fury and Hecla Strait after his two ships

On July 26, aided by four Inuit men hired for the purpose, Rae's men began dragging the twenty-

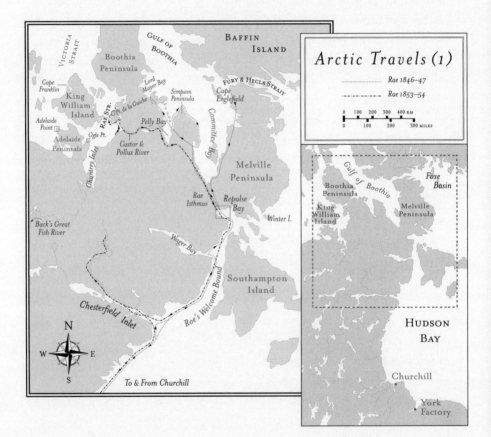

Arctic Travels (1)

.... Rae 1846–47

—·—·—·— Rae 1853–54

0 100 200 300 400 KM
0 100 200 300 MILES

BAFFIN ISLAND

GULF OF BOOTHIA

VICTORIA STRAIT

Boothia Peninsula

Cape Franklin

King William Island

Adelaide Point

Adelaide Peninsula

Ogle Pt.

Chantrey Inlet

RAE STR.

Pt. de la Guiche

Lord Mayor Bay

Simpson Peninsula

FURY & HECLA STRAIT

Cape Englefield

Pelly Bay

Castor & Pollux River

Committee Bay

Melville Peninsula

Rae Isthmus

Repulse Bay

Winter I.

Back's Great Fish River

Wager Bay

Roe's Welcome Bound

Southampton Island

Chesterfield Inlet

N
W   E
S

To & From Churchill

Gulf of Boothia

Boothia Peninsula

King William Island

Foxe Basin

Melville Peninsula

HUDSON BAY

Churchill

York Factory

two-foot *North Pole* up a river through rapids and large boulders. They covered only three miles in fourteen hours but reached a first, small lake. Rae and his men travelled four more days, rowing across lakes and dragging the battered but seaworthy boat over rocky portages. On August 1, they neared Committee Bay at the bottom of the Gulf of Boothia.

Rae had left two men at Repulse Bay to guard the *Magnet*, and now he sent back three more. The following day, sailing past a spit of land in a saltwater lake, Rae spotted two tents. He landed and, with the interpreter William Ouligbuck, called out at the door of one of the tents. Eventually, he writes,

an old woman made her appearance, apparently just out of bed, as she was very coolly drawing on her capacious boots. . . . She surveyed her visitors without showing the slightest symptoms of alarm, although I afterwards learned that I was the first European she had ever seen. An old man soon after popped out his head alongside that of his better half, who appeared to be endowed with a flow of language which set all his efforts to say anything at defiance. A few trifling presents put us all, in a few minutes, on a most friendly footing.

Rae identifies the man as I-il-lak, the woman as Rei-lu-ak, and adds, "From a chart drawn by the woman who, as is usual (at least among the Esquimaux), was much the more intelligent of the two, I was led to infer that there was no opening into the large bay but through the Strait of the Fury and Hecla, and Prince Regent's Inlet." From Rei-lu-ak, then, Rae learned that the deep bay supposed to extend all the way to the Castor and Pollux River, the bay so ardently desired by Sir George Simpson and numerous other armchair adventurers, simply did not exist: Boothia Felix was a peninsula, not an island.

During the next three days, as Rae sailed northwest up Committee Bay, the weather worsened. Realizing that he had no chance of reaching any known points before the ice closed in, he reluctantly turned around. Now he hoped at least to sail north up the west coast of Melville Peninsula to Fury and Hecla Strait before the season ended. Torrential rains made progress difficult, however, and on August 8,

Rae encountered ice: "On pushing out to sea it soon became apparent that we could not proceed on our course, and that there was but little open water in the direction from whence we had come, and even that was fast filling up. As we could neither advance nor remain in safety where we were, there was only one course open to us, and that was to return towards the place from which we had started."

Rae was reluctant to turn back because now he would not complete even part of the survey before winter. If he tried to trace the Melville Peninsula coastline on foot, he would have no time to secure provisions for the looming season of darkness. While heading back toward Repulse Bay, Rae landed at the tents of "our Esquimaux friends, [and] they came running down to the beach led on by the old lady whose fluency of speech I have already remarked, and who appeared determined to sustain her character on this occasion by making more noise than all the others put together, and expressing her joy at our return by loud shouts." The old folk had been joined by two fine, active-looking young men named Arkshuk and Ivitchuk, who told Rae that the caribou had started their annual southward migration. Hunting season had begun.

On August 9, at 6:30 a.m., Rae left three of his men and young Mar-ko with the *North Pole* and, with three others, set out to recross Rae Isthmus. Daylight remained almost continuous and, after a wet, exhausting, twenty-hour hike, Rae arrived back at Repulse Bay, where he found his other five men surviving, as he had hoped, on modest amounts of fish and venison.

Three years had passed since Sir George Simpson had invited him to devise a plan to resolve the mystery of the Northwest Passage, three years of non-stop travel and test after test. That night, as he lay in his tent, Rae would have been justified in thinking that he had passed every test admirably and that now, at last, he was ready to face the final examination.

4

ARCTIC PIONEER

In August 1846, John Rae began preparing to meet a challenge that
no European had yet met: to winter in the High Arctic, hundreds of
miles north of the treeline, while relying for food mainly on his own
resources. Until now, most explorers had tried to carry enough provisions to last; if they ran short, like Franklin in 1819–22, they depended
for survival on native peoples. Some retreated for winter to a base
camp south of the treeline, where game was more plentiful; others
used well-stocked ships as a base. Rae's fur-trade precursors, Samuel
Hearne and Alexander Mackenzie, had wintered south of the treeline
and relied entirely on native hunters. Rae would have the assistance of
the Cree Nibitabo and the Inuit Ouligbuck, but he himself would do
much of the hunting and providing.

On August 10, after arriving back at Repulse Bay, Rae sent most of
his men to help retrieve the *North Pole*. He explored the vicinity for a
long-term campsite and selected a narrow but shallow valley 150 yards
east of the North Pole River, within a few hundred yards of his landing
place. Having yet to discover the superiority of snowhuts, or igloos,
over other styles of Arctic shelter, Rae supervised the building of a
stone house, its walls two feet thick, measuring twenty feet by fourteen. The sloping roof, framed by boat oars and masts and covered with
moosehide and oilcloth, descended in height from seven and a half to
five and a half feet. Rae installed a door made of deerskin stretched
over a wood frame, as well as three windows, each consisting of two
panes of glass he had brought for this purpose. On September 2, Rae
named the finished domicile Fort Hope.

At first, because the men had been forced to use wet clay to cement the stones, the house was damp and miserable. In mid-October, when the clay froze, conditions improved. As the only non-smoker on the expedition, Rae used an oilcloth partition to isolate the small storage area in which he slept. Even so, he would write:

One cause of discomfort to me was the great quantity of tobacco smoke in our low and confined house, it sometimes being so thick that no object could be seen at a couple of yards distance. The whole party, with the exception of myself, were most inveterate smokers; indeed it was almost impossible to be awake for ten minutes during the night without hearing the sound of the flint and steel striking a light. Of course I might to a great extent have put a stop to this, but the poor fellows appeared to receive so much comfort from the use of the pipe that it would have been cruelty to do so for the sake of saving myself a trifling inconvenience.

Rae turned his attention to hunting, fishing, and gathering fuel. The inflatable Halkett boat proved to be useful for setting and visiting nets, and Rae discovered a bog rosemary, *Andromeda tetragona*, that burned well as fuel. While out hunting one day, Rae came upon a covey of ptarmigan, most of them young and strong on the wing. He managed to bag eighteen brace in a couple of hours, just as he had done so often in Orkney with grouse. The party's September bag, much of it his, consisted of 63 deer, 5 hares, 1 seal, 172 partridges, and 116 salmon and trout.

Another morning, while hunting deer before daybreak, Rae spotted a band of animals moving rapidly toward him. He initially supposed them to be deer, but they turned out to be seventeen wolves. They advanced at a gallop to within forty yards, when they slowed and formed a half-circle around him. Rae dropped to one knee and took aim at one of the leaders. Unfortunately, the sun had yet to rise and visibility was poor; Rae's bullet merely grazed the wolf, cutting off a line of hair and skin:

They apparently did not expect to meet with such a reception, for after looking at me a second or two they trotted off, no doubt as much disappointed at not making a breakfast of me as I was at missing my aim. Had they come to close quarters [which they sometimes do when pressed for food], I had a large and strong knife which would have proved a very efficient weapon.

As winter deepened, daylight dwindled and temperatures plunged. Rae visited a nearby Inuit camp and discovered the efficiency of the igloo. Back in the stone house, his pocket edition of Shakespeare's plays had recently frozen solid after getting wet; to thaw it, he had had to take it to bed. By comparison, he found the snowhouse of an old man named Shishak and his wife so cosy and warm that his waistcoat, which had also frozen stiff, actually thawed.

Bent on remaining self-sufficient, Rae studied how the Inuit built igloos. The process was less difficult than he had anticipated, and after a few trials, he and a couple of his men became accomplished ice-masons. By the beginning of December, they had erected four snowhuts, linked by tunnels, in which to store provisions, fuel, luggage, and meat for the dogs. They later constructed two observatories of snow with a pillar of ice in each, one for the dip circle and

Rae studied and adopted Inuit methods of Arctic survival

meteorological readings, the other for a horizontally suspended needle to study the effect of the aurora borealis.

From the nearby Inuit, who kept great numbers of dogs, Rae bought seal oil, deerskin clothing, and a number of sled dogs. He found the people friendly and helpful, though given to pilfering and petty thievery. Using Ouligbuck and his son as interpreters, he enjoyed a good deal of conversation with Rei-lu-ak's friend Arkshuk, who was intelligent and communicative. He learned that the Inuit preferred eating muskox to venison, and bear and walrus to seal and fish. Rae found the senior Ouligbuck rather shy about describing traditional habits, but Mar-ko told him that even in winter, the Inuit stripped off all their clothes before going to bed, the better to warm each other by cuddling. From Arkshuk, Rae also learned about Inuit beliefs:

It is said that many years ago, not long after the creation of the world, there was a mighty conjuror (Esquimaux of course) who gained so much power that at last he raised himself up into the heavens, taking with him his sister (a beautiful girl) and a fire. To the latter he added great quantities of fuel, which thus formed the sun. For some time he and his sister lived in great harmony, but at last they disagreed, and he, in addition to maltreating the lady in many ways, at last scorched one side of her face. She had suffered patiently all sorts of indignities, but the spoiling of her beauty was not to be borne; she therefore ran away from him and formed the moon, and continues so until this day. Her brother is still in chase of her, but although he sometimes gets near, he will never overtake her. When it is new moon, the burnt side of the face is towards us; when full moon, the reverse is the case.

Christmas Day was stormy and cold, reaching a high of −36 degrees Fahrenheit. The resourceful Rae, mindful of maintaining morale, organized a game of European-style football for the brief daylight hours. The men dashed around furiously, rubbing at their faces to avoid frostbite while shoving each other and kicking at the deerskin football. Frequently, a man would lose his footing and sprawl onto the icy pitch, his legs splayed above him. Rae found the scene so ludicrous that he tumbled laughing into a snowbank.

New Year's Day saw better weather: sunny, breezy, and, with a high of −24 degrees Fahrenheit, almost balmy. After an excellent breakfast of fat venison steaks, the men spent some hours at yet another spirited game of football. The snow was hard and slippery, and again the players fell often, roaring and laughing and threatening each other with revenge. After dinner—hare, venison, and reindeer tongue, with a currant pudding for dessert—the non-drinker Rae served brandy. On the whole, he wrote, "I do not believe that a more happy company could have been found in America, large as it is. 'Tis true that an agreeable companion to join me in a glass of punch, to drink a health to absent friends, to speak of by-gone times and speculate on the future, might have made the evening pass more pleasantly, yet I was far from unhappy. To hear the merry joke, the hearty laugh and lively song among my men, was itself a course of much pleasure."

On January 8, 1847, Rae awoke to the lowest temperature of the winter: −47 degrees Fahrenheit. During the ensuing week, while battling the cold, he helplessly watched gales and blizzards destroy both observatories and bury the two boats under twelve feet of snow. He husbanded the cooking fuel as best he could and waited impatiently for the arrival of some Inuit, who had promised to deliver four sealskins full of seal oil. When the men finally turned up, they brought a single sealskin. To save fuel, Rae reduced cooking to one meal a day. Like the rest of the men, he sometimes remained in bed fourteen hours a day to keep warm. Time dragged endlessly and, as he perused *Hamlet*, *Macbeth*, and *King Lear* in the faintest light, Rae thanked his lucky stars that he had remembered to bring his Shakespeare.

February brought better weather. Inuit arrived with surplus venison, and toward the end of the month, deer began migrating north. One day Nibitabo spotted thirty deer and ten partridges but managed to shoot only two of the partridges. The deer roamed around in the middle of a large plain and took care to keep out of gunshot range, much to the annoyance of the eager hunter.

Toward the end of February, Rae roughed out a design and directed the carpenter, Richard Turner, to build two sledges with iron runners from the battens that lined the insides of the boats. The finished products measured six or seven feet long, seventeen inches wide, and, for maximum stability, only seven inches high. Early in March, when the game returned, Rae began bagging partridge and deer. He hoped to set out overland on the first of April, but the night before, Ouligbuck returned from a hunting trip badly wounded in his right arm: he had tripped and fallen on a dagger. Rae delayed his departure to treat the injury.

To aid the expedition, John Rae hired Ivitchuk, a cheerful, enthusiastic young man who had helped drag the *North Pole* back across Rae Isthmus to Repulse Bay the previous August. Now Ivitchuk arrived with his extended family, including his wife, his brother, his father, and their wives, all come to say goodbye: "Our intended travelling companion having received a coat from one, inexpressibles from another, leggings from a third, etc., was soon completely dressed *à la voyageur*, not certainly to the improvement of the outer man, but much to his own satisfaction. Ouligbuck's arm being now in a fair way of recovery, there was no cause of detention."

Rae had undertaken to begin his coastal survey at the mouth of the Castor and Pollux River on Boothia Felix, the farthest point reached by Dease and Simpson after they sailed east through a strait south of King William Island. Unlike Sir George Simpson but like Sir John Ross, the unlucky veteran who had blundered in designating Lancaster Sound a dead end, Rae believed that Boothia Felix was part of mainland North America, a peninsula rather than an island. Now he would see for himself. On April 5, 1847, he set out with five men, among them Ivitchuk and the young translator Mar-ko. They travelled on snowshoes while guiding two sledges, each pulled by four dogs harnessed not in the rows that Europeans favoured, but in the traditional Inuit fan shape.

Heading north, Rae chanced upon the snowhuts of two Inuit families who were fishing for trout. He invited one of the men, Kei-ik-too-oo, to help haul supplies for two days in exchange for a dagger. The man harnessed his dog team, took on a heavy load, and glided rapidly over the snow. Rae immediately noted the superiority of the man's iced runners over the bare iron ones he had been using himself and adjusted his practice accordingly. Ever after, like the Inuit, Rae coated his sledge runners with a mixture of moss and damp snow. He had started along the path that would make him the foremost European exponent of Inuit methods of travel in the Arctic:

Our usual mode of preparing lodgings for the night was as follows: as soon as we had selected a spot for our snow-house, our Esquimaux, assisted by one or more of the men, commenced cutting out blocks of snow. When a sufficient number of these had been raised, the builder commenced his work, his assistant supplying him with the material. A good roomy dwelling was thus raised in an hour. Whilst the principal mason was thus occupied, another of the party was busy erecting a kitchen, which, although our cooking was none of the most delicate or extensive, was still a necessary addition to our establishment, had it been only to thaw snow.

Travelling north and periodically caching provisions beneath piles of stones for the return journey, the men arrived at Committee Bay and followed the coast for four days. Rae then led them directly westward overland toward a large bay that Ivitchuk had visited. The blazing midday sun softened the snow and made travelling difficult. Rae responded by starting the day's hike at 2:30 a.m. and stopping early in the afternoon. Bad weather slowed progress, but on April 15, Rae reached Pelly Bay and camped on an island. He rested for one day, then left the dogs with the two Inuit and an Orkneyman named Adamson, instructing them to obtain food by hunting, fishing, or trading with locals.

With George Flett and John Corrigal, Rae continued north. Using his instruments, he deduced that he was nearing Lord Mayor's Bay, where early in the 1830s John Ross and James Clark Ross had spent two winters trapped in ice. The slightly older Flett was showing signs of fatigue, and finally Rae left both companions to prepare lodgings. Alone in the barrens, he hiked four miles farther, climbed a rise, and looked out at a glorious expanse of Arctic landscape: "From the spot on which I now stood, as far as the eye could see to the north-westward, lay a large extent of ice-covered sea studded with innumerable islands: Lord Mayor's Bay was before me, and the islands were those named by Sir John Ross the Sons of the Clergy of the Church of Scotland." Gazing westward, Rae saw that his geographical instinct had proven correct: a narrow isthmus connected Boothia Felix to the mainland, making it a peninsula.

Returning to camp, Rae rested in the roomy igloo his men had made. Then, to mark his discovery, he built a small cairn and placed a note in it. Carrying thirty-five pounds on his back, the explorer led the way back along the coast, naming inlets, points, and bays as he went. On April 20, leaving the frozen bay, Rae and his two companions struck out overland toward where they had left the other three men.

This became one of the most tiring and ludicrous marches Rae ever led. Because the route lay across several ranges of ice hills, the men no sooner climbed one hummocky ridge than they had to slide and bounce down another. Descending was not always easy, for large boulders often stood in the way: "Corrigal appeared to be an old hand at this sort of work, and I had had some practice, but poor Flett, who

Ridges and ice hummocks made for a difficult march

had begun to suffer much from inflammation of the eyes, got many queer falls, and was once or twice placed in such situations with his head down hill, his heels up, and the strap of his bundle around his neck, that it would have been impossible for him to get up by his own unaided exertions."

Travelling at his own pace, Rae pressed ahead and, quite alone, came upon a party of Inuit. Area residents had a reputation for violence, and the explorer found these men "more forward in their manners and dirty in their persons and dress" than those of Repulse Bay. Nonetheless, he managed to make friends and urged them to visit the island near the bottom of the bay where he had left the rest of his men.

When, not long after Rae, these Inuit arrived in camp, they traded him seal meat, blubber, and dried salmon. In answer to his questions about local geography, and specifically whether any waterways or passages led out of the bay, they said flatly, no. They communicated that by climbing to the top of the highest hill on this island, he could see for himself. The next day, in the sunshine, Rae took his instruments and did as the locals suggested. He could scarcely believe the spectacular view: he could see the whole bottom of the bay. Rae took readings and named the bay in honour of the HBC's John Henry Pelly, an important London-based partner of Sir George Simpson.

On April 24, 1847, Rae set out for Repulse Bay. For the sake of creating accurate charts, he followed the coastline of Simpson Peninsula, which he had cut across on the outward journey and which he now named after his powerful sponsor. After eleven days of slogging, Rae and his men reached their stone house. Their faces were so black and charred from the combined effects of oil smoke and frostbite that their companions at first feared they had been the victims of a gunpowder explosion. Having travelled almost non-stop for thirty days, Rae and his men "thus successfully terminated a journey little short of 600 miles, the longest, I believe, ever made on foot along the Arctic coast."

Rae now said goodbye to Ivitchuk. The young man had been hardworking, obedient, and, when not exhausted by the pace, generally lively and cheerful. He had adjusted well to his fellow travellers, living as they did, though occasionally he would swallow a piece of

In 1821–22, the Hecla *and the* Fury *wintered near Repulse Bay*

seal blubber as a delicacy. What surprised Rae most was how little Ivitchuk ate, often the least of the party. The Inuit man had, however, learned to savour tea and chocolate and to smoke a pipe as if he had been accustomed to it all his life.

Ivitchuk had also picked up a few words of English, which he used whenever he thought they were applicable, and had expressed a keen interest in reading and writing. Because he, like the rest of the party, had returned thinner than when he left, he proposed to spend the rest of the spring eating, drinking, and sleeping. Rae gave him a gun and some ammunition as a reward for his services, along with a few trinkets for his wife. She was "one of the best-looking of the fair sex of Repulse Bay," the explorer observed, "although it was said that the lady had not behaved very well to her liege lord during his absence, having taken unto herself another husband named Ou-plik; but probably the good man knew nothing or cared little about it."

For one week, Rae rested. He had successfully completed half his intended expedition: although he had not reached the mouth of the Castor and Pollux River, he had reached another known point to the west—Lord Mayor's Bay—and so demonstrated that Boothia Felix was a peninsula. He had not lost a single man and he had survived a winter in the Arctic. Now he would chart the western coastline of Melville Peninsula to another known point: Fury and Hecla Strait, which Edward Parry had discovered in 1822 while wintering nearby.

At latitudes this far north, winter means almost continual darkness. In December and January, for long weeks at a stretch, the sun scarcely rises above the horizon, usually managing only to turn the sky a whiter shade of grey. The advent of spring signals a welcome reversal. The days grow gradually longer until, at the height of summer, the sun never sets but merely dips near the horizon before reascending. Even in spring, however, the sunshine is constant enough to turn the snow so wet, heavy, and sticky that it clings to sled runners and snowshoes, making travel difficult.

Analyzing the second leg of his ambitious expedition, Rae decided to resolve the problem of wet snow by travelling at night, breaking camp at 8 or 10 p.m. and stopping at 6 or 7 a.m. when the rising sun began to thicken the snow. On May 13, he again left Repulse Bay with five men, among them the senior Ouligbuck, his arm apparently healed, and John Corrigal, the latter the only repeater. A fatigue party of three men with a sledge and dogs accompanied these five for three days, hauling supplies. Crossing the isthmus to Committee Bay, Rae realized that Ouligbuck was not sufficiently healed to maintain the pace and reluctantly sent him back with the fatigue party.

On May 16, leading four men, Rae started up the west coast of Melville Peninsula, embarking on what he would later describe as the most difficult of all his journeys. The weather soon turned ugly, with strong winds and drifting snow. Walking became difficult. At one point, the men sank nearly waist-deep in snow; at another, they sloshed ahead through salt water up to their knees. Then they ended up on a great slab of ice so slippery that, with their wet and frozen shoes, they found it impossible to keep from falling. Sometimes they had to crawl out of a hole on all fours, like strange-looking quadrupeds; at other times, they fell over backwards, so hampered by the weight of their loads that they could not regain their footing unassisted without shucking them off.

Still the men pressed on. They were running low on food when Corrigal wounded a deer. The buck ran too fast to be overtaken, and Corrigal was about to give up the chase when Rae arrived. The two men continued the pursuit together. After travelling a considerable distance, the deer finally lay down. It rose up again before they could get within range and was trotting off quickly when, by way of giving it a parting salute, Rae dropped to one knee, aimed, and fired—and sent a bullet through the animal's head. The deer's horns were already a foot long, and the venison was in excellent condition for so early in the year.

On May 25, with food again running low, Rae left two exhausted men at a campsite on the coast and carried on with Corrigal and Matheson. Two days later, their provisions almost gone, Rae calculated that he had enough food left to advance for only half a night more. Rae left a weary Matheson and set out with Corrigal in a heavy snowstorm at 9:30 p.m. Unable to see more than fifty yards, he was forced to hug the coast. At four in the morning, the sky cleared long enough that he was able to take some readings and see the coastline for another dozen miles.

Contemporary readers question the arrogance of naming and renaming every geographical feature, especially when sites have already been named by indigenous peoples. But in the mid-1800s, even the progressive Rae showed a passion for naming every uncharted landmark he encountered, in this respect a product of his times. The headland on which he stood became Cape Crozier, after Sir John Franklin's second-in-command. And to the most distant visible point he gave the name Cape Ellice, after the prominent Whig politician Edward "Bear" Ellice, a force in the governing councils of the HBC.

According to Rae's calculations, Cape Englefield, which Edward Parry had discovered at the western end of Fury and Hecla Strait, lay about twenty-five miles north of Cape Crozier, where Rae now stood. He decided that this position would have to do: "Finding it hopeless to attempt reaching the Strait of the Fury and Hecla, from which Cape Ellice could not be more than ten miles distant, we took possession of our discoveries with the usual formalities [building a cairn and placing a note within it] and retraced our steps, arriving at our encampment of the previous day at half past 8 a.m."

On May 28, just after 10 p.m., Rae and his two fittest men began the long trek back to Repulse Bay. Early the following morning, they reached the other two men, Folster and Mineau, who had killed only two marmots (Arctic ground squirrels) and were extremely hungry. If Rae hadn't arrived within another twelve hours, they had intended to boil a piece of parchment skin for supper and to keep a small piece of pemmican for travelling provisions.

Rae led the four men south two days later, proceeding in a straight line where previously he had hugged the coast. The next day, the party reached the first of several caches of venison and other supplies and Rae began spotting and shooting ptarmigan. The return journey was difficult but uneventful, and the expedition arrived at Repulse Bay in good health and spirits. The men were thinner than before, but not nearly so black and charred as the returnees from the previous journey had been. In his *Arctic Narrative*, Rae summarized the exhausting trek:

I have had considerable practice in walking, and have often accomplished between forty and fifty, and, on one occasion, sixty-five miles in a day on snow shoes, with a day's provisions, blanket, axe, etc. on my back; but our journey hitherto had been the most fatiguing I had ever experienced. The severe exercise, with a limited allowance of food, had much reduced the whole party, yet we were all in excellent health; and although we lost flesh, we kept up our spirits, and marched merrily on, tightening our belts—mine came in six inches—and feasting our imaginations on full allowance when we arrived at Fort Hope.

Although he could not know it, Rae had established his own "farthest north" in reaching Cape Crozier. He had become the first European to winter in the High Arctic while living off the land and had explored 655 miles of new coastline, delineating the entire coast of Committee Bay and the southern half of the Gulf of Boothia, excepting only a tiny area in the south of Pelly Bay.

Rae had entered the history of Arctic exploration. By travelling from

Lord Mayor's Bay virtually to Fury and Hecla Strait, he had linked the discoveries of Sir John Ross, made in 1829–30, with those of Sir Edward Parry, made in 1822. Even more significantly, he had established that Boothia Felix was a peninsula, not an island: no channel connected the Gulf of Boothia, discovered by the Rosses from the east, with the mouth of the Castor and Pollux River, reached from the west in 1839 by William Dease and Thomas Simpson.

John Rae had proven, in short, that no Northwest Passage existed in this vicinity.

His mission accomplished, a satisfied Rae awaited the breakup of the ice. Game became abundant around Repulse Bay, and the men hunted with great success. But some of the party had time on their hands— young Mar-ko, for example. During the few days of his father's absence at the outset of the expedition's second leg, he had twice been caught with the old man's bale open. He had also filched tobacco and removed the buttons from the trousers of most of the men. Rae made him restore the buttons and later described young Ouligbuck as both a superb interpreter and "the greatest rascal as yet unhung."

On July 25, 1847, the anniversary of his arrival, Repulse Bay remained frozen solid. Thick ice prevented Rae's departure until August 12, when finally the explorer sailed south through stormy seas. He reached Chesterfield Inlet six days after leaving and arrived at Fort Churchill on August 31 with eight bags of pemmican and four bags of flour—a pointed response to those doubters who had glibly predicted that the men who travelled with him would starve to death.

At Fort Churchill, Rae said goodbye to the Ouligbucks, only one of whom he would see again. A gale detained him briefly, but he resumed sailing south on September 3 and reached York Factory three days later, between 9 and 10 p.m. The entire party looked so hale and hearty that they amazed the good people of the settlement, many of whom had expected them to come crawling back.

Arctic veterans were astonished not only by this early return, mission accomplished, but that Rae had wintered above the treeline without relying on outside help for food and fuel. They recognized that he had pioneered a new approach to Arctic exploration and regarded his feat as almost miraculous. Decades later, Vilhjalmur Stefansson, the twentieth-century explorer, observed:

It was contemporaneously admitted and is now proclaimed . . . that Rae made better use of local arctic resources than any of his competitors and that his journeys excelled most if not all of theirs in miles, speed and comfort. But it has been said that in a combination of these with the other qualities of his work he was not sufficiently an innovator to be considered the founder of a new school in the method of arctic travel. This can easily become a semantic dispute on how new is new. But we think of Darwinism as rightfully named, even as we lay down without dissent a book . . . that traces part of the idea's slow development. Rae was as new as Darwin.

York Factory provided a surprise of its own. On August 30, one week before Rae returned from the Arctic, twenty men—fifteen sappers and miners and five Royal Navy seamen—had arrived with the annual HBC supply ship. They had also brought four sturdy but light and transportable boats to use in searching for Sir John Franklin, who had disappeared into the Arctic with two ships and 128 men. A letter from

Sir John Franklin had disappeared
while seeking the Northwest Passage

Sir George Simpson informed Rae that the British public, having heard nothing of Franklin since he had sailed in 1845 to complete the Northwest Passage, was growing increasingly concerned. Sir John Richardson, a surgeon and naturalist who had accompanied Franklin on Arctic expeditions in 1819–22 and 1825–27, was organizing an overland search-and-rescue operation. These British servicemen, recently arrived at York Factory, would eventually go with him.

As he read Simpson's letter before a fire, Rae paused and gazed into the flames. Knowing the ferocity, treachery, and sheer expanse of the Arctic, and knowing also that Franklin had long since shown himself to be badly overmatched in any contest with these northern wilds, Rae could not help but fear the worst: that Sir John Franklin would never be seen again. He shook off this dark thought and resumed reading.

Simpson informed Rae that he had been promoted to chief trader, one step below chief factor. In this capacity, Rae would be expected to attend the Company's next annual council meeting in June of 1848 at Norway House, a flourishing inland post known for its thriving vegetable garden. Until that time, Rae was welcome to travel whenever and wherever he pleased, on business or on pleasure. The explorer smiled grimly on reading this. The tight-fisted Sir George had not expected Rae to complete his unprecedented expedition this early and had believed this grandiose offer of free time to be relatively meaningless, a gesture that would allow Rae a trip to Red River, perhaps.

The explorer could not help chuckling. He had lived abroad for more than fourteen years. But on September 24, 1847, less than three weeks after emerging from the Arctic and while still assimilating the news about Sir John Franklin, John Rae boarded an HBC supply ship and sailed for London, England, the centre of the universe as he knew it.

5

IN SEARCH OF FRANKLIN

During the past three and a half centuries, northern Europeans, led by Great Britain, had spent huge sums of money searching for a navigable sea route across the top of North America, believing, initially, that such a route would give them trading access to the fabled riches of China. Since the 1570s, when Martin Frobisher identified two possible Atlantic entrances (Hudson and Davis straits), the quest for this Northwest Passage had proven fatal to hundreds. In 1611, for example, Henry Hudson had been set adrift in a lifeboat by a mutinous crew, never to be seen again; eight years later, Jens Munk lost all but two of his 63 men to scurvy and starvation; and in 1719, James Knight disappeared into the Arctic forever with two ships and 37 men.

Those it did not kill, the Passage frequently destroyed in other ways. In the 1740s, Christopher Middleton saw his reputation demolished by armchair experts after he failed to find a waterway leading west out of Hudson Bay; in the next century, after mistaking an Arctic mirage for a non-existent mountain range in Lancaster Sound, John Ross not only suffered relentless derision, but failed to receive another naval commission.

This last debacle was part of a renewed campaign that arose after 1815, when Britain defeated France at Waterloo. In 1809, at the height of the Napoleonic wars, the British navy was the most powerful in history, with 773 ships, 4,444 officers, and 140,000 sailors. By 1818, however, the Admiralty could use only 121 ships and 19,000 crewmen. Regular sailors were discharged, but what to do with all those excess naval officers, most of whom continued to draw half-pay?

John Barrow, second secretary to the Admiralty, renewed the quest for the Northwest Passage. Commercial interest had long since evaporated, but Barrow—a visionary who would guide British exploration from 1804 to 1845—justified the endeavour as advancing scientific knowledge and also on the grounds of national pride: would it not be a scandal if, after the English had tried for centuries, those arrogant, upstart Russians were the ones finally to solve the mystery?

John Barrow guided Arctic exploration for more than forty years

By the early 1840s, largely as a result of Barrow's obsessive drive, but also because the Hudson's Bay Company began mapping the Arctic coastline of North America, the Passage had taken shape as two parallel channels extending respectively from the Atlantic and Pacific oceans and needing only to be linked by a short, vertical third channel. The Lords of the Admiralty felt that the final discovery lay within easy reach, especially given recent advances in technology. One more expedition would almost certainly resolve the mystery—but who should lead it? Who should be given the opportunity to shower glory on himself and England?

Discussion, debate, and ferocious lobbying narrowed the field to half a dozen candidates, among them—though near the bottom—Sir John Franklin, who had recently returned to England after a six-year stint as governor of Van Diemen's Land (now Tasmania). A veteran Royal Navy officer with a surprising literary flair, Franklin had turned his disastrous Arctic expedition of 1819–22, during which he lost eleven of twenty men, into a best-selling book. Famous as "the man who ate his shoes" in the Arctic, he became a British hero and, in 1829, received a knighthood.

Now, however, Franklin was 59, overweight and famously ruled by his formidable wife, Lady Jane Franklin. Having been recalled from Van Diemen's Land after being censured for incompetence—though perhaps unjustly—this fading hero, bent on restoring his tarnished name, would by all reports "die of disappointment" if he failed to gain the leadership of the vaunted expedition. But what of that? Others would die of disappointment if he succeeded.

The odds ran heavily against Franklin. Those odds, however, neglected to factor into account the hidden resolve and invisible puppeteering of Lady Jane Franklin. Suffice to say that in May of 1845, when England sent the most expensive naval expedition ever mounted down the River Thames and westward across the Atlantic to solve the final riddle of the Northwest Passage, Sir John Franklin was at the helm.

Franklin's two state-of-the-art ships, the *Erebus* and the *Terror*, had been reinforced against the pack ice and fitted with twenty-horse-power steam engines, hot-water heating systems, and retractable screw propellers. Both vessels carried daguerrotype cameras, libraries of 1,200 books, hand organs that played fifty tunes, and enough provisions for three years. These supplies included canned soups and meats that, hastily prepared by an unscrupulous merchant who had cut every possible corner, would almost certainly bring on lead poisoning and botulism—though nobody could have guessed that at the time.

Following the usual practice, Franklin stopped at Stromness to draw fresh water from Login's Well. He dined with leading Orcadians, among them members of John Rae's family, including his mother. He stayed overnight at the home of Rae's sister Marion and her husband, a doctor named John Hamilton. He then crossed the Atlantic to Disko Island, Greenland, and from that sheltered haven sent home four men, mainly for illness. He had left England two months earlier with 132 men; on July 12, he left Greenland with 128.

Toward the end of July, while he waitied at the entrance to Lancaster Sound for the pack ice to melt, Franklin tethered his ships to a massive iceberg, where he exchanged greetings with two whaling captains.

Franklin sent four men home from Disko Island, Greenland

After that, Sir John Franklin disappeared.

By 1847, his friends, relatives, and fellow naval officers had grown worried. They began discussing search-and-rescue operations. Sir John Richardson volunteered to lead a small party down the Mackenzie River to the Arctic coast. He had served with Franklin on his two overland expeditions (1819–20 and 1825–27) and had married a niece of the lost captain, Mary Booth (she died in 1845 after giving him seven children). The Admiralty approved Richardson's plan and sent four boats and twenty men to York Factory—the sappers, miners, and sailors John Rae had encountered when he arrived there in 1847 after wintering in Repulse Bay.

Now fifty-nine, Richardson had not expected ever to return to the Arctic, which he had last seen in 1827. For years he had lived sixty miles south of London, near Portsmouth, where he was chief medical officer at Haslar, the largest hospital in the world, and, incidentally, the largest brick building in the British Empire. Richardson knew he needed a competent travelling companion to serve as second officer. He found himself sifting through applications from hundreds of gentlemen of various ranks and professions, all of them eager, none of them especially qualified. On the first of November, 1847, Richardson read a report in the *Times*, a report written by the fur-trading doctor John Rae, who had recently returned to England after fourteen years in the wilds.

In that report, written originally for the HBC, Rae described in pedestrian, matter-of-fact prose how he had led a dozen men north to map the last remaining section of unexplored North American coastline. He had wintered at Repulse Bay, living off the land rather than relying on imported provisions, and then charted 655 miles of new land and coastline, incidentally demonstrating that Boothia Felix was a peninsula not an island and that no Northwest Passage flowed west out of the Gulf of Boothia.

On reading this report at his home, a separate residence situated within the hospital grounds, Richardson jumped to his feet and cried out to his wife, "I have found my companion, if I can get him." He arranged to meet Rae, marvelled at his enterprise—doctor, fur trader, Arctic explorer, and only 34 years old—and invited him to serve as second officer. For his part, as a young man of science, Rae knew Richardson to be England's finest naturalist; and as a lover of exploration literature, he had read about the older man in Franklin's first published narrative and vividly remembered the courage and generosity Richardson had demonstrated. For form's sake, Rae briefly considered the invitation. But already the search for Franklin had become a national obsession: Who could refuse?

While Richardson secured the necessary permissions from the Admiralty and the HBC, Rae visited friends and relatives in Orkney. Most of his time he spent with his mother, to whom he regularly sent part of his income, and who in turn could never quite conceal that, of her eight children who had lived beyond infancy, John had always been her favourite. To his original sponsor, Sir George Simpson, Rae wrote apologizing for having accepted the expeditionary appointment without first consulting him. Rae well knew that Simpson might have demurred, preferring "that I should not be employed in the way of discovery unconnected with the Fur Trade."

He softened the disclosure by sharing confidences, observing that the "great men at the House [of Commons] speak to a poor fellow from Hudson's Bay more as if he was a dog than a fellow creature; indeed, Governor Pelly said when I happened to mention that I was coming to Town in the latter part of January that he supposed it was 'to be shown about like a wild beast,' a compliment which I fully appreciated coming from so high a quarter."

In conversations, Rae observed that Franklin and his men had taken enough provisions to last until July of 1848. No aid could now reach them before that date, and the men would soon be on short rations unless they had managed to obtain fresh provisions from the sea, from the land, or both.

Rae heard one distinguished gentleman, who had once been on an Arctic expedition on which there was no need for the men to obtain their own food, assert, "Wherever the native can live, there the civilized man can also maintain himself." He could only shake his head. Such statements, he knew, might reassure the public, but they were true only in a limited sense. To anyone who cared to listen, Rae would explain that reindeer, or caribou, and muskox are not easily hunted because they are shy of hunters, especially if they have migrated from the south. In winter, they are still more difficult to approach because snow fills the ravines and hollows, leaving even an expert hunter no means of concealing himself. The natives had learned to trap deer in pitfalls dug in the snow, a highly specialized technique. With seals, Rae would add, the problems for "civilized man" were still greater. At Repulse Bay, while the Inuit were bringing in one or more seals a day, the excellent Cree hunter Nibitabo could not obtain even one: the animals always managed to plunge under the ice and swim away, even if they were mortally wounded.

Rae knew well that Franklin was probably facing far worse difficulties than the British public could imagine. But where? Some naval officers believed that Franklin might have sailed north up Wellington Channel after entering Barrow Strait. But at meetings of the Arctic Council, most argued that he had probably become trapped after turning south in the vicinity of Prince of Wales Island. This meant that his ships would be found somewhere within a vast, unexplored quadrilateral whose four corners were bounded roughly by Cape Walker and regions then known as King William Land, Wollaston Land, and Banks Land—an area of seventy thousand square miles.

Late in 1847, the Admiralty modified Richardson and Rae's

At meetings of the Arctic Council, experts debated the whereabouts of Franklin:
Sir John Richardson points at the map

Mackenzie River expedition by adding two additional searches by sea. One ship, the *Plover*, would enter Arctic waters from the west through Bering Strait and send boats eastward along the top of the continent toward the mouth of the Mackenzie River. The other search would include two ships, the *Enterprise* and the *Investigator*, under veteran mariner James Clark Ross, who in 1831 had reached the north magnetic pole, a slowly moving point then located near the west shore of Boothia Peninsula. Now, his two ships would proceed through Lancaster Sound and follow different routes south. Rae and Richardson were to leave provisions in various coastal areas for the use of naval parties detached from these vessels.

Before leaving London, Rae received a Scottish plaid from Lady Richardson and a sewing kit and a book of sacred verse from Sir John Franklin's daughter, Eleanor. Lady Jane Franklin, a well-experienced traveller in her fifties, had volunteered to join the expedition, but

Richardson had convinced her that her presence would place the party "in a number of disagreeable situations during long and rough voyages."

On March 25, 1848, Rae and Richardson sailed out of Liverpool on the mail steamer *Hibernia*. They reached New York on April 10, travelled north to Montreal by steamship, and spent three days with Sir George Simpson at his stone mansion in nearby Lachine. Anxious to begin their search, they left separately for Sault Ste. Marie. Richardson travelled in the steamer *British Empire* and Rae took passage in the *Canada*, supervising eleven Iroquois and French Canadian *voyageurs* who would form the backbone of a canoeing crew of sixteen.

On May 4, Rae and Richardson, reunited, paddled northwest out of Sault Ste. Marie, hugging the coast of Lake Superior, the so-called King of Lakes, which Richardson rightly described as occupying nearly as much space as the whole of England. The two leaders travelled in separate canoes, each with eight *voyageurs*, and followed the usual fur-trade route. Rae would have found this journey easier than the last time he passed this way, just three years before, when, heading north to York Factory after learning surveying in Toronto, he paddled alone during a more dangerous season.

This time, a typical day would begin at first light, around half past three in the morning. Rae would roust the men, who would quickly roll up their blankets and trudge to the water's edge. The chief *voyageur* and the *gouvernail*, or helmsman, would put the canoes into the water. The men would stow the luggage, climb in, and set out paddling by four o'clock. If the wind was moderate and the sky clear, a *voyageur* who could carry a tune would launch into a song, the others joining in on the chorus.

Around eight or nine o'clock, when he spotted a favourable spot, Rae would signal the breakfast stop. The men would land and unload the canteen: kettle, plates, knives, spoons, teapot, cups. From the surrounding forest, they would chop down two or three small trees. Having reduced these to firewood, they would cook breakfast over a

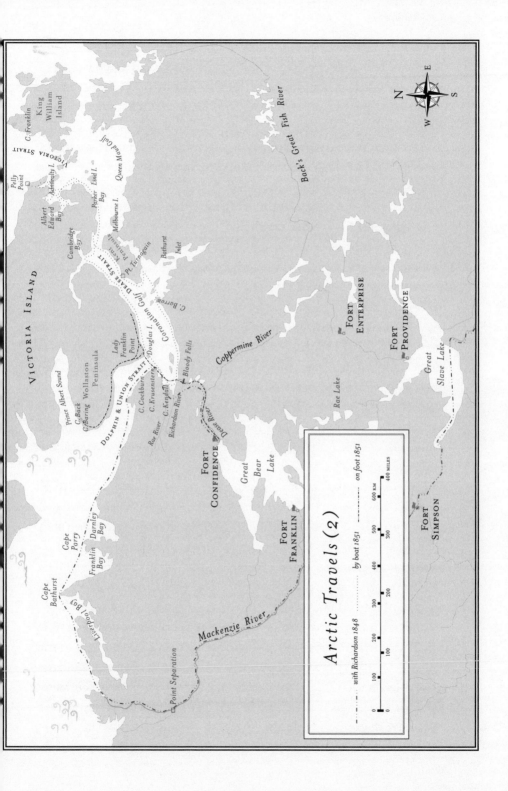

Arctic Travels (2)

— · — · — with Richardson 1848 ⋯⋯⋯⋯ by boat 1851 — — — — on foot 1851

| 0 | 100 | 200 | 300 | 400 | 500 | 600 KM |
| 0 | 100 | 200 | 300 | 400 MILES | | |

N · E · S · W

VICTORIA ISLAND

King William Island

C. Franklin

Pelly Point

VICTORIA STRAIT

Admiralty I.

Albert Edward Bay

Parker Bay

Lind I.

Queen Maud Gulf

Back's Great Fish River

Cambridge Bay

Melbourne I.

Kent Peninsula

Pt. Turnagain

Bathurst Inlet

DEASE STRAIT

C. Barrow

Coronation Gulf

FORT ENTERPRISE

FORT PROVIDENCE

Prince Albert Sound

Lady Franklin Point

C. Back

C. Baring

Wollaston Peninsula

Douglas I.

C. Cockburn

C. Krusenstern

C. Kendall

Bloody Falls

Coppermine River

Rae Lake

Great Slave Lake

DOLPHIN & UNION STRAIT

Rae River

Richardson River

Dease River

FORT CONFIDENCE

Great Bear Lake

Cape Parry

Darnley Bay

Franklin Bay

FORT FRANKLIN

FORT SIMPSON

Cape Bathurst

Liverpool Bay

Mackenzie River

Point Separation

blazing fire. For all this, Rae allowed one hour. Then it was back into the canoes. At about two o'clock, Rae would call for a second break on shore—just half an hour this time, for a cold lunch.

At seven or seven-thirty in the evening, Rae would give the signal to stop and camp for the night. Certain men would carry the lading ashore, then remove the canoes from the water and make any necessary repairs. Others would pitch tents, laying floors with the small, flat branches of the endlessly abundant fir trees. Still others would cut wood and get a fire blazing, over which they would cook supper, usually ham and eggs, biscuit and butter, washed down with copious amounts of steaming hot tea. Rae and Richardson would sit around the fire chatting with the *voyageurs* before retiring to write in their journals and read by lantern light, Richardson turning to the Bible, Rae (most often) to Shakespeare.

After eight days and nights of this relatively comfortable routine, the men reached Fort William (now Thunder Bay) and turned north up the Kaministiquia River. Now the journey became more arduous, with the *voyageurs* making forty portages in the ascent to the head of the Lake Superior watershed and almost forty more while canoeing downriver to Lake Winnipeg. Rolling granite hills gave way to woods of white-barked birch and weeping willow, to forests of dark green pine and tapering larch alive with crimson flowers. Through this rugged wilderness, Rae pushed the men to unusual speed by the force of his example.

The party travelled up treacherous Lake Winnipeg without incident and then made the trip from Norway House to Cumberland House on the Saskatchewan River in eight days, arriving on June 13. At last, having travelled 2,880 miles from New York City—including 1,390 from Sault Ste. Marie in forty-one days—they caught up with Chief Trader John Bell and the twenty British servicemen who, having descended from York Factory, would accompany them on their search expedition. Rae gathered these men, asked a few questions, and grew concerned at their lack of preparedness: This was the crew? These the men with whom he was to confront the fierce and unforgiving Arctic? The next day, when he led the party north and west toward Methy

Portage and saw how the servicemen conducted themselves on the river, Rae felt his initial concern deepen almost to alarm.

One sunny day early in July, John Rae climbed to the highest point at Methy Portage, called the Cockscomb, and stood looking out over the valley of the Clearwater River. He had never passed this way before but had long known that Methy Portage, also called Portage La Loche after the lake at its east end, was the longest, most challenging carrying place in Rupert's Land—essentially a twelve-mile marathon winding past two small lakes with a difficult descent into the Clearwater Valley at the northwest end.

Here, standing on the ridge that separates the Churchill and

HBC employees would enjoy little respite,
even at major portages

Athabasca river systems that flow, respectively, east and north, Rae found that the famous view was all he had expected. He found a shady spot and sat down with his journal, quill pen, and ink, his back against a stump. Looking out, he reached, uncharacteristically, for eloquence: "The beautiful effect of light and shade on the variously coloured foliage, the undulations of the sides of the valley and the pure water showing itself here and there over and between the branches of the trees looking like sheets of polished silver produce a scene which I have seldom or never seen surpassed."

Never mind the mosquitoes, hovering in clouds around his head.

But even this spectacular view, the finest in Rupert's Land, failed to quiet Rae's uneasiness. While still at Cumberland House, Rae had written a confidential letter to Sir George Simpson expressing his misgivings. Neither the men nor the four boats sent from England were well-suited to the work that lay ahead. Also, Rae and Albert One-Eye, an Inuit interpreter in his early twenties (who had both eyes), were expected as the expedition's only hunters to provide enough food for more than a dozen travellers.

Now, hearing the sound of men cursing and grumbling, Rae watched with impatience as a group of servicemen staggered up the broad slope, struggling under loads that most *voyageurs*—and, indeed, he himself—could easily have doubled. They were so ragged and dirty-looking that he had complained to Richardson about it: "A party of wretched Orkneymen is more respectable-looking!" The older man had explained that the servicemen were issued only a single suit of clothes each year, and Rae, on their behalf, felt disgusted with the Royal Navy.

He fretted about the men's appearance mainly because it suggested a more general lack of preparedness. During his fifteen years in Rupert's Land, Rae had worked with First Nations, French Canadians, Métis, and Scottish half-breeds, all of them accustomed to the hard labour of the fur trade. He had internalized a set of standards against which he could not help measuring the recently arrived servicemen. These miners and sappers might understand fortifications, but they knew nothing of canoes, boats, and portages. True, they had covered the 600 miles from Cumberland House in fourteen days, an average of forty-three miles per day. But that was an easy run, and now they had spent seven days at Methy Portage when Rae knew for a fact that a first-class crew of this size could easily have transported the provisions and four boats in half that time, with or without horses.

Worse, Rae had not yet seen the Coppermine River, but he knew both from reading and from first-hand reports that it was one of the most tumultuous and treacherous rivers that flowed to the Arctic coast. He and Richardson were to explore that coast east of the mouth of the Mackenzie and then ascend the lower part of the Coppermine. With a group of experienced hands, like those who had accompanied him on his first expedition, Rae would have felt no qualms. But with these sappers and miners? Batting away mosquitoes, shaking his head, he started back down the trail to camp.

After eight days at Methy Portage, Rae led the expedition through Fort Chipewyan on Lake Athabasca to Fort Resolution on the Slave River, arriving on July 15. There he divided the party, sending Chief Trader John Bell with several men due north to Fort Confidence on Great Bear Lake, there to prepare winter quarters for the entire party.

Rae and Richardson, with the remaining eighteen men and three boats (not counting the inflatable Halkett boat), crossed Great Slave Lake and started northwest down the mighty Mackenzie River. Worried by the lateness of the season—at the Arctic coast, the onset of freezing would terminate any boat travel—Rae demanded speed. The Mackenzie is one-half mile wide at its narrowest, and so he felt safe in pressing on through fog and darkness, landing only to cook supper and trusting the current to carry the three boats clear of shoals and low islands. Rae used these supper stops to deposit provisions along the riverbank for the possible use of naval search parties.

Forced by a racketing lightning storm to camp ashore one night, the explorer found himself rudely awakened when a gale-force wind blew down the tent he shared with Richardson. He had to shout some servicemen awake to help him restore it. Otherwise, the expedition rolled along without incident, reaching the Arctic coast on August 3, 1848. From Sault Ste. Marie, averaging an astonishing forty miles per day, Rae had completed the 3,616-mile journey in ninety days—one of the fastest long-distance canoe-and-boat journeys ever recorded.

The British Admiralty had expressed a hope that if Rae and Richardson reached the Arctic coast early in August, they would explore the western and southern shores of Wollaston Land (now known to be a peninsula adjoining Victoria Island) while travelling east to the mouth of the Coppermine. As they left the Mackenzie River bent on doing precisely that, more than 150 Inuit arrived in kayaks and multi-person oomiaks. They overtook and stormed the slowest of the three expedition boats and began to steal anything that was not tied down. Rae turned around and headed back. He ordered his men to fire their muskets in the air, and the thieves fled—though some followed at a distance for an hour, making sure the white men had departed.

Rae later addressed the differences between the Mackenzie River Inuit, who "have always been so turbulent and aggressive," and those who lived farther east in the vicinity of King William Land. He surmised that the former were hostile not only because their greater numbers made aggression feasible, but also because the only Europeans they encountered regularly provided guns to their bitter, hereditary enemies, the Loucheux. Nevertheless, "These Eskimos are the most daring and impudent scoundrels I ever saw, and I could not help longing to punish some of them; but prudence prevented this as it was most requisite to consider what would be the consequences of such an act, should some less well-armed white people fall into their hands."

Rae and Richardson travelled east along the coast of what is today called Tuktoyaktuk Peninsula. Luckily, they encountered no ice until August 11, when they passed Cape Bathurst, roughly one-quarter of the way to the Coppermine River. As the party continued eastward and Richardson the naturalist drew plants, Rae tried his hand at pen-and-ink landscapes, capturing Cape Parry (from inside a bay) and then the foreboding Cape Lyon. Except for a view of Fort Confidence, these would become the explorer's only surviving sketches.

Now broken ice made progress slow, and Rae went ashore to hunt

Inspired by Richardson, Rae sketched Cape Lyon (above) and Cape Parry

deer. Richardson observed, "In this quarter a skilful hunter like Mr. Rae could supply the whole party with venison without any loss of time." One afternoon, nine friendly Inuit paddled alongside, and Rae wrote, "They told us through our good interpreter Albert (who although brought from the east coast of Hudson Bay some thousand miles distant perfectly understood them) that they were out for the purpose of catching whales. They had evidently abundance of food, for each kayak had a quantity of fresh venison on deck."

As August wore on and the short Arctic summer neared its end, ice conditions worsened and dispelled any notion of crossing Dolphin and Union Strait to Wollaston Land. To make progress, the British servicemen were compelled to portage, carrying provisions and dragging the boats across large ice floes and boulder-strewn outcroppings of land. Never a patient man, Rae grew increasingly irritated as the sappers and miners habitually carried light loads—certainly not half of what an HBC man would carry—thus doubling the distance to travel and wasting precious time:

I felt so annoyed at seeing a great strong man walking off with perhaps one or at most two oars on his shoulder, that occasionally I used to take up all the oars, the mast, and poles of a boat at one time, not a heavy load, and carry them over the portage with ease. This had some little effect but not much. At length, however, pure fear of being frozen in or snowed up caused them to exert themselves and they did sometimes work with energy.

On August 28, travelling through a snowstorm, Rae and Richardson reached Cape Krusenstern and cached eight blocks of pemmican. The previous day, at a likely spot on the coast, they had left one of their three boats along with ten blocks of pemmican, hoping against hope that these would serve survivors of the Franklin expedition. By the time they reached Icy Cove, eight miles short of Cape Kendall, the two remaining boats were badly damaged, barely seaworthy—just as Rae had anticipated. Thick pack ice prevented further progress by water. The expedition had run out of time. On September 1, Rae reluctantly accepted that he had no choice but to abandon the two boats and proceed overland.

While a light snowfall swirled around them, Rae and Richardson discussed the implications of this action. Rae reiterated that during the coming winter, Inuit hunters would almost certainly discover and dismantle the abandoned boats for their valuable iron. That would leave the expedition with a single boat, the one in which Chief Trader John Bell and his men had travelled to Fort Confidence. To complete the stated objectives the next summer—portaging overland and then crossing the strait to Wollaston Land—would require at least six men. In a single boat, that left room for one officer. Who would it be?

As Richardson wrote later, "Setting all personal considerations aside, and looking solely to the means of providing for the examination of as large a portion of the Arctic Sea as could be accomplished, I had no hesitation in deciding in favour of Mr. Rae. His ability and zeal were unquestionable; he was in the prime of life and his personal activity and his skill as a hunter fitted him peculiarly for such an enterprise."

*

Rae spent two days organizing the overland march to winter quarters at Fort Confidence. He divided the requisite supplies into roughly equal loads of thirteen days' food, mainly pemmican, plus cooking utensils, hatchets, astromical instruments, a few books, ammunition, two nets, and the inflatable Halkett boat. On Sunday morning, after everybody had breakfasted, Sir John Richardson led a six o'clock prayer commending the expedition to the care of the Almighty. Rae found the brief service impressive. Standing with his head bowed, a gun on his shoulder and a load on his back, he thought of the Covenanters of old and how they worshipped in the glens and on the hillsides, prepared at a moment's notice either to fight with or flee from their persecutors.

The prayer finished, Rae led the way south toward the Coppermine River. He had distributed the seventy-pound loads by lot to preclude grumbling and warned the men to be careful of the pemmican because they did not have a day's ration to spare. At the outset, Rae carried almost as much as the labourers—roughly fifty-six pounds of instruments and ammunition. But after trudging three or four days over snow-covered hills and half-frozen swamps, he toted more, because most men carried provisions that were slowly consumed. In addition, Rae often killed game which he and Albert One-Eye lugged to camp.

To start, even Richardson, inspired by Rae, carried a light load. But then the sixty-year-old suffered heart spasms and cramps while climbing a hill dotted with half-frozen holes of water. This dropped him to his knees, and for a while Rae feared the older man could not continue. After a short rest, however, Richardson resumed hiking, and Rae distributed his burden among the servicemen.

Rae had issued leather to all the men so that they could repair their moccasins and save their feet. He handled his own repairs and Richardson's, and he saw Albert One-Eye doing the necessary. But he noticed that the servicemen didn't bother to mend their footwear, which only increased his disdain for them: Would they never learn?

The expedition arrived at a large, unknown river. Richardson, showing a fine sense of occasion but no awareness that native peoples might already have labelled the entire area, dubbed it Rae River after his "active, zealous and intelligent companion Mr. Rae, as a testimony of my high sense of his merits and exertions." On the far side of the river, a party of Inuit had erected ten tents. Rae and Albert One-Eye went to the riverbank and attracted attention. Several Inuit men paddled across the wide, fast-flowing river and, when Albert addressed them in their own language, happily landed. They proved to be extremely friendly and at once retrieved four kayaks. They lashed these together in a time-tested manner, two by two, and made five separate trips hauling the Halkett boat and ferrying Rae, the men, and all the luggage to the other side.

The party spent the rest of the day hiking to the Richardson River. With no Inuit in the vicinity, Rae decided to make camp for the night. The fast-flowing Richardson River, over 150 yards wide, is far too deep to ford. In the morning, Rae loaded his gear into the inflatable Halkett boat and, dragging a rope and using tin plates for paddles, started across. On reaching the far shore, he discovered that one of the servicemen, in fastening ropes together, had used a slip knot, which had come apart. As a result, young Albert One-Eye, who had come with Rae, was obliged to paddle back out into the river to regain the line. He found the water so cold on his hands that he had a terrible time making it back.

When the rope was secured, Rae ordered the men to haul the Halkett boat back and forth, carrying as much as two men and one hundred pounds of provisions with each crossing. This worked well but took time, so Rae did not reach the Coppermine River until September 5. By then, snow covered the ground. The explorer had come prepared, however. Donning snowshoes, he led the way a short distance up the Coppermine to the Kendall River. There, surrounded by woods, he ordered a raft built. He used this to cross the Kendall and then led the way west toward Fort Confidence. Gradually ascending, the expedition entered a thick fog that reduced visibility almost to zero. Rae led using his compass, the other men following in single file. In his journal, Richardson described the trek:

I kept rather in the rear, to pick up stragglers; but though we walked at a much brisker pace than usual, there was little loitering. The danger of losing the party made the worst walkers press forward. On the hills the snow covered the ground thickly; and it is impossible to imagine anything having a more dreary aspect than the lakes which frequently barred our way. We did not see them until we came suddenly to the brink of the rocks which bounded them, and the contrast of the dark surface of their waters with the unbroken snow of their borders, combined with the loss of all definite outline in the fog, caused them to resemble hideous pits sinking to unknown depth.

Although the party was slowed by snow showers, Rae forged ahead through the treeless, granite landscape until half past five. Arriving at a large convex rock from which the wind had swept the snow, he gave the signal to make camp. Without fuel to build a fire, the men went to bed supperless, complaining of hunger. Rae and Richardson slept side by side on their plaids, covered by two blankets and an oilcloth. Some of the men had even less bedding.

The next day, the party entered a small forest. While everybody else rested, Rae bagged geese, partridge, and even a deer. The venison, especially, was in fine condition. It afforded a pleasant change from the never-ending pemmican and put an end to the campfire grumbling. Rae could have shot more deer, given time, because they were not particularly shy. He concluded that the Inuit did not hunt them in this neighbourhood.

During the ascent of the Coppermine, Rae was amused one evening by a conversation he overheard among some servicemen:

A fat young fellow named Dodd, whilst toasting himself over a good fire, made of a stick or two of weed we have fortunately picked up, express[ed] to a companion with much feeling the fear he entertained ... of catching rheumatism from having got his feet or rather the soles of his moccasins slightly wet whilst standing on the ice. To one who had been wet for days together without intermission, the croaking of the young man was irresistibly ludicrous. This feeling of taking immense care of themselves was very general among the men ...

Now, after a long day's march, Rae was less amused to discover that a block of pemmican, a full day's ration for the entire expedition, had · been deliberately left behind in the woods as too heavy. "Too heavy?"

he cried in front of the campfire, looking skyward and commencing to pace back and forth. "I don't believe this! I will tell you men one thing: if anything like this should happen again, I will take Sir John and Albert One-Eye and leave the rest of you to your own devices. You can starve to death for all I care. I can easily support the three of us through hunting, and you already know we can easily outwalk you. We will simply depart and leave the lot of you to make your own way to Fort Confidence, if you can."

6

NORTHERN REVERSALS

At Fort Confidence, situated on a rise thirty feet from the north shore of Great Bear Lake, John Rae could look out through a parchment window at a large island about three-quarters of a mile distant—a large, well-forested island, roughly 120 feet high at its centre—that provided plenty of wood for both burning and building. On arriving at the fort in September 1848, Rae had been pleased to discover that his fur-trade lieutenant, Chief Trader John Bell, had overcome unexpected obstacles to construct comfortable winter quarters. Competence, at last!

With characteristic foresight, Rae had sent the methodical chief trader here in mid-July, from Fort Resolution on the Slave River. Bell had arrived to find that most of the original buildings, constructed by William Dease and Thomas Simpson in 1837–38, had burned to the ground. A cabin for the men remained standing, along with two great chimneys from the main dwelling house. Lacking nails, the resourceful Bell had set his men to work using little-known dove-tailing techniques.

First they built a good-sized storehouse out of squared logs, filling the spaces with tempered clay; next, around the existing chimneys, they constructed a main dwelling that measured forty feet by fourteen. It had a central dining hall (fourteen feet by sixteen), a storeroom, and three small sleeping apartments. The great hall served as both dining room and meeting area and also accommodated any visiting natives.

Even with the separate loghouse for the labourers, Fort Confidence could not accommodate forty-two souls, and numbers were sure to rise during the winter when old and infirm natives would seek shelter. As a result, Rae sent three of Bell's men and thirteen of the British service-men to winter at Big Island on Great Slave Lake. He then dispatched two HBC men south carrying mail. That left twenty-four men to winter at the fort.

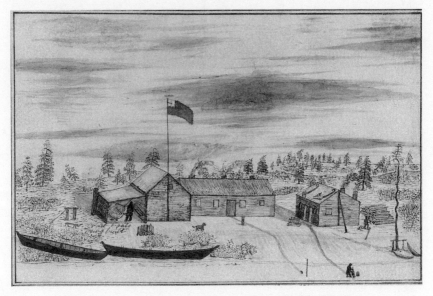

Fort Confidence, winter view, 1850–51—pen and ink by John Rae

Rae assessed the provisions, judged them plentiful, and allowed two meals a day: breakfast at 8 a.m. and supper at 4 p.m. The men ate white-fish, trout, venison, partridge, and hare, either roasted, boiled, or fried. On Thursdays and Sundays they added a dessert of plum, currant, or cranberry pudding, and on festive occasions they feasted on bread, pies, and tarts before dancing to fiddle music.

Rae employed four men as firewood cutters, each responsible for chopping one cord per day. Two men he assigned as sawyers, four as fishermen, and several others as haulers. He gave the reliable Albert One-Eye the task of maintaining the fire in the dwelling house where he lived with Richardson and Bell. To haul firewood, the expert Inuit man iced the runners of his sledge. Rae remarked that the icing enabled him to transport loads twice as heavy as those of the other men, "who very soon were glad to coax the fine young fellow (whom they previously rather treated with contempt) to prepare their sledges in the same manner."

The men also constructed a small observatory in which Rae and Richardson took meteorological observations every hour from seven in the morning until midnight. Richardson later wrote:

During the winter, Mr. Rae and I recorded the temperature hourly, sixteen or seventeen times a day; also the height of the mercury in Delacroix's barometer; the degrees of the aneroid barometer, the declinometer, and dipping-needle. Once in the month a term-day, extending to thirty-six hours, was kept, in which the fluctuations of the magnets were noted every two and a half minutes, and various series of observations were made for ascertaining the magnetic intensity with the magnetometer, the vibration apparatus, and Lloyd's dipping needle. Mr. Rae ascertained frequently the time and rates of the chronometers by observation of the fixed stars; and a register of the winds and weather and appearances of the aurora was constantly kept.

Over a century later, weather historian Tim Ball would observe that "no one kept more precise records than John Rae, the Arctic explorer."

Every day, between six and seven in the morning, Rae also checked a fox trap he built two miles from the buildings, calling the strenuous, four-mile hike a comfortable walk before breakfast. He stored the fox furs for the Company, while from the less desirable rat skins he fashioned a warm winter cap with ear flaps, which he wore outdoors constantly.

Men on snowhoes carried mail throughout the HBC territory, and from Sir George Simpson they brought a letter putting Rae in charge of the vast and challenging Mackenzie River District. The explorer received the news of this promotion with mixed feelings. Thirty-five years old, still unmarried, and acutely aware that Chief Factor Murdoch Macpherson had run that district for twenty-five years, Rae wrote to the governor, "I hope it is not your intention to keep me very long in Mackenzie River District, as I am becoming quite a grey-headed old fellow and it is high time for me to be thinking of looking out for a better half."

Over fifteen years earlier, Simpson had infamously evicted his country wife, Margaret Taylor—a woman who had given birth to several of his children—from her home at Red River Settlement after he married his teenage cousin and brought her unexpectedly from England. Exploiting that knowledge, and professing a cavalier attitude that was alien to him, Rae suggested that although he had enjoyed sexual relations with native women, he did not wish to marry one of them and spend the rest of his life in Rupert's Land.

He continued, "The womankind of the family have done their part in supplying her majesty with subjects and I do not wish that the male portion should be so far distanced in this respect. My brother Tom has got only one legitimate little Rae, Dick none, and myself not one either on the right or wrong side of the blanket that I am aware of." Indeed, Rae had begun to dream not only of taking a wife, but also of crossing the Atlantic to find her: "If permitted to visit England after returning from the sea next summer, I should like to proceed through Canada or the States, government of course paying the expense."

In the meantime, Rae invested energy in choosing the six men who would accompany him the following spring. Reports differ, but Rae's *Arctic Correspondence* indicates that he selected two Scots, Neil McLeod of Stornoway and Halcrow Humphrey of the Shetland Islands; two Protestant-educated Cree who regularly attended Richardson's Sunday sermons, namely James Hope, an experienced steersman who had travelled with Dease and Simpson, and his younger brother, Thomas Hope; a Canadian *voyageur* named Louis Lebrule or Dubrill; and the Inuit interpreter Albert One-Eye, whom Rae described to Sir George as "a very fine lad, fit for any of the usual duties of a labourer, and whom I intend to engage in that capacity for Mackenzie River District, should you have no objections. He would be useful in the event of it becoming desirable to have any negotiation with the Esquimaux at the mouth of the Mackenzie."

In December, Rae made a nine-day trek to discover a shorter route from Fort Confidence to the confluence of the Kendall and Coppermine rivers. In January, he repeated that exercise and believed he had succeeded. He shot ten deer on the first trip and four on the second.

In 1848–49, James Clark Ross searched Somerset Island,
leading sledge parties from HMS Enterprise

Spring arrived late that year, and in April, Rae sent two men ahead to place a depot of provisions, which included two bags of flour, ten pieces of pemmican, and some ammunition.

Meanwhile Richardson prepared to return to England, his spirits rising. Rae had enjoyed his company during the long winter, and marvelled at the older man's memory for poetry. Richardson could quote Burns and other authors by the hour, Rae wrote, and was "conscientious, honourable, with strong and warm feelings concealed under a cold exterior. He was a serene and true Christian without any bigotry or cant and composed during the expedition one or two of the best sermons I ever heard. . . . A perusal of his various narratives of Arctic travel will give the reader more scientific and useful information than the writings of all other Arctic travellers put together." By May, he would write, "I am happy to say that Sir John and I have been on the most friendly terms since we came here, and I shall much regret parting with him."

On May 7, 1849, Sir John Richardson and Chief Trader John Bell left Fort Confidence with all of the men but eight, leaving two to guard Fort Confidence and six to travel with Rae. Before Richardson departed, Rae elicited written instructions to seek Franklin along the shores of Wollaston Land and Victoria Land, to explore the strait believed to separate these places, to help any sailors who arrived from the *Enterprise* under James Clark Ross—and to abandon the quest, no matter what, at season's end. The hunt for Franklin notwithstanding, Rae never forgot the quest for the Northwest Passage:

Whilst attending to these primary objects, I hope, if moderately fortunate, by surveying some degrees of Latitude of the shores along which we pass, to simplify in great measure the question of a northwest passage, for should I get so far as the north coast of Banks Land, and find deep enough water all the way for ships of some hundred tons burden, it is evident that there is nothing but ice to prevent a passage being effected. . . . I think it will yet fall to the lot of the HBC to accomplish this long-attempted undertaking.

*

On June 9, 1849, Rae left one man at Fort Confidence and set out with seven others, one of whom would return to the fort with dogs and sleds. Spring had arrived later even than usual, and much of the Dease River remained frozen. The party had to haul the boat thirty miles over ice and land before reaching the Kendall River on June 21. Rae led his men down that river the next day, portaging and wading the boat through rapids, only to find the Coppermine still covered in ice.

After a week, as the ice broke up, Rae began to descend the Coppermine, reversing the route he had taken the previous fall. Game was plentiful. Rae himself shot ten deer, eight of them large bucks, two of which he killed with a single ball at a distance of 190 yards. One of the men shot three deer and the Hope brothers shot three more. In mid-July, Rae carefully navigated the treacherous Bloody Falls, so designated by Samuel Hearne in 1771 after the savage massacre there of twenty-two Inuit by his Chipewyan travelling companions.

Approaching the mouth of the river to which Richardson had given his name the previous autumn, Rae encountered ice blocking the way forward. With Albert and a local Inuit man, one of those who had played ferryman, Rae spent two days tracing the river westward for thirty miles. When he arrived back at camp, he found Coronation Gulf still clogged with ice. The following day, a fringe of open water appeared along the coast, and Rae embarked for Cape Kendall, hugging the shore.

On reaching the two boats he had abandoned in early September, Rae found them broken up for their iron, as expected—though the tents, oilcloths, pemmican, and other supplies remained untouched. Rae took two tents and the oilcloths and pressed on to Cape Krusenstern, where on July 30, a northeast breeze drove great chunks of ice forcibly against the shore, obliging him to unload the boat and haul it up onto a snowbank to save it from being destroyed.

From Cape Krusenstern, Rae hoped to cross the fast-flowing Dolphin and Union Strait to Wollaston Land; Douglas Island, halfway across, would serve as a convenient resting place. He set up camp on top of the cliffs and waited anxiously for the ice to clear. One tedious week went by and then a second. Every once in a while, a large pool of water would appear and Rae would prepare to embark, only to be thwarted when the wind and current drove ice back into the path.

Finally, on August 19, spying more open water than ever before, Rae and his men pushed out into the swirling floes. After sailing about one mile, they reached open water, applied their oars, and made rapid progress. They pressed on through a soupy fog, but after about eight miles, they came up against a driving stream of rolling ice floes that not only halted progress, but threatened to carry them past Douglas Island, now lost in the fog.

With visibility approaching zero, Rae gave the order to turn back.

The men rowed for their lives. One hour, two hours, three. Eventually, they emerged from the fog to encounter pack ice driven up against the coastline. At Rae's command, they debarked and hauled the boat half a mile, attaining the mainland several hundred yards south of their former camp. They had spent ten hours in this vain attempt to cross the strait, and driving masses of ice had nearly wrecked their boat several times. Hoping still to try again, Rae waited two more days, but a northeast gale blew up and jammed "our cold and perservering opponent in large heaps along the shore."

Tracking a canoe or a boat could be a dangerous enterprise

Finally, open water appeared to the south and southeast. Rae's orders stipulated that by August 25, the expedition should be back on the mainland. Two days before that deadline, Rae acknowledged that he had run out of time. Amid howling winds and driving rain, he gave the word to retreat: even if Sir John Franklin waited just across the channel, nobody was going to reach him on this occasion.

Rae led the way back to the Coppermine River and started up it.

At Bloody Falls, the steersman, James Hope, proposed to haul the boat through the whitewater rapids, saving the wear and tear of dragging it over a portage. Four men waded ashore, seized a line, and began tracking the boat upstream. "We had with ease surmounted the parts where there appeared any difficulty," Rae wrote later, "and had come to the upper end of the rapid where the current was strong but so perfectly smooth that it was the general opinion that a loaded boat might be safely taken up it; so little indeed was thought of there being any danger that the small line [not the large one] was given out to track with."

Halfway up the rapids, the steersman inexplicably panicked. Calling to the trackers to stop, he leapt ashore. Naturally, the bowsman followed. The light rope snapped as the boat swung broadside into the current and capsized. Thinking that the craft would get caught in one of the eddies, Rae raced downstream along the bank to a point of rock near which the boat might pass. Albert One-Eye followed his lead. By chance, the boat swirled to the bank where Albert stood and he managed to hook it by the keel with an oar. Rae ran around to assist him, jammed a pole into a broken plank in the hull of the boat, and cried, "Hold on! I'm coming round."

In the roar of the rapids, Albert may have misunderstood, or perhaps he believed he could achieve more by leaping onto the bottom of the boat—and so he did. The current immediately whirled the craft into a small bay. For an instant, Rae believed the worst was over. Not so, however, because the current now spun the boat into a whirlpool. While the vessel took water and quickly sank, Albert leapt for the safety of the rocks. He slipped, tumbled into the water, and spun beneath the surface.

Rae, horrified, stood knee-deep in the current and called, "Albert!"

He threw off his jacket, prepared to plunge into the river at the first sign of his friend. But the young interpreter never broke the surface. Rae and the other men raced up and down the river, increasingly desperate, looking for signs.

Albert One-Eye had disappeared.

*

The death of Albert One-Eye—the only man he would ever lose and a young man for whom he had cherished great hopes—haunted Rae to the end of his days. Rightly or wrongly, he never forgave the steersman, James Hope, for having precipitated the accident. And he never forgave himself for not having prevented the tragic mishap, although how he could have done so is difficult to imagine.

Rae had intended to retain Albert One-Eye and to groom him for long service with the Company. Now, withdrawing into the woods, he sat on a fallen tree and wept for the young man—for his eagerness and good humour, for his foolhardy bravery. Rae wept for the stupid accident that had cost Albert One-Eye his life.

With his expedition a failure, his last boat wrecked, and his best man lost, it was a morose John Rae who carried on to Fort Confidence. As always, he sought solace in activity. On September 2, the day after he reached the fort, he climbed into a York boat that had arrived from the south and, heavily laden with furs, set out for Fort Simpson on the Mackenzie River. Delayed en route at Cape McDonnell, Rae completed his report to Sir George: "I am sorry to say that we have been quite unsuccessful in the object of our voyage and I have to regret the loss of our excellent Esquimaux Interpreter Albert who was drowned at the Bloody Falls."

Rae's orders had expressly stated that the search expedition was not to be extended beyond the summer, and so he turned his thoughts to Company business—though he never forgot the Northwest Passage. While travelling up the Mackenzie, Rae responded to a letter from England in which Sir John Richardson offered to send him anything he might want. Besides several "volumes of useful and entertaining works," including a new collected Shakespeare, the explorer asked for a telescope, an aneroid barometer, an astronomical chart of the stars, and a good general atlas with all the latest discoveries.

Late in September 1849, Rae arrived at Fort Simpson and took charge of Mackenzie River District. The following week, somewhat to his dismay, Lieutenant W.J. Pullen of the Royal Navy turned up with seven men, having left six others at Fort McPherson while making his way up the Mackenzie. Pullen and his men were searching for

Franklin from HMS *Plover*, which had entered the Arctic from the west through Bering Strait. Rae welcomed them warmly, though he wrote to Richardson in England that the seamen, having expected to be away from their ship for no more than a month, had arrived in tattered rags, none of them carrying so much as a blanket.

Rae sent five of the new arrivals to winter at Great Slave Lake with the five men who had accompanied him north, whose presence now reminded him painfully of the absence of Albert One-Eye. Together with two marines, Pullen remained at Fort Simpson. Rae initially described the naval officer as a most agreeable man and a welcome addition to the small group wintering there; later he would observe that Pullen "seemed to expect too much and had a peculiar abruptness of manner and peremptoriness of tone which is not over agreeable to us half savages of the north."

Fort Simpson itself was even less comfortable than Fort Confidence. The house was the coldest Rae had ever lived in, excepting only his stone house at Repulse Bay and the miserable log shack on Charlton Island in which he had spent his first winter in Rupert's Land. The explorer observed that even having burned enough wood to keep a 300-horsepower steamer going for six months, the ink he used to write had frozen solid on the mantelpiece. During the Christmas season, the men had tried to make merry but faced a shortage of wine, grog, and women: "There were only three of the latter commodity and these were none of the best-looking, but I must do them the justice to say that they endured a power of dancing and tea."

Rae did not settle easily back into the business of fur trading. He got the district running more smoothly than before, but found the accounting and record-keeping tedious. As always, he was more interested in learning about the peoples around him—in this case, the Loucheux. Like the Esquimaux, with whom they had a difficult relationship, the Loucheux wintered in snowhuts, although they piled snow only halfway up the outside walls and lined the inside walls with fine branches. Many of them relied on bows and arrows instead of guns, and so remained independent of the white man. "These people continue to prefer their skin dresses and deerskin robes to woollen coats and blankets," Rae wrote, "showing I think great good sense in thus adhering to their old customs."

Rae had already written to Sir George requesting a leave of absence, during which he hoped to visit England and Orkney; after his recent hard work in the North, he had reason to believe this would be granted. Late in May 1850, as head of district, Rae travelled down the Mackenzie River to the Arctic coast to gather the furs collected during the winter at the lower forts. When he arrived back at Fort Simpson on June 10, he learned that two Company clerks had arrived a couple of days earlier with a shocking story to tell.

After dinner that evening, with the other senior men—the recently returned John Bell and the naval officers William Pullen and William Hulme Hooper—Rae sat down to hear the tale. James Stewart, an HBC man based at Fort Selkirk more than 1,100 miles away, had set out on snowshoes for Fort Simpson to determine why he had received no annual supplies—a quest that, to John Rae, made perfect sense. With three-quarters of the trek accomplished, Stewart called in to visit the small HBC station at Pelly Banks, where Pierre Pambrun was in charge. What Stewart discovered had clearly disturbed him.

Pambrun, whose father had been a chief trader, picked up the tale.

Late the previous November, while Pambrun and his two men were out hunting and fishing, Pelly Banks Station had burned to the ground. The blaze destroyed not only the buildings, but also furs worth over 800 pounds, leaving only three bales of furs and a bit of powder without shot. The men rebuilt the cabin into a rough shelter, but without food and clothing, suffered bitterly through a freezing cold December, living mostly on baling cord, leather, and marten furs—these last valuable but, as Rae knew, especially low in nutrition. The men even ate their own moccasins.

John Rae vaguely remembered having met Pambrun before, and having judged him a self-centred blowhard. He struggled to keep an open mind. Through the long, dark days of December, when the sun barely rose above the horizon, the three HBC men at Pelly Banks benefitted occasionally from the help of a native man encamped nearby—a man reduced to supporting his wife, young brother, and two small daughters by snaring rabbits and digging roots.

In January, Pambrun, a burly, active man and an experienced outdoorsman, decided out of compassion—he said—to leave what remained of the skins for his two companions and test whether he could survive by fishing in a lake that lay some days away.

Rae felt his mind spinning: had Pambrun actually deserted his men?

But Hooper, an inquisitive naval officer, wanted to know what Pambrun had eaten at the lake. Surprisingly, the man had kept a record. During fifty-seven days, while encamped nearby, he had devoured twenty fish, eighteen rabbits, eight partridges, ten squirrels, one fox, one raven, and one owl. Toward the middle of March, with spring on its way, he had made his way back to Pelly Banks Station and, to his dismay, found only one man still alive—William Foubister, a twenty-eight-year-old Orkneyman, who had been reduced to skin and bones. His companion, a French Canadian named Hyacinth Dubois, had died of starvation just eight days before.

Pambrun asked Foubister where the body was. He replied that he had cached it beneath some stones and the wolves had dragged it away. Pambrun noticed some bones in the hearth and young Foubister, catching his glance, hastened to explain that they were old caribou bones he had picked up while gathering firewood. Pambrun doubted this but decided to take the younger man at his word. With a view, he said, to acquiring some food, he visited the native man encamped two days away. This man told Pambrun that he, too, had seen the bones in the hearth—and that they were not caribou bones, but human: "The live man has eaten the dead."

When, after an absence of five days, Pambrun returned to Pelly Banks, he found William Foubister lying before a guttering fire, scarcely able to move. He chose not to confront him. During the next few days, he went hunting every morning, trying to loop partridges with a long pole and snare. He was usually gone for hours. But one morning, using a piece of birch fungus as tinder and a pointed green stick as shot, he managed to shoot a squirrel. Hurrying back to the cabin, he found a kettle boiling on the fire: "What's this?"

Foubister said, "I'm boiling water for tea."

When Pambrun checked the kettle with a spoon, however, he discovered not water for tea, but a thick, chunky broth—and in that broth, to his horror, something unmistakably human.

Now, at Fort Simpson, Pambrun said that this hideous discovery had paralyzed him, rendering him speechless. William Foubister, caught out in his unspeakable deed, cowered on the hearth, unable to meet the larger man's eyes.

Finally, Pambrun demanded, "Will you now confess?"

Foubister began to tremble.

Standing over him, Pambrun roared, "Will you confess that you have been eating poor Dubois!"

Trembling, the starving young man admitted that he had.

"Pierre, you don't understand," he blurted, bursting into tears. "I wanted to live not for myself but for the sake of my old mother, back home. I'm the only support she has, the only way she has of living."

Pierre Pambrun would not listen to another word. He would not remain in the cabin with this miserable wretch. Outside, he piled two days' worth of firewood and then, though Foubister pleaded with him to remain, he strode off into the woods.

When he returned to the cabin two days later, Pambrun found William Foubister lying dead on the hearth, his body stiff and cold, little more than a skeleton. Beside the corpse lay an open Bible and a kettle, empty and overturned.

John Rae had heard such stories before. He well knew that starvation could reduce even the strongest man to desperate measures. The last resort, when death became the only alternative, was to eat the flesh of dead human beings. Not long ago, he had talked with an old native fisherman who recalled a particularly harsh winter. He had visited Fort Norman seeking food, carrying the hands of his dead brother-in-law in his game bag—all that remained of the man.

Nonetheless, Rae found this latest tale distressing. Toward William Foubister, a fellow Orcadian, he felt far more compassion than outrage—though he perceived that some of the other men, William Hooper, for instance, reacted differently. What troubled Rae most, though, was his suspicion that this harrowing tragedy could have been averted. If the steadfast and generous James Stewart, instead of the selfish Pambrun, had been based at Pelly Banks, probably none of this would have happened. While he hesitated to condemn a man who had survived such an ordeal, Rae felt that Pambrun's conduct came perilously close to dereliction of duty—that the man had saved his own life at the cost of two lives for which he had been responsible.

And here, in response to Hooper's avid probing, Pambrun grew more self-righteous, his tale increasingly lurid. Rae felt repulsed: two HBC men had lost their lives! Poor, miserable wretches. He felt a desire to punish Pierre Pambrun—though any attempt to do so, he knew, would be futile. During the next few days, he would have to write a brief official report. Now he rose abruptly to his feet: "Gentlemen, I leave you to your catechism."

"What? Adjourning so early?"

"I work in the morning."

Glaring pointedly at Pambrun to communicate that one man, at least, had discerned the truth, Rae spun on his heel and strode out of the room.

In the HBC's northern district, the arrival of summer signalled the end of the annual fur-trading cycle. Traders stationed along the Mackenzie River had to begin transporting their furs upriver in June to catch the ships sailing for England from York Factory. Above Fort Simpson, in order to reduce the impact of blockages and traffic jams, those in charge would split the "Mackenzie Brigade" into two, giving half the boats a head start of several days.

On June 16, Rae sent Chief Trader John Bell up the Mackenzie with four well-laden boats. Four days later, he and Pullen followed with five more boats. The upriver journey, which involved endless portaging and tracking, inspired the navy man Hooper to assert that the poor HBC middlemen worked like dray horses: "I never saw toil

to equal, for endurance and severity, that of the Hudson's Bay
Company's servants during the
summer season." For nine days,
from two o'clock in the morning
until eight or nine o'clock at night
and sometimes later, Rae led his
men up the Mackenzie, halting
briefly for breakfast, eating dinner
only after landing at night, snack-
ing on pemmican when possible.

Sir Francis Beaufort
urged John Rae to still greater exertions

Rae anticipated that once
granted his requested leave, he
would keep right on travelling,
first across the continent to New
York City and then to England,
where perhaps he would find a
wife. On June 25, however, one day shy of Great Slave Lake, Rae
encountered two native canoeists carrying an "extraordinary express."
He went ashore to accept delivery, then sat on the banks of the broad,
fast-flowing river to read three communications.

The first came from Sir George Simpson at Lachine. Searchers had
found no trace of Sir John Franklin. England grew increasingly
alarmed. Both Rae and Pullen were to renew their searches immediately. Pullen was to return to the Arctic coast, "the manner and direction of any search being left to his discretion and judgement." As for
Rae, Simpson wanted him to travel farther north than ever before.

Reeling, Rae turned to the other two letters. From London, England,
Lady Jane Franklin expounded on this new directive in a friendly,
respectful, and indeed flattering manner:

[My anticipations were not] so extravagant as other people's, for it has been the
custom of people to throw upon you everything that others failed to accomplish—
'oh Rae's in that quarter, Rae will do that'—as if you and your single boat could
explore hundreds of miles NSE & West and as if no obstacles of any kind could

interfere.... Myself, I think that your quarter is by far the most promising of any, for it is the quarter to which my husband was most distinctly . . . directed to proceed, and where I have no doubt he directed his most strenuous efforts.

Also from London, Sir Francis Beaufort, the Admiralty's chief hydrographer (England's official mapmaker), contributed the final letter:

I cannot let the mail go without telling you how intensely fixed all eyes are upon you . . . [and] upon what is yet in your power, and in yours alone, to do next season. . . . Let me then, my dear Doctor, add my voice to the moans of the wives and children of the two unfortunate ships, and to the humane and energetic suggestions of your heart, and implore you to save neither money nor labour in fulfilling your holy mission. Two ships will sail in ten days for Bering Strait—others in spring for Baffin Bay. The Americans are preparing an expedition but to you I look for the solution of our melancholy suspense.

Having read the letters once through and exchanged a few words with Pullen, who was ecstatic about having been promoted to captain, Rae walked alone along the banks of the Mackenzie. He felt as low as he had ever felt in his life. His last expedition had ended in disaster. He had failed not only in his main objective, finding Franklin, but even in his secondary one of reaching Wollaston Land and perhaps discovering the final link in the Northwest Passage. Worst of all, he had lost Albert One-Eye—a fine, active young man, the loss of whom haunted him still.

About Franklin, missing now for five years, nobody could hope to discover good news. Rae had been dreaming not of returning to the Arctic but of travelling to England to seek a wife. Instead of strolling around Hyde Park with a pretty girl on his arm, he would soon be battling blizzards in the fierce, unforgiving North. As he stood looking over the Mackenzie River, swiping at the mosquitoes that swarmed around his head, John Rae wondered: Why, oh why, hadn't Franklin stayed home?

7

RUPERT'S LAND REALITIES

E arly in the summer of 1850, standing on the banks of the fast-flow-ing Mackenzie River, surrounded by men and York boats heavily laden with furs, and having received letters that made a mockery of his latest plans and projections, John Rae faced a pressing logistical prob-lem. Both he and Captain William Pullen had been ordered to return to the Arctic coast and resume the search for Franklin. However, Fort Simpson and the smaller trading posts farther down the Mackenzie had been depleted by recent visitors. Those forts could supply one party, perhaps, but certainly not two.

Sir George had promised to send men and provisions from Red River, which meant waiting. But Pullen faced no such obligation and Rae agreed that he should leave immediately. Two navy men injured the previous year were returning to England as invalids unfit for service. Rae replaced them with three HBC men, recommended two native hunters from Fort Good Hope, and loaned the commander an unusually large boat that he had built at Fort Simpson. Nine feet broad and thirty feet long on the keel (forty feet overall), this craft dwarfed the naval vessel. Pullen christened her *Try Again*.

On June 29, at Hay River on Slave Lake, having transferred and reorganized supplies, the two parties separated. Pullen and his second-in-command, William Hulme Hooper, with ten navy men, three HBC men, and two native hunters, started back down the Mackenzie toward the Arctic coast in the mighty *Try Again* and the small whale boat they had taken from HMS *Plover*. Rae generously gave Pullen the sextant, horizon, and chronometer that Richardson had left him in 1849 and

Rae would employ dogsleds in crossing the frozen Dolphin and Union Strait

authorized the navy man to clear the various forts of provisions, taking roughly 4,500 pounds of food and supplies and leaving only the small reserve necessary for Company business.

Pullen, revitalized by his promotion and confident that further exertions would pay dividends, proposed to travel east along the Arctic coast from the mouth of the Mackenzie to Cape Bathurst and then to sail north and explore Banks Land. Within two months, the experienced Rae would write with skepticism and concern,

From others I learn that Commander Pullen intends doing wonders this summer. His object is to reach Melville Island . . . and after that proceed to Port Leopold [on Somerset Island] where he expects to winter. If he does this, he will excel any expedition that has yet visited the Arctic Sea; at the same time I fear that if he attempts to push too far he will never be heard of again, although he has got two Fort Good Hope Indians as hunters.

From Fort Resolution on Slave Lake, on the day after he and Pullen parted company and just five days after receiving his new orders, Rae wrote to Sir George laying out a fully developed—indeed, brilliant—plan for his own next expedition. That autumn, with the men and supplies he received from Red River, he would travel north to Fort Confidence on Great Bear Lake. During the winter he would build two small boats. In the spring, having secured enough provisions mainly through hunting and fishing, he would undertake a two-part expedition.

First, before the ice thawed, Rae would lead a few men with dogsleds to the Arctic coast. He would cross the Dolphin and Union Strait on foot and explore the shores of Victoria Land and Wollaston Land, seeking the strait (the final link in the Passage?) that supposedly lay between them. Before spring thaw, he would recross the strait and travel not back to Fort Confidence, but to a provision station on the Kendall River near the coast. There he would meet a contingent of his men who would have brought the two boats that far.

Then, with a larger party, he would undertake the second part of the expedition by boat. He would descend the Coppermine River and, as the ice broke up, sail into Coronation Gulf and beyond. Rae expressed the hope that should he accomplish this double search, "neither the great men at the Admiralty nor their Honours in Fenchurch Street [HBC headquarters in London], will think that I

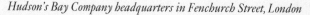

Hudson's Bay Company headquarters in Fenchurch Street, London

have been making a sinecure of my situation as person in charge of the Expedition." He added, "It will be requisite during the winter to renew my acquaintance with snowhouse architecture, to accustom my teeth to munch and my stomach to digest frozen pemmican and lastly to do with as little drink as possible."

Rae informed Sir George that for his second-in-command he had hired Hector Aeneas Mackenzie, an HBC man about to retire from Fort Norman, where he had been in charge: "He is very active and an excellent shot, and much liked by the men, whom he at the same time keeps in excellent order."

Rae proceeded south from Slave Lake to Methy Portage with his boatloads of furs. Travelling through lakes and rivers and over portages, he averaged thirty miles a day over the nine hundred miles from Fort Simpson. On July 20, 1850, during a relentless rainy spell, he arrived at the great fur-trade crossroads and found much of it reduced to a muddy bog. The oldest *voyageur* in his party had never seen the twelve-mile stretch in such deplorable condition.

Five days later, with the rain still pouring down, the fourteen promised men turned up. Hoping to receive some well-experienced hands, Rae was bitterly disappointed to discover neither a Scot nor a carpenter nor an interpreter nor even a sailor among the newcomers. Times were changing. Red River had become a flourishing, multiracial community, but many Métis, Scottish half-breeds, and natives had begun to resist the HBC monopoly on the fur trade, thus reducing the pool of skilled workers.

Now, faced with a shortage of horses but with a huge quantity of supplies to transport quickly, Rae ordered the newcomers to carry cargo to the middle station, only to discover that they had been explicitly exempted by contract from this onerous chore. When some of them flatly refused to go beyond their contractual obligations, Rae could hardly believe it. He discharged two men, transferred a third, and hired two new men on the spot: a Mackenzie River District interpreter, John Hebert dit Fabien, and an Orcadian boat builder named George Kirkness.

To Sir George, Rae fretted that "the amount of wages given was too small to induce the best class of men to engage; however, since these have come I must try and do the best I can with them, altho' I fear that will not be much." Rae also wrote to Chief Factor James Hargrave at York Factory—with whom, far from the man's wife, he had become quite friendly—and asked him to send several items, among them an inflatable Halkett boat and instruments to replace those he had given Pullen, as well as an Inuit interpreter if one were available in Churchill (none would be).

At Methy Portage, Rae had received an apologetic letter from Sir George acknowledging that he was "not yet to be released from this arduous service," while also informing him that he had been promoted to chief factor, effectively doubling his income. Rae was not assuaged. On the first of August, just before he departed for the Arctic, he wrote to thank his sponsor, but also to renew his heartfelt request for a leave of absence: "I will not pretend to be in bad health for I am not, but the continued anxiety which my various and ever-changing duties has caused me has affected my mind and memory so much that even I feel a great change for the worse in myself, so that if you cannot grant my request, I fear I shall be obliged to leave the service."

Rae sugarcoated what was essentially an ultimatum. He assured Sir George of his everlasting gratitude regardless of what the governor decided, but left no doubt that he was serious: "It is true that my means are not very great, and I cannot settle down as an idle gentleman to live on my property, but I have my profession and am not too lazy to attend sick people if I could find any foolish enough to trust me. If you can permit me a leave of absence I would try to come out to Red River on snow shoes after returning from the coast next summer."

On August 2, 1850, Rae left Methy Portage with Hector Mackenzie, fourteen men, and two women, the "country wives" of the interpreter and of Joseph Roy, another Mackenzie River District servant, originally from Quebec. Always flexible, Rae permitted the women to come, at least as far as Fort Confidence where he proposed to winter, because as well-adapted natives they would help rather than hinder the expedition. Still, he fretted that the party as a whole would prove extravagant, wasteful, and unable to endure privation: "I have little hope of doing much either for the credit of the company or myself unless circumstances are more than usually favourable—this however will not prevent me making every effort in the good cause and if the navigation is at all open on the coast in summer, we may be able to penetrate pretty far to the northward. 'Tis the spring journey over ice that I am doubtful of."

Rae's complaints about the men sent to him from Red River eventually earned a mild rebuke from Sir George. The explorer's dissatisfaction, expressed also in a letter to Sir John Richardson, found its way into *The Times*, which according to the governor "mortified [the HBC's John] Ballenden not a little, as he did his utmost to procure the best men that could be got—sparing neither wages nor fair promises. When fault must be found ... it is better that [it] should be done under private cover to the competent authority in the Country rather than to a stranger, who gives it publicity in the newspapers, without any explanation or modification & without affording us the opportunity of giving the requisite explanation."

John Rae reached Fort Simpson in mid-August and spent a week organizing before departing for Fort Confidence. On his arrival on September 10, he found the three familiar log houses needing only windows, doors, and a fresh coat of mud to make them habitable. Rae sent a few men to collect logs for boat building. He sent others to establish two fisheries half a dozen miles away by putting nets into Great Bear Lake; soon these would yield fifty to seventy fish a week, most of them trout, which could be packed away in ice for use during the winter.

Two days after he arrived, Rae set out for the Coppermine River, hoping to retrieve eighty pounds of pemmican he had cached near Bloody Falls two years earlier. On his third day out, still twenty miles from the Coppermine, he happened upon the tents of a dozen familiar native families "who set up a perfect yell of delight as they rushed out of their tents to shake hands with us." The natives accepted a present of tobacco and told Rae that they had found the cache and eaten the pemmican, and that a group of Inuit had removed the tent and other articles. Concerned now about securing enough provisions to last the winter, Rae returned to Fort Confidence, shooting deer along the way.

Back at the fort, the log party had found the necessary logs, crooks, and stem and stern posts. Rae designed the craft he wanted and ordered George Kirkness, the carpenter, to build two of them. By the end of October, Rae could write that one of the boats was completed except for a few fittings and that it looked very fine:

Its dimensions are 22 ft. keel, 6 ft. 6 ins. broad, and two feet 3 ins. high amidships, the boards being 1/2 or 3/8 in. thick and the timbers bent birch 1 in. by 5/8. The build is clinker [using overlapping planks fastened by "clinched" nails, their protruding tips bent over] and the rigging is to be two lug sails. The wood here although knotty is sound and so tough that not one of the boards split in bending, notwithstanding that many of them were fitted in without being steamed.

To Sir George he would add with pride that even though the wood was green, the boat was so light that two persons could lift it with ease and four carry it without inconvenience: "Being a sort of 'Jack of all trades' (no recommendation I am sorry to say) I made the draught of it, as the carpenter had never before built a boat of the mould required. Of course there are none of my men that know anything about rigging a craft properly, but this I can easily manage, having practised a little some years since, at splicing ropes and roping sails." When both vessels were finished, he pronounced them "fine craft, handsome looking, strong, light and well-adapted for shallow water, whilst they are sharp enough forward and aft to make them pull and sail well."

Winter arrived early, even for Fort Confidence. On September 22, the temperature fell to zero degrees Fahrenheit and the channel to the island opposite froze over. Soon a foot of snow covered the ground. Rae worried that conditions would worsen, but the weather turned mild, the hunting remained good, and by the end of October, he had stored two months of provisions for a party of eighteen persons and thirteen dogs. He wrote to Richardson that "we live much in the same style as when you were here, having a roasted deer croup generally for Sunday's dinner with a very diminutive plum pudding."

Rae continued campaigning with Sir George for a leave: "My trip towards the Coppermine was a very pleasant one," he wrote in November, "but it let me into a secret of which I had not previously been fully aware, i.e., that a walk of 25 miles was quite as much for me now as 40 or 50 miles would have been some years since." Further on he stated flatly, "I am still desirous of coming out to Red River in winter 1851/2 and thence to England if you will grant me permission."

By early January, despite having reduced the party's rations, Rae faced a food shortage. Windy weather had driven much of the game eastward and had also affected the nearby fisheries. Meanwhile, thirty starving Slavey had become dependent on the fort: "How these poor people were to have passed the winter, had we not come here, I am at a loss to know unless they had taken themselves to some good fishing station, for they had very little provisions and still less ammunition."

The local Slavey were quite unlike the Cree and Ojibwa from the Moose Factory area. Among those tribes, women enjoyed both respect and power—though lately, perhaps as a result of too-long familiarity with Europeans, the women had begun manifesting unusual aggressiveness. Not long before, Rae heard, two Cree women had engaged in a physical fight so fierce that men jumped in and separated them. The two, who loved the same man, had insisted on finishing their battle, explaining that only then could they become friends again. Finally, after a desperate and bloody contest that involved kicking, scratching, and biting, one woman defeated the other. The loser withdrew but returned soon afterwards and shot her rival dead. Clearly, these Cree women acted autonomously, if ill-advisedly.

In the Mackenzie District, by comparison, the Slavey and Hare men exploited their women so that they themselves could hunt and fish as the spirit moved them. The women not only did all the domestic work—making clothing, constructing tents, carrying baggage during migrations—but could be disposed of without consultation. Not long before, one man had coveted his neighbour's wife. A wrestling match ensued. All the men wore their hair long and flowing, and these two seized each other by the locks. They grappled furiously until one man cried , "Uncle!" or signalled that he had had enough. The victor, the covetous man, then paid twenty made beaver (standard beaver skins), roughly the price of a gun, and the woman became his to exploit.

At Great Bear Lake the previous winter, John Richardson had observed that the local Slavey esteemed good hunters who aspired to excel. However, "as in other communities, there are many indolent people among them also, who are content to be looked down upon, while they live by the labours of the more active." This did not make for prosperity. Now John Rae wrote that the HBC would, according to common custom, feed all those native people unable to catch fish for themselves:

In Mackenzie District, native women constructed tents and made clothes; men hunted when the spirit moved them

I am determined that none are allowed to die of starvation as long as we have anything eatable in store. At the same time, those that are able are made to exert themselves in setting hooks (for which they receive lines and baits) for trout, and spearing herrings. The latter mode of taking fish altho' very common near Fort Franklin had never been attempted in this part of the Lake, until a short time since when learning from the fisherman that he had seen a number of small fish near the ice whilst setting a net, I made a small spear, and killed 70 herrings in a very short time. Yet this work, easy and simple as it is (for a child might do it), does not suit the thoughtless natives here, and it is only by threatening to give them nothing to eat that they can be prevailed upon to attend to it at all.

Fortunately, some Slavey couriers arrived in mid-January to report that they had cached a supply of venison six days' journey away. Rae sent a party to retrieve the food. The hard work involved in dragging heavy loads for a long distance over a rough track wore out the sled dogs and rendered them less fit for the looming trek. Still, Rae now had enough provisions to last until spring.

During the winter, Rae received a printed copy of his book about his first expedition, which had finally appeared in London the previous year: *Narrative of an Expedition to the Shores of the Arctic Sea in 1846 and 1847* (usually shortened to *Arctic Narrative*). An editor had had his way with the work—no doubt by necessity—and Rae pronounced it "so re-modelled that I did not know my own bantling when it reached me."

On January 21, the temperature reached the lowest point of the year—a bone-chilling seventy-two degrees below zero Fahrenheit. After that, the winter slowly improved, bringing few storms, an abundance of snow, and a number of days that were merely cold. Rae would snowshoe alone out onto Great Bear Lake almost every night and stand looking up at a billion twinkling stars, feeling like the last man on earth.

March brought a warm spell. Temperatures soared and lingered for days in the high thirties and low forties. No matter what the weather, however, the indomitable Scot thrived on hard work: "Nothing from the securing of the buttons and seams of my travelling breeks [breeches], to the splicing, fitting and servicing of our boats' rigging but I had my hands at. Such duties and occupations for a C.F. [Chief Factor] may be thought *infra dig* by my brother officers, but I care little about that as long as the work is done."

John Rae expended much ink on HBC business and recommended several individuals for advancement. He also received word that Commander Pullen, who had left Slave Lake intent on making exploration history, had run into pack ice while sailing east along the Arctic coast and failed to get beyond Cape Bathurst. He had returned up the Mackenzie and, with his men, wintered again at Fort Simpson and Great Slave Lake. He would leave the following June and travel to England from York Factory.

Rae felt vindicated about Pullen. Ambition had blinded the naval man to the harsh realities of Arctic service, which he had once dismissed as a mere bagatelle. Now, apparently, he viewed it as awful work—the most severe and harassing duty he had ever experienced during his twenty-two years as a seaman. He complained about never eating a proper meal. He was sick and tired of the North, he said. Referring to the reversal of the previous year, he hoped to go straight to England this time.

As for his own looming expedition, Rae remained concerned about the men's lack of experience as sailors. Nevertheless, his crew had improved wonderfully over the winter. By spring, he would be ready to go.

Before he left Fort Confidence, Rae heard that William Hulme Hooper, Pullen's right-hand man, was writing a book about life in Rupert's Land—a book that would paint an unflattering portrait of the HBC. This did not sit well with Chief Factor Rae. Having spent all his adult life working for the Company, progressing steadily through the ranks from surgeon and clerk to chief trader and now to chief factor, Rae had become something of a Company man.

Remembering how Hooper had interrogated the self-aggrandizing Pierre Pambrun over the tragedy at Pelly Banks, Rae anticipated the worst: accusations that the HBC had mismanaged its operations and starved its own men, perhaps, or else damaging allegations about the Company's treatment of native peoples, which over the years had become an issue.

Certain of a sympathetic audience in Sir George Simpson, and feeling honour bound to defend the Company, Rae made, in a private letter, what the circumspect medical man R.L. Richards would later summarize as "scathing remarks about naval officers and others." Rae's observations cry out for more complete quotation, however, because they reveal so much—not only about conditions in Rupert's Land, but about the relationship between the HBC and the Royal Navy:

Whilst the *Plover* wintered on the Asiatic coast, [Commander T.E.L.] Moore kept an Esquimaux girl in his cabin for purposes that were but too evident, thus giving a fine precedent of morality to his officers and men, who were no way loath to follow so laudable an example when they had the opportunity. When the captain and fair lady took an airing in a dog sledge or cariole, they had a running accompanyment of officers, at least one before and another behind, who did all the duties of labouring men in this country when during the winter a person travels *en bourgeois*, a luxury by the way that I have not yet enjoyed, having never had my foot in a cariole except when it was standing still with no animals tackled to it.

The *Plover*'s men, Rae wrote, overcharged native people for muskets and sold them watered-down spirits, "cheating them as much or more than the most rascally fur trader ever heard of." He added that near Point Barrow, Commander Pullen had gone aboard the American yacht the *Nancy Dawson*: "During his absence Hooper [his second officer] and nearly all the men scattered themselves among the Esquimaux women on the floes, when an opportune rupture of the ice took place, and caused a number of very ludicrous exposes. This circumstance I suspect Pullen is not aware of, as he is himself strictly guarded in his moral conduct."

Rae wrote that he would not have mentioned these trifles if he did not expect Hooper to attack the H B C on moral grounds. Anticipating a verbal skirmish and seeking to supply Sir George with ammunition, he also noted the hypocrisy of criticizing conditions in Rupert's Land while a potato famine devastated Ireland. Between 1846 and 1851, that famine reduced the population of the Emerald Isle by twenty per cent, forcing the emigration of one and a half million people. Meanwhile, Rae wrote,

These self-sufficient donkeys come into this country, see the Indians sometimes miserably clad and half-starved, the cause of which they never think of enquiring into, but place it all to the credit of the Company quite forgetting that ten times as much misery occurred in Ireland during the last few years, at the very door of the most civilised countries in the world, than has happened in the Hudson Bay Cos. Territories during the last quarter of a century.

Rae must have felt some chagrin when he eventually discovered himself mentioned in flattering terms in Hooper's 1853 book, *Ten*

Months among the Tents of the Tuski, with Incidents of an Arctic Boat Expedition in Search of Sir John Franklin, as Far as the Mackenzie River, and Cape Bathurst. Hooper mentions meeting Rae, "the well-known Arctic voyager," on the Mackenzie River: "I cannot forbear to offer a tribute to his courteous and delicate attention; further acquaintance engendered sentiments of great esteem for his many excellent qualities."

The book does justify some of Rae's concerns, however. Hooper deplores the wretched living conditions in the northern wilds, noting, for example, that the unappetizing diet included dry boiled meat, fish roasted with its scales, reindeer tongues, bear meat, and beaver tails so fatty as to be almost indigestible. He also expresses revulsion at the sight of a fox caught by its bleeding paw in a trap: "Sure am I that few fair ones who now wear muff and tippet could resume them without a pang, had they witnessed the torture of this poor animal."

As far as the tragic events at Pelly Banks were concerned, Hooper had been completely taken in by the slippery Pierre Pambrun, as Rae anticipated. The navy man had failed even to suspect the dereliction of duty at the heart of the disaster. Instead, he remained transfixed by the story's sensational aspects. His was the only published account, for example, to deposit a human liver in the cooking pot.

For poor William Foubister, who starved to death, aching and alone in a dark, frozen hell, repudiated and condemned by the last human being he would ever know, the Victorian Hooper showed no sympathy at all. After describing how Pambrun discovered him with his boiling kettle, regained his power of speech, and demanded a confession, Hooper wrote that the miserable wretch "pleaded that not alone the love of life (and oh! when life is fleeting, then is the love for it the strongest)—not the love of life alone incited him to the deed, but that he wished to live—aye!—mark it well—that his aged mother might not be deprived of her sole support, her only stay."

For Hooper, there could be no justification for Foubister's act.

Even so, reading *Tents of the Tuski*, John Rae would realize that Hooper was not a malicious man—far from it. He was just another British naval officer with little experience of Rupert's Land, shocked to his foundations by the harsh realities of the North.

8

THE THIRD EXPEDITION

O n April 25, 1851, as John Rae stepped out the door of the main hall at Fort Confidence, wet snow slid off the roof of the building and narrowly missed drenching him. The sun was already high in the sky. Reaching up and snapping off a large, dripping icicle that had only now become dangerous, Rae worried that he had delayed too long: this premature spring had begun to melt snow and ice that he desperately needed, threatening to strand him on the wrong side of the strait he meant to cross. Yet Rae knew that he could not have got ready any earlier—not with an undertaking of such complexity.

Two weeks before, at the earliest date that blowing snow and blizzard conditions would allow, Rae had sent four sledges carrying 2,700 pounds of provisions as far as the Kendall River. None of that weight was made up of tents, because Rae had taught John Beads and Peter Linklater how to build igloos during the winter. These two men would accompany him on the first part of the expedition. Rae had also given Hector Mackenzie, his second-in-command, detailed instructions covering every possible contingency, advising him what to do, for example, if Rae himself failed to return, if he sent word of some important finding, or if letters arrived announcing that Franklin had been found.

From behind the main hall, the sled dogs began to bark. As Rae went around the building to investigate, he felt confident that, though they omitted nothing necessary, from an awl to an ice chisel, he and his men would carry no useless weight. While naval officers sledding in the Arctic would haul bedding weighing almost twenty-five pounds per man, Rae had reduced this weight for his overland trio, including himself, limiting them to one blanket, one deerskin robe, and two hairy deerskins to place between themselves and the snow. Writing to Sir George, he had described this as "rather *luxurious*, being 22 lbs. weight for all, but we can easily lighten it if required."

When travelling, Rae wore Inuit-style clothing, the first European explorer to do so. His everyday suit was a fur cap; large leather mitts with fur around the wrist, lined with thick blanketing; and moccasins made of smoked moose skin, large enough to accommodate two or three blanket socks and with thongs of skin stretched across the soles to prevent them from slipping. He also wore a light cloth coat with its hood and sleeves lined with leather, a cloth vest, and thick mooseskin trousers, all of which were "neither so heavy nor so warm-looking as the dresses very commonly used on a cold winter day in England." In addition, he carried "a spare woolen shirt or two and a coat made of the thinnest fawn skin with the fur on, weighing not more than four or five pounds, to put on in the snow hut, or when taking observations." His personal effects consisted of a pocket comb, a toothbrush, a towel, and a bit of coarse yellow soap.

Out behind the main hall, Rae checked the traces on the sleds while one of the men fed the dogs scraps of meat. He was about to embark on the most ambitious small-party expedition ever undertaken in the Arctic. Having been prevented two years earlier from crossing Dolphin and Union Strait by boat, the thirty-seven-year-old explorer would now try to cross it on snowshoes, accompanied only by two much younger men. He was making for territory that no European had ever visited, and he hoped to discover not only the fate of the Franklin expedition but also, perhaps, a strait dividing Victoria Island from Wollaston Land—potentially the final link in the Northwest Passage.

With preparations complete, Rae donned his snowshoes and led four men and four sledges east from Fort Confidence. Dogs hauled three of the sledges, harnessed not in rows, according to British naval practice, but in an Inuit-style fan-out. Two men hauled the third sledge. Another man, now guarding the provisions advanced to the Kendall River, would join them all for a short distance. The "fatigue party" would then return to Fort Confidence to help Hector Mackenzie transport two boats, the *Lady Richardson* and the *Forlorn Hope*, to the provision station

*Rae, who preferred huskies such as these
to other dogs, hitched the animals to sleds
not in rows but using an Inuit-style fan-out*

on the Kendall for the summer part of the expedition.

In designing this complex plan, the ingenious Rae had allowed for contingencies, reversals, and last-minute changes. But he had also drawn on what was, among Europeans, unprecedented experience and knowledge of the Arctic, and so he felt confident of success.

For the overland journey, Rae would carry enough pemmican and flour to last thirty-five days and enough grease to serve as cooking fuel at a rate of one pound per day. Unlike government sledging parties, he would not stop for lunch but only for a moment to take what the Hudson's Bay men called "a pipe," eating a mouthful or two of pemmican before resuming the trek. After much reflection, he had decided to bring along two extra dogs; the animals available from the local Slavey, although hardy, were not as powerful as the usual Inuit sled dogs, the huskies. Including food for the animals, the party's whole equipment weighed only 560 pounds, but even this, Rae knew, would require from the dogs great powers of endurance and considerable strength. After all, he proposed to examine three hundred miles of coast or ice-covered sea before returning to the Kendall River and, when the ice turned to water, taking to boats for the second part of the expedition.

The weather turned bad on April 27 just as Rae arrived at the provision station. After huddling in a crowded igloo through two days of stormy weather, Rae led the men north. The fatigue party travelled to within ten miles of the Arctic coast, doing most of the heavy hauling, and turned back on May 2. Rae pressed on with Beads and Linklater, both of whom had been born in Rupert's Land and were in their early twenties—fit men and ideal travelling companions.

On reaching the Arctic coast at Richardson Bay five miles west of the mouth of the Coppermine River, Rae found the ice ahead free of hummocks and pressure ridges and not unfavourable for travelling. In the afternoon, with the sun high in the sky, the glare off the ice and snow threatened the men with snowblindness, whose victims feel as if sand has lodged in their eyes. They blink incessantly, tears streaming down their cheeks. Continued exposure produces inflammation, a relaxing of the eyelids, and a complete loss of vision. Men have been known to lose their sight.

To avoid all this, Rae decided to rest during the day and travel by night, when visibility would resemble that of twilight at the lower latitudes. Two hours before midnight on May 2, he donned snowshoes and set out across Coronation Gulf toward Wollaston Peninsula on Victoria Island. In order to examine bays, rivers, and inlets while his men drove the dogs straight ahead, Rae hauled a small sledge piled with bedding, instruments, pemmican, a musket, and tools for building a snowhut. After slogging along the coast, he touched land at Point Lockyer and then crossed Dolphin and Union Strait by way of Douglas Island, where he cached provisions for the return journey.

Four days out, near Cape Lady Franklin, Rae reached Wollaston Land, believed at the time to be separate from Victoria Island. Searching for the lost expedition and for a non-existent strait between Wollaston and Victoria, Rae travelled east along the coast. He spotted and named the Richardson Islands "after the distinguished naturalist and traveller" who had accompanied him previously. At one point, between observations for time and latitude, Rae shot ten hares: "These fine animals were very large and tame, and several more might have been killed, also a number of partridges, had it been requisite to waste time or ammunition in following them."

When the temperature plummeted to twenty-two degrees below zero, the men—one of them badly frostbitten in the face—retreated to their latest igloo, finding its shelter more than usually acceptable. Rae found surveying and taking a set of lunar readings to be decidedly unpleasant work. But he persevered, and on May 10 he ventured beyond where Dease and Simpson had reached in 1839 while exploring this coast from the east. No strait lay beyond this point.

Suspecting now that Victoria and Wollaston formed part of the same land mass, Rae debated whether to strike north overland in hopes of reaching open water or to return west toward Cape Lady Franklin, where he had landed, and seek the elusive (in fact, non-existent) strait beyond that point. He chose the latter course, because to head north would mean crossing high ridges of land, most of them already clear of snow, and a few days of warm weather would have made travelling with sledges and dogs utterly impossible.

That night, a snowstorm reduced visibility to twenty yards. Fortunately, the snowshoers had the wind at their backs. Rae found their previous track and so didn't need to stop repeatedly to take bearings: "After a very cold but smart walk of rather more than seven hours duration, we were very glad to find ourselves snug under cover of our old quarters, our clothes being penetrated in every direction with the finely powdered snow."

The storm that raged through the next night made travel impossible, but in the morning, accompanied by the panting of dogs, the creaking of sledges, and the gentle *whump whump whump* of snowshoes, Rae again headed west dragging his sledge, which weighed over thirty-five pounds. He visited Douglas Island, retrieved his cached provisions, and fought his way farther west along the south coast of Wollaston Peninsula, battling rough ice and blowing snow. He followed the shoreline as it swung north, naming Simpson Bay and Cape Hamilton.

The party came upon thirteen Inuit lodges and Rae chatted amicably with the inhabitants. Timid at first, they soon gained enough confidence to sell him seal meat for the dogs and boots, shoes, and sealskins for the men. These Inuit, on the west coast of Wollaston Peninsula, had neither seen nor heard anything of any European ships.

On May 23, having passed (and named) several more bays and islands, Rae realized that he had better soon turn back. Spring thaw loomed

An Inuit winter camp often comprised more than a dozen igloos

and, for certain this time, threatened to trap the boatless party on the wrong side of Dolphin and Union Strait. Resting in the igloo as night came on, scribbling notes by candlelight, the explorer decided to make one last sortie northward, to see what he could see. He would travel light, bringing only Peter Linklater, the faster of the two young men, and leaving the dogs and Beads to rest before their long journey back to the Kendall River.

After midnight, when finally the sun dipped below the horizon, Rae shook Linklater awake. He boiled water and sipped a cup of tea, then donned his snowshoes and led the way north along the unexplored coast of Wollaston Land. The night was clear and beautiful, the sky blazing with stars, and as he strode deeper into the treeless barrens, the silence broken only by the crunch of snowshoes on hardpacked snow, Rae revelled in the knowledge that no European had ever passed this way. Here at the edge of the known world, hundreds of miles from the nearest fur-trading post (which itself lay hundreds more miles from any large settlement), every step he took carried him deeper into the unknown.

This was the essence of exploration.

On the horizon, as if in celebration, the aurora borealis emerged out of nothingness to form a great, shimmering rainbow across the northern sky. While Rae marched into the night, its arch slowly grew larger, filling more than half the heavens before resolving itself into a series of vertical, grass-green rays cascading toward the horizon. Then began a shimmering dance of violet light, folding and unfolding across the sky in a thousand shades of purple, advancing, retreating, and finally shattering in a liquid explosion that ended with a sparkling, multicoloured shower.

Beneath this dance of light, John Rae walked on. Having left camp with only a compass, a sextant, and a musket for protection against wolves and bears, he and Linklater travelled fast. They walked for six hours, stopping to rest only once, briefly, at the younger man's request. At last, as the aurora dispersed and the rising sun turned the sky grey, Rae rounded Cape Baring. Linklater had fallen some distance behind and the explorer forged on ahead, excited now, climbing a promontory from which, in the distance, he could see a high cape. This impressive landmark he named Cape Back after the artist-explorer George Back, who, in 1821, by finding a band of Yellowknife rescuers, saved Franklin and Richardson from starving to death at Fort Enterprise.

Between that cape and the promontory on which he stood, Rae could see a large body of water (Prince Albert Sound), and he wondered whether it might prove to be an east–west strait. Just ten days before, on May 14, 1851, a sledge party from Robert McClure's icebound HMS *Investigator* had reached the other side of the sound, forty miles to the north—though of course Rae couldn't know that. He yearned to keep walking, but he knew that he had run out of time.

On May 24 Rae began to retrace his steps. He verified readings, retrieved caches, and encountered a few friendly Inuit out hunting. None of them had seen or heard of any Europeans. Six days after turning back, Rae and his two men recrossed Dolphin and Union Strait to a high rocky point north of Cape Krusenstern. By June 4, when the party reached Richardson Bay again, a layer of water on the ice confirmed that it was not too soon to conclude their snowshoe and dog-sled journey.

Rae's timing was impeccable. On June 5, he started overland toward the Kendall River. En route, he shot a large muskox bull, pronounced

*At Prince Albert Sound, Rae narrowly missed encountering
a sledge party from Robert McClure's ice-bound* Investigator

the meat excellent, and undertook to preserve the skeleton and transport it to England. The party reached the provision station after travelling five days from the coast, "during some of which we were fourteen hours on foot and continually wading through ice cold water or wet snow which was too deep to allow our Esquimaux boots to be of any use."

The last part of the journey, if not the most fatiguing, was easily the least pleasant. Streams flowed through every hollow and valley, some of them so deep and rapid that the men would have to walk three or four miles out of their way to find a place to ford; even then, they often had difficulty maintaining their footing, and at one point Linklater slipped and lost all the cooking utensils, plates, pans, and spoons. For the last two days, the men had to eat on large, flat stones. They survived mainly on geese, partridges, and lemmings. These last little animals were migrating north in such numbers that the dogs killed enough on the way to support themselves without any other food. For the men, lemmings were a special treat when roasted over the fire or between two stones.

In his official report, Rae noted that "the conduct of the two men who accompanied me has been excellent, and they as well as myself are in a much better state for commencing another such journey than

Melting ice produced increasingly difficult and dangerous conditions

when we left Fort Confidence." He calculated that, starting from the Kendall River, he had covered 824.5 nautical miles, or 942 statute miles, and he speculated, in private correspondence, that this was "perhaps the longest [journey] ever made on the arctic coast over ice."

At the Kendall River station, writing to Sir George from inside a tent, with so much dust and ashes flying about that they dirtied his paper, and with some Slavey camped nearby making a hullabaloo—"there is no keeping the rogues quiet"—Rae observed that he had survived the journey much better than anticipated: "The heart did its work well, and the legs also did not fail me—although when passing among rough ice I had a twitch or two in one of my knees that had been formerly sprained."

Rae asked Sir George to relay his report of the expedition thus far to the Royal Geographical Society, "as I should like to try to obtain the [gold] medal, which I can scarcely expect to receive unless my summer boat voyage is very fortunate, and besides there will be so many competitors from the arctic coast and from other quarters that my chance is but a poor one." He thought to add, "I hope you have granted me leave of absence this fall as I would like much to travel to

Red River in winter." To facilitate that trip south, he would attempt to haul one of the two small boats back to Fort Confidence.

On June 13, 1851, Hector Mackenzie and eight men arrived with the two boats from Fort Confidence at the Kendall River provision station. Two days later, Rae, Mackenzie, and ten men proceeded down the tributary toward the Coppermine. Ice forced them to wait for almost a week at the confluence. They started down the river and, on day three, encountered rapids "so formidable, owing to the great height of the water, that the steersmen, although daring almost to the point of recklessness, would not venture to run the boats down, even without their cargo." Rae waited four days for the water to fall and then, his patience exhausted, proceeded despite the danger.

The Coppermine is a notoriously difficult river, but by portaging around the impossible stretches and running the merely difficult ones while taking on water, the party made it to Bloody Falls. There, by placing a net in an eddy below the falls, they caught forty salmon in fifteen minutes. Rae left the men and spent the better part of an hour sitting alone on the riverbank, sorrowfully, watching large chunks of ice being drawn into the whirlpool in which Albert, his Inuit interpreter, had drowned two years before. A piece of ice several feet thick entered the eddy and went around two or three turns. Suddenly, by a whirl of the stream, it tilted onto its edge and stood upright before disappearing beneath the surface as if sucked under by some unseen monster.

On the hazardous Coppermine River, Rae waited four days and then ran the rapids

On reaching the mouth of the Coppermine, Rae set up camp and waited for the pack ice to melt farther out on Coronation Gulf. A few of his men had sailed boats on large lakes and knew how to steer in a fair wind. On arriving at the coast, however, Rae determined that not a man of either crew knew how to tack or turn a boat when plying to windward under difficult conditions. He spent several hours teaching them the knack, stressing the need to keep the foresheet to windward until the boat had swung far enough in the new direction. More than once, Rae was roused from rest, reading, or writing by cries and shouts, only to look out and see the men having trouble, somewhat to his amusement, while practising with one of the boats.

Early in July, a breeze opened a narrow channel along the shore toward the east, and Rae sailed twenty-two miles by nightfall, when ice made further progress impossible. From that point on, he proceeded eastward along the coast by taking advantage of any open water. Progress was slow and difficult. In many places, the ice lay against the rocks, forcing the men to make portages. This work, though arduous, had fortunately become routine for the steadily improving crew.

The weather remained changeable. On the morning of July 16, as Rae and his men rounded Cape Barrow, they found themselves sailing into a torrent of rain. After they put ashore for breakfast, the weather cleared and Rae climbed a promontory. The highest rocks afforded him a splendid view north and east across the beginning of Dease Strait. The prospect was not encouraging, however: the whole strait, as far as the eye could see, lay covered by an unbroken sheet of ice—ice so thick and strong that hundreds of seals cavorted along its edges.

Rae reboarded the boats and carried on, making slow progress by following crooked lines of water through the ice. Six days beyond Cape Barrow, a stiff southeasterly breeze opened a channel toward Cape Flinders at the western point of the Kent Peninsula. Nearing that cape, which Franklin had named during his first disastrous expedition, Rae spotted three Inuit hunters and put ashore. Half a dozen other Inuit watched from a nearby island.

The explorer approached the hunters, noting that they looked thinner and less well-fed than the Arctic natives he had met to the east.

The men at first appeared alarmed and fearful, but Rae offered them some trinkets, a gesture they rightly understood as friendly, and quickly gained their confidence. These men had never before communicated with Europeans. Using gestures, sign language, and Inuktitut words and phrases that he had picked up, Rae questioned the men for half an hour. They lived in this quarter and had lived here all their lives, but no, they had seen no great ships. They had seen no foreigners, nor any sign of foreigners. Nor had they even heard of any foreigners visiting these lands: Rae was the first.

Disappointed but not surprised, Rae resumed his voyage eastward. He passed Turnagain Point, where in 1821—far too late in the season—Franklin had finally turned around and begun his desperate overland retreat. Rae reached Cape Alexander at the eastern end of the Kent Peninsula on July 24, two days earlier than Dease and Simpson in 1839. From here, where Dease Strait was narrowest, Rae proposed to cross to the southern coast of Victoria Land. Soon afterwards he wrote,

Had geographical discovery been the object of the expedition, I would have followed the coast eastward to Simpson Strait and then have crossed over towards Cape Franklin [on King William Island]. This course, however, would have been a deviation from the route I had marked out for myself, and would have exposed me to the charge of having lost sight of the duty committed to me.

Ironically, indeed tragically, had Rae carried on farther east, he would have discovered the fate of the Franklin expedition early enough to retrieve priceless written records. Along the west coast of King William Island he would have found not only dozens of frozen corpses—some under boats, others in tents, still others face down in the snow—but hundreds, if not thousands, of pages of logbooks, journals, diaries, and final letters. But on July 27, 1851, as the winter ice began breaking up, the dutiful Rae beat north across Dease Strait to Victoria Land.

Cambridge Bay, John Rae discovered, extended several miles farther into Victoria Land than Dease and Simpson had realized, forming an excellent harbour "with a sufficient depth of water for vessels drawing upwards of twenty-four feet, and having a good holding ground of sand or mud. Into the west side of this harbour a rapid river about fifty yards broad of beautifully clear water empties itself." A gale blew up and locked Rae into the bay for two days.

As August began, however, the weather cleared and the wind opened a passage to the east. Rae pushed off, but he had not been travelling for more than ten minutes when the wind chopped around "directly in our teeth and blew a gale, against which, having lowered the masts and sails, we had great trouble in making way with oars. At length we reached a small island in the bay; from thence by plying to windward under close reefed sails, at about 4 p.m. we doubled the point."

With the wind at their backs and aided by a flood tide, Rae and his men reached Cape Colborne in an hour. From that point east, Rae began delineating coastline that had never been charted. He named Anderson Bay in honour of David Anderson, bishop of Rupert's Land, and Parker Bay, sixteen miles farther, in honour of Sir William Parker, admiral of the British fleet. Yet another bay, because of its "resemblance to one of the most frequented and best-known harbours in Orkney," he called Stromness. Rae named Lind Island in honour of the Swedish singer Jenny Lind (1820–67), "whose sweetness of voice and noble generosity have been the theme of every tongue," and Taylor Island after the twelfth American president, Zachary Taylor.

The following day, having travelled over one hundred miles without stopping except to cook, Rae reached an insurmountable ice barrier. The shore lay barren of vegetation and even of driftwood. A tract of light grey limestone had been forced up in immense blocks close to the shore by the pressure of ice. From the north came yet another gale, with heavy squalls and showers of sleet and snow. Finally the wind fell and a lane opened up along the coast, revealing reefs. Rounding these, Rae emerged into open water, set close-reefed sails, and beat west-southwest through an ugly, chopping sea. The slightly built boats strained and heaved as pounding waves washed over them, but eventually Rae entered a snug cove and secured them.

The next day, unable to make any headway using oars, Rae sailed windward until the gale became too violent for even his most reduced canvas. Again he sought shelter ashore. On August 5, Rae passed high limestone cliffs rutted with deep snow. A thick, cold fog came on, encrusting the boats with ice, so he landed and soon had the voyagers snug in their tents. Some of the men, who were searching for something to burn in this rocky and treeless landscape, were surprised to discover driftwood of notable size—the first they had seen since leaving Cape Alexander. Rae identified the wood as poplar and surmised that it came from trees in the Mackenzie River District.

The explorer sailed north along the east coast, naming capes and bays. On the ninth of August, he picked up an eighteen-foot length of pine that provided firewood for several days. He saw no signs of either Europeans or Inuit, but spotted many snowy owls along the shore. As evening came on, the men forced their way forward for another three miles, pulling and poling against thicker and thicker ice. Finally, just north of Albert Edward Bay, they ground to a halt.

For the next two days, a relentless northeast wind kept the ice close to the shore and showed no signs of changing. A less intrepid explorer would have turned back, but John Rae decided to press ahead—not out of the reckless ignorance that in 1821 had cost John Franklin the lives of more than half his men, but out of the calculated and well-informed awareness that he could safely proceed overland. Besides, what if Franklin had reached the coast directly ahead? Or what if the waterway Rae had seen on the west coast of Wollaston Land was in fact a strait that emerged just ahead, a final link in the Passage?

Just before noon on August 12, with three men, his trusty musket, and enough food to last four days, Rae began hiking north:

Hoping to avoid the sharp and ragged limestone debris with which the coast was lined, we at first kept some miles inland, without however gaining much advantage, as the country was intersected with lakes, to get round which we had to make long detours. Nor was the ground much more favourable for travelling than that nearer the beach; in fact, it was as bad as it well could be, in proof of which I may mention that, in two hours, a pair of new moccasins, with thick undressed

Buffalo skin soles, and stout duffle socks were completely worn out, and before the day's journey was half done every step I took was marked with blood.

The party advanced seventeen miles by walking twenty-four, then bivouacked on a spot near the coast, from which Rae saw and named Halkett Island. The next morning, although his feet began bleeding again, he proceeded north for another three miles: "As the travelling continued as bad as ever, and as the whole party were more or less foot sore, I resolved to remain here to obtain observations whilst two of my men travelled ten miles to the north and the other went to kill deer." The two men returned that evening limping. From the farthest north that they had gone, they had been able to see another seven miles to Point Pelly, which Rae named in honour of Sir J.H. Pelly, governor of the HBC.

Rae and his men hiked back to the boats the next day in eight and a half hours, killing two deer on the way. The men left on guard had built two stone cairns as ordered, and in one of these Rae deposited a note encapsulating his expedition and mentioning that he had explored to a distance of thirty-five miles north of this point. Two years later, in May of 1853, a sledging party from HMS *Enterprise*,

HMS Terror, *beset in the Arctic in 1837,*
suffered still harsher treatment a decade later

wintering in Cambridge Bay under Captain Richard Collinson, would find it.

Early on August 15, 1851, with a fierce wind blowing from the north-northeast and the boats in danger if the wind shifted to the east, Rae sailed back a few miles to a safer harbour. There he waited for any favourable change in the wind and ice that would allow him to use the shelter of Admiralty Island (which he had named the previous week) to cross Victoria Strait to Point Franklin on King William Land.

If Rae had managed to cross the strait at this point, he would again have discovered the fate of Franklin: this is the latitude in which the *Erebus* and *Terror* had been beset. It was not to be, however. Late that morning, Rae sailed out into the strait, but the breeze increased to a gale and shifted to the east. Facing a great accumulation of ice, Rae sought shelter in the lee of a point. The following morning, when the wind subsided, he tried once again to push across to Admiralty Island, but the ice was worse than ever.

Four days later and some miles farther south, Rae made a third and final attempt to force a passage eastward to King William Land. But after five and a half miles, he reached a wall of close-packed ice and had no choice but to turn back. Rae could not know it, but the conditions he encountered remain essentially unchanged even today, because pack ice breaking off from the polar cap travels south down the broad McClintock Channel and jams into the narrower Victoria Strait at the bottom. No sailing ship, but only a nuclear-powered icebreaker, could ever effect a passage through these waters.

At the time, John Rae looked longingly east across Victoria Strait and saw land that he could not visit and did not presume to name. But in 1905, during a sledge journey, Roald Amundsen's second-in-command paid tribute to Rae by naming those visible islands the Royal Geographical Islands and giving British names to their most prominent features.

On August 21, 1851, while creeping along the shore of Parker Bay, Rae discovered a length of pine wood and examined it with growing excitement. This was not driftwood but a man-made pole. Almost six feet long, three and one-half inches in diameter, and round except for the bottom twelve inches, which were square, it appeared to be the butt end of a small flagstaff. It was stamped on one side with indecipherable marking, and a bit of white line had been tacked to the pole near the bottom forming a loop for signal halyards. Both the white line and the copper tacks bore the marks of the British government: a red worsted thread, the "rogue's yarn," ran through the white line, and a broad arrow was stamped on the underside of the head of the copper tacks.

Rae was still carefully describing this pole in his journal and had not travelled more than half a mile, when the two boats came upon another stick of wood lying in the water, touching the beach. This one was a piece of oak almost four feet long and three inches in diameter, with a hole in the upper end. This post or stanchion had been formed in a wring lathe. The bottom was square, and Rae deduced from a broad rust mark that it had been fitted into an iron clasp.

Rae anticipated a debate over the sources of these pieces of wood, so he offered his considered opinion in his official report, incidentally becoming the first explorer to rightly suggest that Victoria Land was an island. Citing the flood tide from the north, he argued that a wide channel must separate Victoria Land from North Somerset Island and that these pieces of wood had been swept down this channel along with the immense quantities of creeping ice. In his rough notes, though not in his report, Rae wrote of the two poles, "They may be portions of one of Sir John Franklin's ships. God grant that the crews are safe."

Back in April, before he left Fort Confidence, Rae had written to Sir John Richardson about Franklin's whereabouts. He mentioned a letter he had received from an even more concerned correspondent:

Lady Franklin says that a growing opinion prevails in England that the long-missing expedition is icebound somewhere in the direction of the magnetic pole [this slowly moving point was now located on King William Land], or towards Back's River, and to search in the neighbourhood of these places was the principal object of the small expedition under Captain Forsyth. It is very proper that those parts should be examined, but I have very little expectation that any traces of those looked for will be found in that quarter.

Rae had then suggested that if the lost expedition was not found between Cape Walker to the east-northeast and Cape Bathurst to the west-southwest, then it would probably be found in the vicinity of Melville Island to the north. His discovery of the two pieces of wood did nothing to change his opinion. Unfortunately for history, Rae correctly guessed the direction from which the broken pieces had come but overestimated the distance they had travelled.

In their introduction to Rae's *Arctic Correspondence*, J.M. Wordie and R.J. Cyriax wrote of his findings, "That these pieces were derived from the Franklin expedition has not been proved, but that they were so derived is virtually beyond doubt." Others had found traces of the Franklin expedition—rope, wood, canvas, even graves—from before his ships sailed into tragedy. With these broken pieces of wood, however, John Rae had become the first explorer to discover relics from that expedition *after* it was locked into the ice. In August 1851, of course, as he sailed slowly along the coast of Parker Bay searching for still more relics, Rae had no way of knowing this.

Rae did know, however, that the British Admiralty had sent ships to Barrow Strait. One or more of these might have come to grief after penetrating southward and so yielded the wood he had found. As a man of science, he felt that he had insufficient evidence to speculate about ultimate sources. In his official report, therefore, he confined himself to description. Meanwhile, he had a homeward journey to complete. Having stowed the wood, the copper tacks, and the line— the Admiralty, he knew, would be keenly interested—Rae turned his attention to the wind and the waves.

From Parker Bay, where he found the wood, Rae made excellent time sailing west. One morning three days later, a stiff breeze became a gale. Soon the explorer found himself in the worst seas he had ever encountered. He reduced the sails until the two light boats were scudding under the smallest possible canvas. Heavy waves broke over the vessels, smashing and twisting and threatening to capsize them. Despite hidden rocks, Rae sought the shelter of a harbour—dangerous work because he had to run almost among the breakers to see the shoreline.

Rae hugged the coast to Cape Lady Franklin. On August 29, he crossed Coronation Gulf and found the Coppermine River raging. When the water did not fall for two days, Rae proclaimed confidence in the skill of his men and started up the river. The Coppermine, far higher even than when it stole the life of Albert One-Eye, had never been ascended in such dangerous conditions. The ledges of rock that ran along the base of the cliffs lay hidden beneath the driving current so that tracking meant walking along the top of the cliffs. The men's strongest cord snapped four times, and so they entered the pounding river to shove the boat over the rocks. After five days of furious work, the party made camp at the Kendall River, the worst of the trek behind them.

A few days later, on September 10, 1851, Rae and his men regained Fort Confidence. Finding everything in order and more than 3,000 pounds of dried provisions in store, Rae instructed Hector Mackenzie to close the post and pay the men, specifying generous bonuses and gratuities. Several months later, the associate governor of Rupert's Land, Eden Colvile, would review the accounts: "I find that in several instances the men employed under Dr. Rae in the Arctic Searching Expedition have been overpaid. All these payments were made under Rae's authority and it appears to me that it is not the Fur Trade that should suffer. . . . The matter should be settled between Rae and the Government." True to form, the explorer had rewarded his men well for their work. Colvile didn't pursue the matter, however, and by then John Rae was already organizing yet another expedition for the HBC.

Meanwhile, the day after he arrived at Fort Confidence having completed one of the most remarkable Arctic expeditions ever undertaken, Rae departed on what was, for him, a simple journey. After stowing the Parker Bay poles in one of the boats he had built, he crossed Great Bear Lake and started up the Mackenzie River. Bent on enjoying his long-anticipated leave of absence, he was making for England and Orkney. Certainly he would visit his mother, and perhaps he would meet a woman to marry. This much he knew for certain: nothing, but nothing, was going to stop him.

9

BEST-LAID PLANS

Arctic experts have designated John Rae's Victoria Island expedition his most successful. During his spring sortie from Fort Confidence to Cape Baring and back to the Kendall River, Rae trekked 1,080 miles, one of the longest such expeditions ever made over Arctic ice. Later and under more favourable circumstances, British naval men would exceed Rae's distance: G.F. Mecham travelled 1,336 miles with the advantage of four or five food depots both ways, and Leopold McClintock covered 1,400 miles while passing through country rich in muskox and deer.

Even so, Rae's spring journey was a remarkable physical accomplishment, and he followed it immediately with a second stunning achievement. His summer voyage east and north along Victoria Island, during which he sailed 1,390 miles while charting 630 miles of unexplored coastline, stands comparison with William Dease and Thomas Simpson's 1838–39 voyage, which had set an Arctic standard for smallboat travel. In addition to these physical and geographical successes, Rae discovered the first Franklin relics, those two pieces of wood from one of the lost ships (probably the *Terror*). Despite all this, to call Rae's third expedition his most successful is to mistake subsequent mythologizing for history. It was but a prelude.

Rae now sailed up the Mackenzie River to Fort Simpson, arriving late in September. He proceeded through Great Slave Lake and the Slave River to Lake Athabasca and started up the Athabasca River, eventually to be stopped by ice. At Fort Chipewyan, he waited for the ice to freeze hard and, on November 17, set out on snowshoes with eight men, reaching Fort Garry at Red River on January 10, 1852. He spent a pleasant eighteen days making arrangements, and then Eden Colvile—who had not yet seen the expedition accounts with their "excessive" generosity—took him as far as Pembina on the U.S. border in a dog cariole or sleigh, "a very gay affair neatly painted and well-furnished with warm robes, drawn by dogs ornamented with wool and white leather saddle clothes with bells attached."

Back on snowshoes, Rae travelled the Crow Wing Trail to Crow Island in ten days—the fastest time on record, as this most keenly competitive of men carefully noted. From Crow Island, Rae continued south and east by stagecoach, reaching St. Paul, Minnesota, in mid-February 1852. Calculating from the previous April, when on snow-shoes he set out from Fort Confidence for the Kendall River, Rae had travelled over eight thousand miles without using any form of mecha-nized transport. And he was still going:

Rae travelled from Fort Garry to the U.S. border in a dog cariole

[Between St. Paul and Galena,] our sled broke through the ice on the Chippewa River. The driver had a very narrow escape, having been dragged out of the water by another passenger and myself just as the current was sweeping him under the ice. One of the horses was drowned and my portmanteau got full of water—fortu-nately there was not much in it to spoil.

Late in February, Rae reached Chicago, a bustling city of about 40,000 inhabitants. He journeyed by train through Windsor to Hamilton, where he visited his brothers Richard and Thomas and found them thriving as Rae Brothers and Company, commission merchants and pork packers. From there he headed south to New York, arriving on March 8. Along the way, Rae overtook and travelled with a French count, Charles de la Guiche, who was visiting North America on a hunting expedition: "He is a very agreeable, fine fellow, but he does not come up to my ideas of a great sportsman or traveller, being rather too fond of taking it easy." Nevertheless, a couple of years later, Rae would name Point de La Guiche for this obscure Frenchman.

Rae sailed out of New York on a steamer on March 10 and arrived in London a couple of weeks later. By April 3, *The Athenaeum* magazine would report that "Dr. Rae has arrived in England and testifies in the excelling condition of his health that the perils and hardships of Arctic exploration—a more than ordinary share of which have fallen to his lot—are not very severely trying."

Rae made reports on his latest Arctic expedition to both the Hudson's Bay Company and the British Admiralty. To the latter he delivered sections of the flagstaff and stanchion he had found off Victoria Island. No tangible news of the lost Franklin expedition had turned up, so "my little discovery of the two pieces of wood, one of which at least bore evidence of having formed part of a government ship, was of interest."

During Rae's four most recent years abroad (March 1848 to March 1852), England had grown increasingly obsessed with Sir John Franklin. The clever, connected, and conniving Lady Franklin had exploited the sympathy of the British public, presenting herself as a bereaved widow who stoically refused to accept her husband's death. She had raised public subscriptions and had browbeaten the British Admiralty into sending out one fruitless search expedition after another.

In 1849, a bizarre and decidedly unscientific revelation had produced what would prove to be one of the few accurate predictions about the whereabouts of the lost navigators. William Coppin, a retired sea captain, had informed Lady Franklin that his recently deceased young daughter had appeared before his other children to announce that Franklin and his men were trapped to the west of Prince Regent Inlet near Point Victory, off King William Island. (Rae had established that King William Land was, in fact, an island.)

Lady Franklin subsequently instructed Charles Forsyth and William Kennedy, the captains of two different search expeditions, to search in that area. Forsyth found this suggestion more "surprising than sensible" and returned without pursuing it, to bring news of gravesites and relics discovered on Beechey Island, all of which pre-dated any disaster. Then Kennedy, who had spent three days with Coppin, failed in 1851–52 to penetrate far enough south either to verify or to repudiate the supernatural communications.

By the time Rae arrived in London, Lady Franklin had rejoined the popular consensus: "I am persuaded now that it is pretty well proved that my husband could not have penetrated south west." He was believed instead to have gone up Wellington Channel. The sole dissenting voice remained that of the irascible doctor Richard King, who had descended the Great Fish River with Sir George Back in 1833–35. Having argued at the outset that Franklin was departing to "form the nucleus of an iceberg," King now lobbied to lead an expedition down the Great Fish—but he had been lobbying aggressively to do so for more than a decade and nobody paid any attention.

On April 10, 1852, Rae met Robert McCormick in John Barrow's office at the British Admiralty. McCormick was soon to leave for the Arctic as a surgeon on HMS *North Star*, part of the much ballyhooed "Last of the Arctic Voyages," a five-vessel search expedition to be led by Sir Edward Belcher. McCormick wrote later that he and Rae "had a long chat together over the Arctic chart on which he pointed out to me a spot to the southward and westward of Cape Walker [in Barrow Strait] as in his opinion the most likely spot for discovering the fate of Franklin."

Like most Arctic experts, Rae simply did not believe that the lost navigators would be found anywhere near the coast of the continent. He reasoned that if the ships had iced up anywhere near the western shore of Boothia Peninsula and had to be abandoned, the crews would certainly have followed the example of Sir John Ross and Sir James Ross in 1832 and would have retreated toward Fury Beach on the east coast of Somerset Island. There, where Sir Edward Parry had wrecked HMS *Fury* in 1825, they would not only have found a large depot of provisions and fuel, but would also have been in a position to attract the attention of whaling ships, just as the Rosses had done.

Furthermore, to travel south with a view to reaching some tiny fur-

The wreck of the Fury *had left an enormous stockpile of provisions on Fury Beach,
Somerset Island, making it an obvious destination for shipwrecked sailors*

trading outpost would involve a much longer journey with a far smaller chance of success. What HBC fort could even begin to support so many men? Fury Beach, by comparison, offered an immense stock of preserved vegetables and soups in good condition, as Franklin and his officers must have known and as would later be verified by other British sailors. Again and again, Rae reached the same conclusion: if the lost ships were icebound anywhere within 240 miles of Fury Beach, then, logically, any surviving men would head for that site and nowhere else.

Two months after his arrival in London, on May 24, 1852, the Royal Geographical Society awarded John Rae the Founder's Gold Medal "for his survey of Boothia under the most severe privations in 1848 and for his recent explorations on foot and in boats of the coasts of Wollaston and Victoria Lands by which many important additions have been made to the geography of the Arctic regions." In his citation, Society president Sir Roderick Murchison wrote the following:

With a boldness never surpassed he determined on wintering on the proverbially desolate shores of Repulse Bay, where, or in the immediate neighbourhood, one expedition of two ships had wholly perished, and two others were all but lost, and, in relation to his most recent expedition: 'with a pound of fat daily for fuel' and without the possibility of carrying a tent he set out accompanied by two men only, and trusting solely for shelter to snow houses which he taught his men to build, accomplished a distance of 1,060 miles [actually 1,080] in 39 days or 27 miles a day including stoppages—a feat which has never been equalled in Arctic travelling.

In what must have become one of the lingering disappointments of his life—especially since public recognition would later elude him—Rae was not present to receive the medal. Sir George Back, his nominator, accepted it on his behalf. Rae himself had gone to Orkney, probably in response to a medical emergency involving his widowed mother. On August 18, 1852, three months after the awarding of the medal, Rae wrote Sir George Simpson from Stromness: "My mother holds out remarkably but is quite unhappy unless she can get me to eat and drink something at least five times per day." In January 1853, he would reiterate that "my mother altho' her memory is failing holds out remarkably." She would die, having reached her early sixties, on February 14, 1855.

Meanwhile, back in London in 1852, Rae made up for lost time. In April, Robert McCormick of the Belcher expedition spotted the explorer "walking down Piccadilly with a good looking girl held to his arm. . . . He did not see me, being more intent on the girl." Soon afterwards, on May 1, Rae wrote to the Hudson's Bay Company laying out a proposal for yet another Arctic expedition, "a plan for the completion of the survey of the northern shores of America, a small portion of which along the west coast of Boothia is all that remains unexamined."

Rae suggested equipping a party at York Factory. One officer and twelve men, including two Inuit, would sail north to Chesterfield Inlet in two boats, leaving around June 15, 1853. One boat would be strongly built and somewhat larger than those he had sailed to Repulse Bay in 1846, the other as light as possible. Having proceeded up the inlet, the bulk of the party would transport the lighter boat overland to Back's Great Fish River, then descend that waterway and sail north to complete the survey. The expedition would require three months.

Rae almost certainly submitted this rough outline in response to a request. Powerful HBC directors in London had been studying the latest Arctic charts on which recent Royal Navy explorations had filled in notable blanks. In 1849, Sir James Clark Ross and Francis Leopold McClintock had sledged across Somerset Island and explored its west coast, discovering Peel Sound. In 1851, just a few months earlier, Erasmus Ommanney had charted the other side of that

Sir James Clark Ross had discovered Peel Sound in 1849

channel, the east coast of Prince of Wales Island. News of the discovery of Bellot Strait would not reach England until October.

Still, this much had become obvious to HBC experts: to chart the remaining unmapped coastline of North America, worthy in itself, would probably also mean establishing the final, vertical link in the Northwest Passage. The HBC had entered into the competitive spirit of the quest. The Company wished to complete the survey—and chart the passage—before its archrival the Royal Navy. If that meant sending out another twelve-man expedition under the best leadership it could muster, then so be it.

In his proposal, John Rae observed that many young, enterprising HBC officers would be well-qualified to lead the exploring party, and that he himself, "although much less efficient than I was some years ago," would also be willing to do so. Early in June 1852, back in Orkney, Rae received word that the HBC had approved his plan. Shortly thereafter, in a brief letter to Sir Roderick Murchison of the RGS thanking him for the Gold Medal, he wrote, "I have, contrary to my expectations, been appointed to lead the party!"

Back on the "civilized" side of the Atlantic, Rae had begun to yearn for the Arctic wilds—or at least for the kudos to be won by returning there. He would have welcomed the chance to lead this expedition not only for its own sake, but also because it would enable him to right a geographical wrong involving his first expedition. Back in the summer of 1850, during that terrible rainy spell at Methy Portage, Rae had written to the British hydrographer, Sir Francis Beaufort, protesting the latest Admiralty charts, which had rendered "the most important part of my discoveries" of 1847 null and void.

Rae had determined that Boothia was not an island but a peninsula connected to continental North America. The 1849 chart, however, delineated most of Pelly Bay with a dotted line, implying doubt. Rae hadn't marched along the entire coast of that bay, but he had viewed the whole from the summit of Helen Island and "to confirm the evidence of my eyes if necessary, I had the charts of the natives who had passed their lives in the neighbourhood (their winters on the ice of Pelly Bay and their summers on its shores)."

Certain armchair geographers, thinking wishfully, clung to the notion that a channel might extend from Pelly Bay to the waters west of Boothia and so lead to the west coast. Rae wrote that he found it

extremely hard that, after having with my party passed a winter during which we suffered privations of no ordinary kind, and performing two journeys on foot either of which I believe was as long as any that have been accomplished in those barren regions, my facts should be doubted merely because they differed from the opinions of more influential individuals who had nothing but conjecture and theory to guide them. . . . Besides, I may observe that land seen by Government expeditions from much greater distances than any part of the shores of Pelly Bay were from me, appear in the Admiralty charts by a continuous line. To prove this I have only to draw your attention to Banks and Wollaston Lands.

During his sojourn in Britain, Rae repaired his strained relations with the hydrographer, who offered to provide compasses and other state-of-the-art instruments for his next expedition. Indeed, Rae looked forward to setting the record straight. The forthcoming journey would take him nowhere near Pelly Bay, but by tracing the Boothia coast north from Back's Great Fish River, he would demonstrate in a different way that Boothia was a peninsula.

During the London season, which extended from March or April through July of each year, members of the British upper classes would meet and mingle in the metropolis at theatre events, grand balls, and glittering receptions. Come August, members of this elite would retreat from the London social whirl to the countryside, where their extensive estates, dominated by splendid country houses, often included well-stocked deer forests and grouse moors designed for hunting. There they would entertain guests for extended periods.

In the summer of 1852, while visiting Orkney and doing not a little grouse hunting, John Rae received invitations to visit two such country estates in northern Scotland, one from the earl of Selkirk, who had known Rae's father in Ross-shire, the other from Edward "Bear" Ellice, the member of parliament for Inverness-shire. A vigorous man now entering his seventies, Ellice—after whom Rae had named a cape—was also a Whig power-broker and a major force in the governing council of the Hudson's Bay Company.

The powerful Edward "Bear" Ellice befriended Rae

Rae went first to Ellice's, where he enjoyed himself so much hunting deer and black-cock and playing the drawing-room dandy that he stayed on three weeks and never made it to Selkirk's. "Altho' not in good shooting condition whilst there," he wrote afterwards to Sir George Simpson, "I believe I supported the credit of the concern as a pedestrian, beating all the nobs there to sticks, and keeping pace with the smartest of the gillies on level ground or going up hill, and distancing them all hollow at running down a steep place—the most trying work of all for the legs."

On November 18, 1852, Rae attended the London funeral of the First Duke of Wellington and, through the kindness of a friend (probably Ellice), enjoyed a fine view of the splendid procession. He then crossed the English Channel and visited Paris for the first time before returning to Orkney and his mother for Christmas.

During these months in Britain, the ever-practical Rae kept one eye on business. He reported to Sir George Simpson that the British government had rewarded him most handsomely for his Victoria Island expedition. After twenty months occupied with government affairs, he received pay for two full years at a rate of six hundred pounds per year (totalling, in contemporary terms, roughly u.s. $90,000).

Rae was arguing at the time that experienced Arctic hands should be paid more than novices, at least forty pounds a year, and in some cases fifty, with a bonus of ten or fifteen pounds for good conduct: "For instance, a man such as [John] Beads would scarcely engage for the same terms as those who would have to act as middlemen. I am particularly desirous of this man's services as he is a most cool, able steersman in rapids."

Rae also addressed the question of Inuit interpreters. To William McTavish at York Factory he wrote, "If any other Interpreters could be obtained instead of Ouligbuck and his son I should prefer them. To Ouligbuck I have no particular objection but the boy that I had with me formerly is one of the greatest rascals unhung—and by his falsehood and misconduct made his father sulky and discontented. I should prefer Ouligbuck's son Donald, who, altho' he spoke but little English, was a good tempered hard working fellow." He would later revise his estimate of Mar-ko.

Inevitably, given his outspoken and competitive nature, Rae was caught up in exploration politics. In October 1852, William Kennedy returned from leading a sailing expedition, funded by Lady Jane Franklin, having failed to accomplish both his stated objectives, of reaching the magnetic North Pole (then on King William Island) and of finding traces of the Franklin expedition. Kennedy, a "half-breed" born in Red River to a Scottish father and a native mother, had left the HBC after complaining about the Company's treatment of native peoples. While profoundly sympathetic to this cause, Rae judged that Kennedy's complaints reflected badly on the entire Company—and indeed, however obliquely, on Rae's own reputation.

Rae observed to Sir George Simpson, "The way to get credit here is to plan some impossible scheme, no consequence how absurd, to assert positively that you will do more than anyone else ever did or could do, and after having signally failed, return with a lot of paltry reasons—sufficiently good to gull John Bull—for your failure." He could not contain his resentment: "It is perhaps unnecessary for me to mention that Kennedy has done little; he and his party made a long journey, [the] greater part of it over land, and traced only a few miles of new coast. Like a good fellow he just touched my furthest north point and then struck off west, instead of doing what I would have done—divided the party and sent a portion of it southwards to the magnetic pole."

Rae may have been right to be disdainful, but he also had an unfortunate habit of expressing his views to anyone who would listen. By openly voicing his contempt for the opinions and accomplishments of men like Kennedy and Richard King, Rae made bitter enemies. When he later became vulnerable by defending unwelcome truths, the most eloquent of his enemies would jump at the opportunity to destroy his good name.

In a letter dated November 26, 1852, and published in *The Times*, Rae outlined his latest expeditionary plan. He added a postscript: "I do not mention the lost navigators as there is not the slightest hope of finding any traces of them in the quarter to which I am going." Late the following January, after spending Christmas in Orkney with his mother and extended family, Rae returned to London. He visited Sir John Richardson, his former travelling companion, and dined with artist-explorer Sir George Back, his sometime patron. Then, toward the end of March 1853, he sailed on the steamer *Europa* for New York City. John Rae could not know it, but he had embarked on the most successful of his Arctic expeditions—and, arguably, on the most successful Arctic expedition of all time.

10

BACK TO THE BARRENS

New York City had become not only a gateway to North America, but a bustling metropolis whose citizens, in the spring of 1853, were discussing the establishment of the New York Central Railroad, the American debut of the internationally acclaimed composer Louis Moreau Gottschalk, the spirited defence by Harriet Beecher Stowe of her recently published anti-slavery novel *Uncle Tom's Cabin*, the creation of the great American symbol of Uncle Sam, who had made his first appearance the previous year in a weekly New York comic publication called *Diogenes, His Lantern*, and the growing popularity of matrimonial agencies advertising "wives for poor and deserving young men."

But John Rae stayed only three days after his arrival on April 9: he had a last stretch of coastline to survey—perhaps even a Northwest Passage to discover. He met Henry Grinnell, the American shipbuilder who was sponsoring a second Franklin search expedition that was due to leave, under the leadership of Elisha Kent Kane, the following month. And he had his photo taken by

At age 39, passing through New York, John Rae posed for photographer Matthew Brady

the photographer Matthew Brady, who would eventually become famous for his work during the American Civil War.

Then away he went at his usual whirlwind pace. After taking the train to Montreal, he spent four days visiting Sir George Simpson, once again enjoying elaborate meals highlighted by rare port and Madeira (in small doses). He looked in on his two brothers in Hamilton, as usual, then travelled by steamer to Sault Ste. Marie, arriving on May 6. That same day, back in Montreal, McGill University conferred upon this "renowned Arctic traveller" the honorary degree of doctor of medicine.

Usually such recognition went only to those who had advanced the study of medicine. Rae, who had qualified as a surgeon two decades before but had practised little, observed that the university had made the award "without any examination, which was very fortunate for a few questions on medical subjects would have floored me." His Scottish heritage, his growing eminence, and his exemplary service with the Hudson's Bay Company had carried the day: the founder of the university, James McGill, had immigrated from Glasgow and had made his fortune in the fur trade.

At the Sault, Rae visited his old friends James and Letitia Hargrave, recently retired from York Factory. But he fretted that the canoe he needed to travel farther west had not yet arrived. Lake Superior had been free of ice since May 1, and a delay of eight or ten days could cause the failure of the expedition or force him to winter in the North, neither of which the thirty-nine-year-old explorer anticipated with pleasure: "Some years since I would not have cared much about being forced into the latter alternative, but now much exposure of any kind injures me, and more care will be requisite to keep me in a fit state of health to carry out the work I have to do."

The canoe finally arrived on May 12, and Rae and a few men left the next day, battling headwinds across Lake Superior to reach Fort William (now Thunder Bay) in nine days. From there, Rae announced his intention to retire from the HBC in a letter to Sir George: "It may be as well to mention that I propose retiring from the service as soon as I return from the present tour, for altho' far from having a competence, I may manage to live by some exertion on the means I have saved, small as they are."

As a designated chief factor, Rae received no salary but rather a fraction of Hudson's Bay Company profits (two eighty-fifths of forty designated shares, twice the allotment of a chief trader and usually a tidy sum). By the following spring, his four years of service as a chief factor, dating from June 1, 1850, would also allow him to draw a retirement allowance, receiving one additional year at his current rate and half that percentage for the following six years. Rae also hoped to receive "something extra (as usual on such occasions)" for his current expedition, though he had been dissuaded from seeking to formalize that arrangement with HBC officers in London by his friend Edward Ellice, whose kindness was "a strong enducement to follow the advice given instead of my previous determination."

Loath to accept this resignation—a reaction Rae no doubt anticipated—Sir George would pretend to understand it as a request for an additional leave of absence. He would then try to entice Rae to remain with the HBC by outlining a future of steady advancement, proposing to put him in charge first of York Factory and then of Red River Settlement. But these propositions were to come later.

From Fort William, Rae canoed west to Fort Alexander at the mouth of the Winnipeg River and then north up Lake Winnipeg. He followed the same route as he had in 1848 with Sir John Richardson, but later in the spring so that he encountered no ice. On June 12, he reached Norway House and met the dozen men chosen to accompany him. Rae had asked specifically for certain old hands. Two of his favourites, Corrigal and Folster, were unavailable, but he knew three of the men who had signed on: John Beads and James Johnston had worked with him in 1850–51, and Thomas Mistegan, "a brave Cree Indian and splendid deer hunter," had served with him and Richardson as a steersman (the leader in a boat, as a bowsman is in a canoe). Mistegan now guided one canoe "with extreme skill down some of the very bad rapids 'en route' to York Factory, not touching a stone, whilst my Iroquois guide was sometimes in difficulty and on one occasion got his canoe badly damaged."

The party reached York Factory on June 18, five days behind schedule. Rae judged the two waiting boats to be well-suited for the work ahead. The larger boat, twenty-eight feet long and eleven feet wide, resembled Orkney herring boats and would probably draw more water than was desirable. The smaller one, twenty-four feet long and seven feet wide, was built of light, tough wood—the better for hauling overland—and was well-designed for running or ascending rapids. Both vessels were rigged with a jib and "two standing lugs, that is with the tacks coming down to the heel of the mast, so as to avoid the necessity of lowering the sails in tacking" or changing direction. Rae judged that the smaller boat, which was rather low in the sides, would be less comfortable and harder to handle in stormy weather, so he took charge of it himself. He appointed James Clouston, the only other Orkneyman on the expedition, steersman of the large boat.

Chief Factor William McTavish, brother of Letitia Hargrave, had organized the necessary supplies: pemmican, flour, biscuits, tea, sugar, and preserved milk, but no alcohol except for use as fuel and a small quantity of brandy and wine to be used only as medicine. Rae also loaded the boats with moccasins, blankets, buffalo robes, a good supply of ammunition, fishing nets, several sledges, and snowshoes. For trading with the Inuit, he brought several large cases filled with saws, daggers, files, axes, scissors, needles, beads, and hoop iron.

Although he was packed and anxious to leave, Rae had to wait several days to test the chronometers he had brought (necessary to ensure accurate survey work). Then a fierce snowstorm delayed his departure further. Finally, on June 24, 1853, to the sounds of a seven-gun salute and three hearty cheers, Rae once again sailed north out of York Factory.

The water along the coast as far as Churchill, 120 miles away, proved to be so shallow that when the tide went out, the sea would lie five or six miles from the high water mark. At first, close-packed ice forced the boats to hug the shore so tightly that at ebb tide they were grounded. To keep the boats afloat, Rae began sailing out of sight of land, though this brought its own risks. The driving wind and waves broke the ice floes into large, irregular chunks, some of them rounded by constant friction into great ice balls that ranged in diameter from three to five feet. These rolled and tumbled shoreward at flood tide with "a velocity which may appear incredible to those who have not witnessed it."

Some of the floes were large enough to support a man and, if flowing steadily, would have been quite safe. But they were churning so wildly that even an agile man would be thrown off and crushed or swept beneath the waves. Sometimes the only way to keep the boats from being damaged by driving ice was to anchor them to the largest grounded pieces and then have the men use poles to keep the floating, whirling masses away as best they could, but "notwithstanding every effort, the large boat got two planks stove in, fortunately above the water line, and on three other occasions both boats very narrowly escaped being crushed."

On the third day, while all hands used poles to ward off the churning ice lumps, one of the men in the large boat missed his set, his pole glancing off the floe that he was trying to push. He lost his balance and pitched head first into the frigid water. Luckily, instead of hitting ice, "he popped like a seal into one of the few holes of water alongside and received no injury beyond a very complete dunking, about which he himself was the first to make a joke. The fine fellow wishing to let himself 'drip' a little, although the temperature was at the freezing point with a keen easterly wind, continued at work; but his moccasins being slippery with the wet, before three minutes were past, he repeated the plunge." Rae insisted this time that he immediately change his clothes.

Early in July, the breaking, whirling ice grew so dangerous that Rae resumed hugging the shoreline. During one ebb tide, the two boats were grounded. The explorer waited in vain through two tides for the water to float them free. His patience exhausted, he ordered the heaviest cargo to be carried seaward nearly a mile to the only visible mass of ice. This ice island, large and firm enough to support the weight, was made up of a number of large floes fused together by pressure. Now that the cargo had been transported, the flood tide began. For once, inexplicably, the stiff, easterly breeze brought no ice. All of the men but two, who had remained with the cargo, had regained the boats. The tide was still hours away from floating them free when the two men on the ice island began waving their arms, splashing about in waist-deep water and shouting as loud as they could. But those on the boats could not make out a word.

Obviously, something had gone wrong. Rae and the other waiting men plunged into the rising tide and made for the ice island as fast as they could run, shouting and laughing when waves washed over one or another of them or "some unfortunate sinner put his foot in a hole or struck his toe against a stone and took a header." The men arrived not a moment too soon, for the short, breaking, iceless waves were quickly demolishing the compound ice island and threatened to destroy the expedition's most important supplies.

Rae and several men stood waist deep in the sea for more than half an hour with these heavy valuables on their shoulders, while the rest of the crew fetched the small boat by brute strength, floating it free just in time. The men bundled everything on board even at the risk of sinking the small vessel and were then able, by bailing constantly, and with waves washing over the sides, to reach a larger, more solid ice island a couple of miles farther out. Here they unloaded the cargo and changed their wet clothes.

Rae later observed that "getting wet in a river or lake or any other place the banks of which are lined with wood is no great hardship, but where there is no fire to be had the case is different, and some of the poor fellows looked particularly blue until they got their clothes changed." The men waited twelve hours in considerable discomfort before the rest of the crew finally floated the large boat free and arrived to reload the cargo.

On July 11, 1853, Rae reached the Churchill River and beached the boats on a sandy spot immediately below the ruins of Fort Prince of Wales, once a massive stone structure overlooking Hudson Bay. Rae, who had long since mastered the literature of exploration, recalled with a hint of disapproval that in 1782, Samuel Hearne had seen the guns destroyed and the houses inside the fort blown up by French invaders after he surrendered without firing a shot.

In the shadow of the fort, Rae dried and repacked cargo and repaired the boats. While a gale began, he sent two men five miles upriver to the Company headquarters at Fort Churchill. The officer in charge, his old friend James Anderson, soon arrived in a whale boat. The designated Inuit interpreter, William Ouligbuck, Jr. (Mar-ko), had not yet arrived from hunting porpoises in the North but was expected any day. While still in England, remembering Mar-ko as a young man, Rae had requested some other interpreter. Now he discussed his options with an experienced Company man named Omond, who had served for years as an interpreter and understood Inuktitut well.

Omond insisted that young Ouligbuck, now several years older than when Rae had known him, was easily the best man available, "that in addition to his own language he spoke English, Cree and French passably well, that he could be fully relied upon to tell as nearly as possible what was said, and no more, and give the Eskimo reply with equal correctness." When he had a personal interest at stake, Omond said, young Ouligbuck would not hesitate to lie, but he did this so clumsily that cross-examination would quickly elicit the truth. Rae added, "I

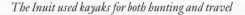

The Inuit used kayaks for both hunting and travel

had an opportunity afterwards of proving this character of my interpreter to be perfectly correct."

On July 12, having written letters reporting his progress so far, Rae waited impatiently for a gale to abate. He was reluctant to proceed without an interpreter, and seeing no sign of young Ouligbuck, Rae took aboard an Inuit named Munro, whose linguistic skills were merely passable. At thirty minutes past midnight, in a moderate wind and after a hearty farewell, he resumed his journey.

Forty miles north, four Inuit came off shore in kayaks to report that the porpoise hunters were not far behind, William Ouligbuck among them. Before long, Rae found himself watching, amused and surprised, "at the smart manner in which the Eskimo steersman brought his boat within a few yards of ours, luffing up, lowering the sail and dropping the anchor at the proper moment, with all the accuracy of a practiced boatman."

Within five minutes, having seen for himself that Munro couldn't compare linguistically, Rae had engaged young Ouligbuck as interpreter. Within ten minutes more, Mar-ko had arranged for the disposal of his share of game and had transferred his possessions. Rae made a present of tobacco to the other Inuit, shook hands all round, and sailed on up the boulder-strewn coast.

The ice cleared under the blazing July sun, and the party made rapid progress, sometimes under close reefs and again with full sail. Eighteen miles south of Knapp's Bay, the boats came to where Munro's wife and family were camping. Since the Inuit man wished to leave some property and say goodbye, Rae sent him ashore with a canoe and two men, all of them ordered to return as quickly as possible. The visit extended to five hours.

When the men returned, Rae learned that Munro's wife had been absent, having gone to fetch the venison of a deer shot by their young son. The visitors had been received with great hospitality and treated to a meal of choice deer meat. The parting of Munro from his children and his wife (who arrived back) "had been most tender and affectionate, and when he came on board he looked in very low spirits. Some good venison was added to our stock of provisions, and another kind of supply far less acceptable, in the form of clouds of mosquitoes."

Despite this delay, the party travelled 400 miles in 110 hours by sailing day and night through the now open waters—a five-day marathon that would have exhausted most voyagers. Rae, however, meant to regain lost time: he still hoped to accomplish his objectives in a single season and pushed himself and his crew to that end. By July 17, when he reached Chesterfield Inlet, he was just five days behind schedule. He proposed now to sail the light boat to the head of the inlet, transport it overland to Back's Great Fish River, descend that waterway to the coast, and sail north.

In Chesterfield Inlet, fog reduced visibility and while Rae slept, the steersman inadvertently sailed into a deep, uncharted river. The explorer faced a difficult decision on waking. The unknown river, as large as the Coppermine, flowed from the northwest—the direction in which he wished to proceed. Should he continue up it? Rae reasoned that the small land mass between this river and the next could hardly generate so large a stream. After running north some distance, this river would almost certainly swing west, taking him where he wanted to go. Rae decided that instead of returning to the inlet, he would continue up the river with eight men in the light boat.

Rae named the river the Quoich after the highland glen where he had hunted deer with the Edward Ellices, father and son. Leaving half the men with the large boat, Rae travelled up the crooked, fast-flowing stream, portaging around rapids and covering 210 miles in ten days. The twisting, torturous river never did turn west, but instead slowly diminished in size.

Halted seventy miles from Back's Great Fish River—Chesterfield Inlet would have got him no closer than ninety—Rae sent two parties to explore the area westward within a fifteen-mile radius. The men returned to confirm what he had surmised: the country was so rugged—"a bed of rocks and stones thrown together in the most confused manner"—that even if they could transport the light boat overland and sail down Back's River, they would arrive at the Arctic coast too late in the season to sail north and not in a promising place to winter. Nor did he now have enough time to descend the Quoich and sail up Chesterfield Inlet as originally planned.

Rae had no choice but to head back. But first he went hunting for food, shooting five muskox and four reindeer. He preserved five of the skeletons to send to England, and later he could not refrain from noting the contrast between his proceedings and those of a Lady Franklin–sponsored search expedition led by Edward Inglefield that ventured up Smith Sound in 1852 and killed sixty muskox. Despite having on board numerous naturalists and 120 officers and men, "yet not a single skeleton was brought home, although known to be of great value and much required in museums."

To Edward "Bear" Ellice, Rae wrote that the animals he shot were in poor condition, probably because the countless mosquitoes in the vicinity afforded them no leisure to feed. The explorer had never seen so many bloodsucking insects. They sounded like an army of swarming bees, only far more numerous. They invaded the men's ears, noses, mouths, and eyes. They got into the soup, the tea, the pemmican—into

Rae hunted muskox for food and preserved their skeletons for scientific study

anything, in fact, that could be got into. At night, they knocked on the sides of Rae's tent like the pattering of a small shower of sleet. Nothing but a gale or a temperature near freezing kept them at bay, and most of the men, without tents, got little sleep.

Bitterly regretting that he had deviated from his original plan, which might conceivably have enabled him not only to reach the Arctic coast but even to discover the remains of some of the sailors from the Franklin expedition, Rae returned to the spot where he had left six men and the large boat. What now? The explorer decided to sail north, winter at Repulse Bay, hire some Inuit dogs, and complete the survey of the west coast of Boothia early the next year, travelling overland before spring breakup.

Rae judged the existing party to be too large to maintain. On August 9, he sent six men back to York Factory in the light boat with James Clouston in charge, and a seventh, the homesick Munro—"a good lad, but of little use as an interpreter"—as far as his home near Fort Churchill. That left him in the large boat with seven men: four half-breeds (John Beads, Jacob Beads, John McDonald, and James Johnston), one Scottish highlander (Murdoch McLennan), the Cree Thomas Mistegan, and the Inuit William Ouligbuck.

On August 15, 1853, in a cold, drizzling rain, John Rae sailed into Repulse Bay. The last few days had produced a lot of thick fog and little excitement. In Roe's Welcome Sound, the party had come upon 300 walruses lying on rocks a few miles from shore. The men had wounded a number of these agile creatures, and Rae had managed to actually kill one, "an immensely large fellow" whose fat would provide enough lamp oil for the entire winter.

Repulse Bay looked more bleak and dreary, more forbidding, than Rae remembered. For mid-August, it also wore a more wintry and Arctic aspect than he had expected to face so early. Thick masses of ice clogged the shoreline, and immense snowdrifts filled every ravine and every steep bank with a southern exposure. A mass of ice and snow several feet deep covered his old landing place. Proceeding slowly up the North Pole River, Rae located a new, more amenable landing spot and moored the boat.

Jumping ashore, awash in memories, Rae went directly to Fort Hope, the dwelling he had constructed in 1846. He found the stone walls exactly as he had left them. The little mud oven, although exposed to the weather, was still in perfect condition. Some Inuit had used it to cache meat. In the woods, he found the path where every night before going to bed, he had paced back and forth to warm his feet. Around the stone house, in the hard-packed mud, he found footprints tracing the outlines of his men's British-made shoes, the marks as clear and fresh as if they had been made seven days rather than seven years before.

Everything looked so familiar and yet so different. Rae completed his reconnaisance with mixed feelings—the winter he had spent here had not been easy—then returned to the river. He found the boat moored, the tents pitched, and the cargo partly unloaded. This gratified him enormously, "my fellows being all so well up in their work that they did not require my superintendence."

During his preliminary inspection, the eagle-eyed Rae had detected no signs of recent visits by Inuit hunters. He was disappointed. From them, he hoped to acquire sled dogs. Without dogs, the expedition would be reduced to man-hauling, which he knew to be brutal work. What is more, the absence of hunters suggested that perhaps the caribou had adopted a different migration route. Rae had brought enough food to last three months. Would he be able to find enough game to provide for the other six? Finally, Rae had noticed that little of his favourite fuel—the heather-like plant *Andromeda tetragona*—had blossomed in this unusually cold season. Would his men be able to gather enough to last the winter?

Rae allowed himself two weeks to answer these questions.

On September 1, 1853, immediately after breakfast, John Rae gathered his seven men around a campfire. As a responsible leader with a democratic streak, he refused to risk the lives of his men without consulting them. The party had spent the past two weeks hunting, fishing, and gathering fuel. The time had come to decide. Should they try to survive nine long, dark, freezing months here in the Arctic barrens? Or should they abandon their objectives and retreat to York Factory?

Rae had spent the previous evening in his tent reviewing their situation and their prospects. Now he told the men that, personally, he would prefer to remain. But he was reluctant to expose them to the risk not of privation—"I know you would not much mind that"—but of starving or freezing to death. Refusing to minimize the dangers, Rae laid out the facts as he understood them. In theory, they had brought enough provisions for three months; in fact, two-thirds of those supplies would be required for the spring sledge journey. Wintering here would almost certainly mean subsisting on reduced rations.

During the past two weeks, the men had shot thirteen caribou, one muskox bull, ten ptarmigan, and three marmots. (Rae himself had accounted for most of the larger animals, including the bull and nine deer; Mistegan had shot three deer and Jacob Beads, one). In addition, fishermen had netted 136 salmon with an average weight of four pounds.

During this time, however, nobody had seen any signs of Inuit people, which raised questions about caribou migration patterns: Had they changed? How much more game would there be to acquire? As for fuel, they would have none for warmth. The men had gathered enough *Andromeda tetragona* for careful cooking for four months. This would mean eating one or two meals per day, taking care to cut the venison (excluding bone) into small pieces, having the kettles filled and perfectly ready before lighting the fire, and boiling for not a moment too long.

Having explained all this at the campfire, Rae reiterated his own desire to stay and finish the job and that he felt he had neither the right nor the desire to expose the men to danger without their approval. He would need their decision at once, however, because if they chose instead to return to York Factory, the party would have to leave within the next couple of days or risk getting frozen into the ice.

Not surprisingly, these hand-picked men gave their leader a full vote of confidence. They declared themselves ready and willing to remain, to work as hard as possible in obtaining food and fuel while opportunity lasted, and to live cheerfully on quarter allowance if necessary. With the vote unanimous, the party resumed their vigorous preparation for the Arctic winter.

By the end of September, the men had gathered enough fuel and shot enough game to last until the anticipated spring caribou migration. Provisions now included 109 deer, 1 muskox, 53 brace of ptarmigan, and 1 seal. Rae had shot 49 deer and the muskox, Mistegan had bagged 21 deer, and Ouligbuck 9.

October brought freezing temperatures. Ice formed on nearby lakes to a depth of four to six inches. This increased the mobility of the migrating caribou, enabling them to cross the country in all directions instead of only through certain passes, and so made hunting more difficult. Even so, by mid-month, when the annual migration ended, the expedition had added another twenty-five deer.

Since his first sojourn here at Repulse Bay, Rae had learned a great deal, mainly from the Inuit, about wintering above the treeline. He never even considered reoccupying Fort Hope, the stone house he had constructed seven years earlier. Instead, he and the men pitched tents.

Winter increased the mobility of the caribou
and made hunting more difficult

When the snow made it possible, they would erect and inhabit much warmer igloos, which Rae had long since learned were incomparably superior to any other option.

Meanwhile, finding his regulation sheet tent rather cold during a gale of north wind, Rae converted it into a stove room and moved into a leather tent that was less pervious to the wind. With the temperature hovering around twenty-two degrees below freezing, Rae applied himself to describing, in his grammatically rough but evocative style, his unheated living quarters:

The tent is one of those in common use among the prairie Indians; [it's] made of buffalo skins, ten in number and is supported by five oars, two boats' yards, the main boom, five poles, two canoe paddles, one piece of plank, one boat's thwart and two ice chisels. It has an opening at the top to let light in or smoke out as the case may be, which can be shut or nearly so at night or when it rains by two wing-like appendages, one of which may also always be placed on the windward side. The door is low and is shut by means of a skin suspended over it and faces the south-east as the prevailing winds are from the opposite direction.

At the back of the tent is my bed consisting of three blankets and a couple of buffalo robes in lieu of a feather bed—a very snug sleeping place to one who never, until within the last year or two, carried more than one blanket when travelling. At my head is placed the arms chest and at my feet the canteen and provision basket; on the left is my cassette of clothing; and on the right is a miscellaneous mass of articles such as moccasins, socks, pieces of leather, writing desk, ammunition, waterproof bag and warm garments, etc....

Over the head of the bed within reach of my hand is my double rifle (always ready loaded) suspended on branches of deer antlers. To one side are fastened my powder flask, shot pouch, large leather mitts, warm cap and small telescope, that latter being very useful in discovering animals, the deer being difficult to see in rocky ground. At one of the tent poles near, a lamp hangs which by means of a line and pulley can be lowered to a convenient height when required.

John Rae loved such naturalistic detail. Years later, when he tried to shape his notebooks into a publishable narrative, his passion for it frequently led him astray. Few non-specialist readers would want to read twenty pages on the subject of ice formation, for example, but Rae launches into just such a reflection after briefly describing how he ended up huddling in his blankets in his cold, fireless tent. He had returned to camp with his clothes soaking wet to the hips and his Inuit boots, full of water, frozen so hard they had to be cut off his legs.

This damage had occurred two miles north. Rae, while hunting, had forded a small stream ten or twelve inches deep that lay just below a large pool covered with thin ice. During the day, instead of rising, the temperature fell. Late in the evening, when Rae arrived back at the stream, he found it swollen to a depth of nearly three feet but had to cross it. Now, as he lay in his tent, Rae wrote copious notes on how his wetting and freezing had come about as a direct result of ice forming in the pool above the stream. Years later, he added another dozen pages on the subject, and he eventually turned the whole speculation into a scientific essay.

At the end of October, as soon as the snow was sufficiently hard-packed, Rae built himself an igloo with the expert help of Ouligbuck. It was an oval dwelling, nine feet by eleven feet, seven feet high at the centre. For a window, Rae inserted a two-inch-thick pane of ice that measured twelve inches by twenty-four. Later, because the igloo was so large for a single person, he reduced its size and added a double window.

Rae speculated that this igloo, half a mile south of Fort Hope, was probably the coldest dwelling in which ever a man passed a winter:

I say this advisedly because the Eskimos invariably live together two, three or more in the same Igloo, and sleep in the same bed under the same fur covering. I was quite alone for the simple reason that my men were all great smokers, whilst I did not use tobacco in any form, and a houseful of tobacco smoke would have been more unpleasant than 15 or 20 degrees of temperature, which was about the usual difference of temperature in the two houses.

The colder it was, the greater the difference. In Rae's igloo, ink froze regularly. He would take it to bed to thaw it. The seven smokers, meanwhile, shared a circular snowhut fifteen feet in diameter and nine feet high at the centre. Finding snow to be a bad conductor of sound, Rae pushed a long pole from his dwelling through to that of the men and devised a signal code. Two taps meant breakfast, three taps, dinner, "that is when we had the luxury of two meals a day."

November brought fine weather and a mean temperature of −18 degrees Fahrenheit. December, however, except for a few days, provided a continual gale with snow and drift and a mean temperature of −23. In February, the mean fell to −39 degrees as temperatures ranged from −20 to −53. And though the sky would turn light grey, the sun never rose above the horizon.

With the hunting season finished and most fuel-providing plants buried under several feet of snow, the cold and deserted habitat offered little to induce the men outdoors. As a medical man who had read countless exploration narratives, however, Rae understood the importance of keeping his party not just well fed, but active and alert.

With nothing like the resources of Royal Navy ships, which carried libraries and even theatrical props, Rae prescribed a certain amount of exercise and spent a few hours each day teaching reading, writing, and arithmetic. A couple of the men proved to be avid scholars. Rae regretted the paucity of his library, whose half-dozen books included his water-stained works of William Shakespeare and a book of sacred verse given to him by Eleanor Gell, daughter of Sir John Franklin.

The months passed rapidly and not unpleasantly. Far from the comforts and conviviality of civilization, Rae did his best to recreate the spirit of the Christmas season, choosing a meal of choice venison and deers' tongues with a small allowance of biscuit, plum pudding, and even a bit of brandy. The men worked up an appetite by playing football. On New Year's Day, 1854, they again amused themselves with football, though they left off sooner because a freak warm spell had briefly raised the temperature to eighteen degrees above zero Fahrenheit, which felt far too warm for such antics.

The New Year's meal resembled that of Christmas, with the additions of some very curious-looking cakes, some tins of mock-turtle soup, and even some attempted mince pies, though these turned out to be a failure: "My fine fellows were again as merry and happy, drinking their small allowance of brandy and singing their songs, as if they had been in the midst of their friends instead of surrounded by a desolate wilderness of snow." Rae, who rarely succumbed to nostalgia, imagined himself talking convivially in the festooned drawing rooms of Orkney and England. But later he observed: "One great comfort in being with the halfbreeds of Hudson Bay is that one seldom or never hears a word that could offend the most sensitive or delicate lady."

In January 1854, the meticulous Rae began preparing for the looming spring journey. Before Christmas, the priority had been the collection of black lichen for fuel. Now he redeployed his men. In a workshop built of snow, he had the carpenter Jacob Beads take apart the party's four sledges, reduce their framing woodwork, and put them back together more securely than before. Acting on Rae's advice, Beads narrowed the runners and reduced the sledges' weight by a third.

Later, Rae would revel in describing how his methods of exploration differed from those of the Royal Navy. The most cost-efficient explorer who ever lived—his first Arctic sojourn had cost 1,400 pounds, less than one-tenth of the average naval expedition—he enjoyed contrasting the simple equipment of his little party with "the expensive and elaborate get-up of our great Government Expeditions."

Rae's refurbished sledges, for example, rode lower than British government sledges, which had runners seven inches high and would often get stuck in anything but hard-packed snow. When Rae's sledges traversed hummocky ice, they could not dive into the loose snow lying in the hollows like the high-runner sledges did, so they would not strain the men or require the removal of weight.

As expedition leader, Rae expected to leave the direct route often to take sightings. He might have gone sledless, but instead he proposed to drag a smaller, one-hundred-pound sledge carrying instruments, books, gun, clothing, some provisions, and a small saw in case he became separated from his men and needed to build a snowhut. Such efficiency had become critical now that the party faced the prospect of man-hauling.

The previous year, Captain Henry Kellett had written to John Barrow that, despite his many years at sea, he had never seen such arduous work: "Men require much more heart and stamina to undertake an extended travelling party than to go into action. The travellers have their enemy chilling them to the very heart, and paralyzing their limbs. . . . I should like to see the travelling men [and their leaders above all] get an Arctic medal."

Early in the twentieth century, the courageous but hapless Robert Falcon Scott, who regarded man-hauling as a test of virility, would lead his men to their deaths in the Antarctic after being reduced to crossing an icy barrens by this means. The experienced Rae, with no doubts at all about his manhood, entertained no illusions about man-hauling. He knew the Inuit used sled dogs for a reason and that dragging even well-designed sledges weighing hundreds of pounds across an endless expanse of jagged ice, with hands and shoulders rubbed raw by ropes, while blizzards raged or the glare of reflected sunlight burned eyes to watering, was killing work. But it was clear that he could not now avoid it.

In mid-January, to cache food for the looming expedition and to test his equipment, Rae set out man-hauling with three men, John Beads, Murdoch McLennan, and Thomas Mistegan. A violent snowstorm compelled the party to shelter in an igloo for four days. Eventually, they reached Cape Lady Pelly, eighty-five miles from camp, and there, under a great heap of stones, cached 230 pounds of supplies, safe from any visitor but man or polar bear.

Back at Repulse Bay, the explorer resumed his preparations.

John Rae's attention to detail has been rivalled only by that of his foremost emulator, Roald Amundsen, the man who, early in the twentieth century, would not only defeat Scott in a race to the South Pole, but would also return alive. Now Rae calculated provisions for a sixty-day journey. Supplies included 390 pounds of pemmican, 128 of flour, 70 of biscuit, 35 of preserved potato, 5 of tea, 40 of sugar, 5 of chocolate, 12 of condensed milk, and 135 of cooking alcohol and tallow, for a total of 820 pounds.

The bedding, guns, and ammunition, not counting what Rae carried,

Man-hauling provisions required both courage and stamina

added another 176 pounds, bringing the total to 996 pounds. Rae would haul 70 pounds of that himself, leaving 926 pounds, or 232 pounds for each large sledge. (Rae later reduced this total.)

Other supplies included three guns (one double-barrel and two single) with ammunition, a small box of beads and cutlery for trading, and much else besides: needles, thread, screws, buttons, Inuit-style snow goggles, pieces of moose skin for repairing moccasins, and deer-skin thongs for mending sledges. The bedding consisted of one and a half blankets sewn together and five straps of lightweight deerskin with the hair still on to place between the men and the snow. The whole of this bedding for five persons weighed less than twenty-five pounds.

To locate weaknesses and determine the speed at which he might travel, Rae timed his men hauling loaded sledges over a measured mile. He too practised over that distance, hauling his sledge with 120 pounds on it. He set aside the fixed ration he proposed to use and, along with the men, tested it for four days. He carefully examined his "six-inch sextant by Dollard, which had been my companion for five of the eight springs and summers I had been on Arctic service . . . [and found that] this excellent instrument required no adjustment of any kind." And he adjusted his two chronometers, which he wore inside a thick blanket belt around his waist to protect them from cold.

Spring showed signs of arriving. Still hoping against hope to buy sled dogs to handle the heavy hauling, Rae sent three men to search one final time for any sign of Inuit people. They found none, and the explorer resigned himself to man-hauling. He would leave three men—Thomas Mistegan, Murdoch McLennan, and John Beads—to guard the boat and other property. Next to himself, Mistegan was the expedition's best hunter, so those who stayed behind would not starve. Rae put Beads in charge, however, because during the winter he had taught the young man to read and write well enough to keep a rough journal.

At the end of March, having lived off the land through yet another Arctic winter, John Rae was ready to complete the mapping of the northern coast of North America. By connecting the discoveries of Dease and Simpson with those of Parry, Kennedy, and Joseph René Bellot, he proposed to link the known navigable sea routes from east and west—the north and south channels—and so to resolve, not incidentally, the centuries-old mystery of the Northwest Passage.

THE TWO DISCOVERIES

On March 31, 1854, forty-year-old John Rae left Repulse Bay leading four men more than a decade younger: Jacob Beads, James Johnston, John McDonald, and William Ouligbuck. These five began their journey in bright sunshine and, despite the travail of man-hauling, in excellent health and spirits. Two of the men who would remain at winter quarters accompanied them for eight miles. All told, the party was hauling 865 pounds of provisions, which, with those already deposited at Cape Lady Pelly, would last them sixty-five days.

Rae at first headed northwest along the same route as he had taken in 1847. He would cross Boothia Peninsula and chart its western coast from the mouth of the Castor and Pollux River, the farthest Dease and Simpson had reached, to Bellot Strait. The four men with him were "all active and able young fellows, but one or two of them perhaps a little too light" to haul a sledge that, on departure, weighed nearly two hundred pounds and whose weight would increase substantially at Cape Lady Pelly.

Two days out, Rae realized that the spirited but slight McDonald, already suffering fatigue and pains in his chest, would be unable to keep the pace. He sent McDonald back to Repulse Bay in favour of Thomas Mistegan, who had been bitterly disappointed at remaining behind. In addition to his other qualities, Mistegan was an admirable snowshoe walker and sledge-hauler, and he had great powers of enduring cold. The Cree hunter caught up with the party on April 4. The men prepared him a special supper, to which he did justice after his rigorous hike of about thirty-five miles.

Two days later, after struggling through rugged terrain, Rae retrieved the cache at Cape Lady Pelly. He left some supplies for the return journey and resumed the northern advance across the dreary, snow-clad country, still following the route he had taken seven years before. The trek was more difficult this time because of the greater weight of the sledges (Rae's now weighed 110 pounds) and a greater quantity of rough ice.

Rae travelled Inuit-style, building igloos as he went. These snow-huts remained impenetrable to stormy winds. Although they required, on average, one hour to build, an igloo remained ready with its door blocked up with snow for the return journey. Also, a traveller would not have the trouble of pitching, taking down, packing on a sledge, and hauling a cumbrous tent, which, like bedding, would keep gaining weight from moisture. Another advantage was that moisture from the men's breath adhered firmly to the igloo's walls, instead of condensing and dripping onto the bedding as it did in a tent.

John Rae travelled Inuit-style, building snowhuts as he went

Later, Rae would observe that although government-backed Arctic explorers hired natives, when they had the opportunity, to build igloos for them and publicly acknowledged the superiority of snowhuts over tents, they never learned to build these comfortable dwellings for themselves, offering the most frivolous excuses and reasons for not doing so, the chief one being, bizarrely, that it was difficult to get snow for the purpose.

Also unlike these naval explorers, who cooked twice a day and stopped for lunch, Rae travelled non-stop, usually breakfasting on fruit, a piece of frozen pemmican, and half a biscuit: "We never stopped to eat or drink, but put a small piece of our breakfast allowance of pemmican in our pockets, which we munched at our pleasure." Supper usually consisted of still more pemmican, boiled with flour and preserved potato into a porridge called *rababoo* and served out with the most scrupulous impartiality both as to quantity and quality. The men would enjoy their smoke, and then the whole party would go to bed:

There were five of us, and we all lay under one covering taking our coats off, so that our arms might be more closely in contact with our bodies. This and the changing of our moccasins was all the undressing we went through. I always occupied an outside place, and the cook for the next day the other. Those inside were warm enough, but when either of the outsiders felt chilly on the exposed side, all he had to do was turn round, give his neighbors a nudge and we'd all put about, and the chilly party was soon warmed. We got so speedily accustomed to this that I believe we used to turn over from one side to the other when required without waking.

Rae had started out as early as he dared in the travelling season, but now the weather turned wintry again. Gale-force winds and heavy, drifting snow confined the men to snowhuts or reduced them to travelling as little as six miles a day. The temperature fell to sixty-two degrees below zero, and Jacob Beads froze two of his toes. By April 10, when the party reached the point on the coast of Committee Bay from which the explorer intended to travel due west across Boothia Peninsula, all the men, including Rae, had endured some degree of snow-blindness, their eyes stinging as if filled with sand.

The following night, Rae and his men found themselves hauling sledges through drifting snow under a full moon, sinking nearly ankle-deep at every step. The party managed eight and a half miles in six and a half hours, then built a small igloo and enjoyed some tea and frozen pemmican. They rested three hours, then resumed slogging through country so flat and snow-covered that it was difficult to tell where lakes began or ended. On April 14, Rae led the men forward through the zero visibility of a violent snowstorm, steering by compass. After two and a half hours, the party took shelter, having covered only one and a half miles.

The next day brought clear skies and relatively balmy temperatures (eight degrees below zero), though the heavy snowfall made trekking difficult. Rae mentions this in his autobiography, which then ends abruptly in mid-sentence: "It was impossible to keep a straight course and we had to turn to the northward out of our course, so as to select the. . . ."

Some readers have suggested that Rae suppressed the remainder of the manuscript because of what it revealed. His story is picked up in his own words, however, in D. Murray Smith's landmark volume, *Arctic Expeditions from British and Foreign Shores*, published in 1877. There, Smith introduces unpublished notes containing "fresh particulars in connection with this most interesting episode in Arctic Exploration. These valuable notes have, in the kindest manner, been supplied by Dr. Rae for the present work. We give Dr. Rae's communication, so courteously sent, in the form in which it has come to hand." Rae, who hated copying even more than writing, obviously scrawled a few introductory sentences, appended the final part of his autobiography—and simply never received it back.

At Pelly Bay, Rae encountered a dense fog and again had to travel by compass. Confronted by impassable mountainous terrain, he veered southwest across Boothia Peninsula and came across the fresh footprints of an Inuit person hauling a sledge. Rae sent Ouligbuck and Mistegan to find the traveller. After eleven hours, they returned with seventeen Inuit, among them five women. Rae had met some of these people at Repulse Bay in 1847, but others had never seen Europeans before and behaved aggressively.

"They would give us no information on which any reliance could be placed," Rae wrote in his official report to the HBC, "and none of them would consent to accompany us for a day or two, although I promised to reward them liberally." The Inuit objected to the party's travelling farther west, which puzzled Rae until he realized that they had cached provisions in that direction. "Finding it was their object to puzzle the interpreter and mislead us," he wrote, "I declined purchasing more than a piece of seal from them, and sent them away, not however, without some difficulty, as they lingered about with the hope of stealing something; and, notwithstanding our vigilance, succeeded in abstracting from one of the sledges a few pounds of biscuit and grease."

The following day, an incident occurred that would prompt considerable speculation. Early in the afternoon when the party stopped to cache seal meat, Ouligbuck slipped away and tried to rejoin the Inuit he had met the previous day. Rae noticed his absence and immediately gave chase, determined not to lose his excellent interpreter. He and Mistegan overtook the Inuit after a sharp race of four or five miles. The young man, crying like a baby, pleaded illness as an excuse for his attempted defection. Rae accepted this, suggesting in his report that Ouligbuck had "eaten too much boiled seal's flesh, with which he had been regaled at the snowhuts of the natives."

This explanation would fail to satisfy many of Rae's contemporaries, and also some of his later readers. Perhaps the young man, while being entertained for several hours at the snowhuts of the locals, had become intimate with one of the women and wished to rejoin her. Perhaps Rae suspected or even knew this and chose not to report it.

Years later, one of the most reliable and articulate Inuit men, In-nook-poo-zhe-jook, would explain that the Pelly Bay entourage had deliberately frightened young Ouligbuck by claiming that hostile Inuit living farther west would almost certainly murder the entire expedition. Nothing of the kind had ever occurred, however, and the only Inuit people who had ever shown any serious aggression lived over one thousand miles away, near the mouth of the Mackenzie River.

Why the fabrication? Rae had already deduced that the hunters had cached meat to the west and did not want it discovered, so they frightened Ouligbuck hoping he would persuade the party to change course. In this interpretation, certainly, the young Inuit man's credulity accords with his reputation as too naive to tell a believable lie. In any case, once overtaken, Ouligbuck wept and expressed his readiness to rejoin the expedition. And the falseness of the assertion about hostile Inuit would be demonstrated almost immediately, because two Pelly Bay men joined the expedition in travelling west, evidently quite without fear.

Rae had just resumed travelling when he encountered an Inuit man named See-u-ti-chu driving a team of dogs with a sledge laden with muskox meat. This man agreed to hire out himself and his dogs for a couple of days. He cached his provisions on the spot and recommended heading west along the route he had just travelled.

The party had no sooner loaded up the dogsled and left than a second communicative local man, the aforementioned In-nook-poo-zhe-jook, who had been away seal-hunting the day before, arrived with more dogs and offered to accompany the party.

The ever-observant Rae noticed that In-nook-poo-zhe-jook wore a gold cap-band and asked him where he had got it. The Inuit man replied that it came from the place where the dead white men were. He had traded for it. Rae proceeded to interrogate him with the help of William Ouligbuck. Later that day, he recorded field notes:

Met a very communicative and apparently intelligent Eskimo; had never met whites before but said that a number of Kabloonas [white men], at least 35–40, had starved to death west of a large river a long distance off. Perhaps 10 or 12 days journey. Could not tell the distance, never had been there, and could not accompany us so far. Dead bodies seen beyond two large rivers; did not know the place, could not or would not explain it on a chart.

With hindsight, we can surmise that the Inuit informant, himself unclear about what happened where, might have confused events and locations. The remains of thirty-five or forty sailors would eventually be found at Terror Bay on the west coast of King William Island. More remains would turn up on the coast near Starvation Cove. The discussion of what happened, where exactly, and when would continue into the final decades of the twentieth century and beyond.

Rae bought the man's cap-band on the spot. He wondered fleetingly whether it might have come from the lost Franklin expedition but quickly dismissed that notion as impossible. Half a dozen ships were searching the waters and islands far to the north. That, everybody agreed, was where the Franklin expedition would be found. Besides, what did he have to act upon? Some white men had died ten or twelve

Sledging over hummocky ice, by S. Gurney Cresswell;
John Rae faced similar conditions with fewer men

days away in a spot these Inuit hunters had never visited that now lay under a thick blanket of snow. The information was far too vague. Rae told In-nook-poo-zhe-jook that if he or his companions had any other relics from white men, they should bring them to his winter quarters at Repulse Bay, where they would be well rewarded.

Both dog teams were tired, and the party made slow progress along a river to Simpson Lake. After a couple of days, the two Inuit men wanted to head home. See-u-ti-chu feared that wolverines might plunder the cache of muskox meat he had stored when he encountered the expedition. Rae paid the men well, repeated his promise regarding any relics, and said goodbye. On resuming his journey, he noticed deer tracks and traces of muskox and realized that the surrounding tundra, frozen and snow-covered, was a hunting ground in which game abounded.

Some weeks before, Jacob Beads had frozen two toes. On April 25, after a hard day's hike of more than eighteen miles, he was scarcely able to walk. The slightly built Johnston also showed signs of fatigue.

Rae decided to allow these two men to proceed at a slower pace to some rocks that lay ahead, where they could build an igloo and wait. The following day, with his two sturdiest men, the Cree Mistegan and the Inuit Ouligbuck, Rae took four days worth of provisions and set out for the mouth of the Castor and Pollux River—the farthest point ever charted from the west, fifteen years earlier.

On April 27, 1854, Rae reached sea ice: a coastline. He passed several heaps of stones, evidently Inuit caches, before discovering a pillar of stones clearly intended more as a marker than as protection of property and whose top had fallen down. He sent Mistegan to trace what looked like the frozen bed of a small river immediately to the west, while with Ouligbuck he dismantled the pillar in search of a document. He discovered none but, checking his latitude, found himself within a quarter mile of Thomas Simpson's 1839 reading on a cairn he had built at the mouth of the Castor and Pollux River. Mistegan returned and affirmed that the frozen bed was indeed a river. Rae had reached his first goal.

Now he prepared to carry out the main objective of his expedition. He would travel north and west along the coast of Boothia Peninsula and King William Land to Bellot Strait, and so complete the mapping of the northern shore of the continent, not incidentally connecting the discoveries made by Simpson in 1839 and by William Kennedy and J.R. Bellot in 1852. He and his two men retraced their steps. After a tiring fifteen-hour march over thirty miles of rough terrain, they arrived at Beads and Johnston's snowhut. The two had shot nothing and had gathered little fuel. Beads could scarcely move, and, despite their protests, Rae insisted that the two men remain where they were. At two o'clock in the morning on April 30, having loaded provisions for twenty-two days onto sledges for Ouligbuck and Mistegan, and himself dragging a third sledge piled with instruments, books, and bedding, Rae set out to trace the last uncharted coastline of North America.

Through fierce winds and heavy, blowing snow, John Rae forced his way north along the coast of Boothia Peninsula. He named Shepherd Bay, Cape Colville, and Stanley Island. Opposite Stanley Island, looking west across the ice during a clear period, Rae spotted a distant promontory and called it Matheson Island (later amended to Matheson Point). To his surprise, the coastline showed no sign of turning west, as the charts suggested it should, to encompass King William Land. Rae continued north and, on May 6, arrived at a promontory he named Point de la Guiche (latitude 68°57'72", longitude 94°32'58"). There, Rae, Mistegan, and Ouligbuck stood gazing out over the ice of a frozen channel where naval charts had indicated they would find land.

Fog and stormy weather had slowed their progess to this point. Given the time left before spring thaw, the distances involved, and the condition of his men, Rae realized that he would not be able to complete the whole survey of the coast as he had intended—not without risking lives. But, with growing excitement, he also glimpsed something else, a possibility: Was this channel before him the final link in the Northwest Passage?

Discoveries tend not to arrive as revelations. Perhaps Archimedes really did discover water displacement when he stepped into his bath, and maybe he did cry, "Eureka! I have found it!" Perhaps Isaac Newton really did discover gravity while sitting under an apple tree at Cambridge. More likely, both stories are fanciful after-the-fact elaborations. More likely, both discoveries emerged slowly, products of painstaking observation and study, arriving not like bolts of lightning but like glorious dawns.

Now, on the west coast of Boothia Peninsula, the ever-practical John Rae put Ouligbuck to work building a snowhut. Taking out his instruments and charts, he sent Mistegan north across the ice beyond Point de la Guiche. The hunter hiked five or six miles and climbed a hill of rough ice to gain a vantage point. The land was still trending northward, while to the northwest, at a considerable distance across a channel of rough ice—perhaps twelve or fourteen miles—more land appeared: "This land, if it was such, is probably part of Matty Island or King William Land, which latter is also clearly an island."

Rae had reached a point where except for the unknown strait before him, his survey matched that made by Sir James Clark Ross in 1830, providing "a very singular agreement ... considering the circumstances under which our surveys have been taken." Rae was being generous. In snowy weather, Ross had missed the strait and charted the area as an enclosed bay—albeit with a dotted line and a question mark. His uncle Sir John Ross, who had discovered the non-existent Croker Mountains, closed the line while preparing the final copy of the expedition map and called the strait Poctes Bay.

Rae contemplated the frozen passage before him. It contained "young ice" radically unlike the much rougher ice he had encountered three years before on the other side of King William Island. Clearly, the island protected this channel from the impenetrable pack ice that flowed from the north. This passage would be navigable when Victoria Strait was not.

Rae looked north toward where James Clark Ross had traversed the ice by dogsled; Ross had surmised, though with some hesitation, that no passage existed in this vicinity. Rae looked south down the strait. In 1835, George Back had looked north, wondering, before reluctantly retreating to the mainland. Four years later, Thomas Simpson of the HBC—an unstable thirty-one-year-old contemptuous of native peoples—had sailed past the entrance. Bent on returning to investigate further, Simpson had died the following summer under mysterious circumstances—as if the Passage had reserved its ultimate secret for a man of different character.

Now, even if he couldn't prove it, John Rae knew he had discovered, running between Boothia Peninsula and King William Island, the hidden gateway link in the Northwest Passage. This was it!

Half a century would elapse before Amundsen would prove him right.

As he looked out over the final link in the Passage, Rae knew that he could still chart perhaps half the remaining distance to Bellot Strait, but that he certainly could not complete the whole trek without great risk to his men. In any case, he had already discovered what he really sought: the channel that would eventually be named Rae Strait.

That night, having built a small cairn just south of the tip of Point de la Guiche to affirm his discoveries, a satisfied Rae and his two hardiest men, the Cree and the Inuit, began the long journey back to Repulse Bay. On reaching the two men he had left waiting, Rae felt confirmed in his decision to turn back. Both were worn down, and Beads was losing one of his big toes at the joint. On other occasions, farther south, Rae had treated frostbite with great success by applying a poultice made of the inner bark of the larch fir. Now, under more difficult conditions, he could do little.

Beads insisted on limping along, stoutly refusing to be hauled. The weather had cleared, the snow was hard-packed, and the men made better time than coming out. They reached their Pelly Bay snowhut on May 17, shortly after midnight, with the bright sun low on the horizon.

John Rae meets Inuit with Franklin relics at Pelly Bay,
from a painting by Charles Comfort

Noticing traces of Inuit, Rae sent Mistegan and Ouligbuck, after they had rested, to follow the tracks. Eight hours later, the two returned with a dozen Inuit men, women, and children.

One of the Inuit people produced a silver fork and spoon, which Rae promptly bought: "The initials F.R.M.C., not engraved but scratched with a sharp instrument on the spoon, puzzled me much, as I knew not at the time the Christian names of the officers of Sir John Franklin's expedition." Still convinced that Franklin had become lost far to the north, Rae speculated about Captain Robert McClure, who had sailed with a search expedition in 1850, and wondered whether the initials might be his, with the small *c* omitted—perhaps F. Robert McClure?

Two of the Inuit, one of whom Rae had met in 1847, offered, for a price, to accompany the party for two days with a sledge and dogs. Always anxious to spare his men, Rae accepted the offer. When the two visitors left them, he bought one of the dogs. He used it to help him chart the coastline of Pelly Bay, so settling once and for all the geographical questions—was Boothia really a peninsula? did no hidden channel lead west?—raised after his 1847 expedition. Then he continued south.

John Rae arrived at Repulse Bay at five o'clock in the morning on May 26, having covered in twenty days the distance (less forty or fifty miles) which, going out in rougher weather, had taken thirty-six days. He found the three men he had left behind living on friendly terms with several newly arrived Inuit families who had pitched tents nearby. "The natives had behaved in the most exemplary manner," wrote Rae, "and many of them who were short of food had been supplied with venison from our stores, in compliance with my orders to that effect."

These Inuit had arrived from Pelly Bay with relics to trade and stories to tell. At last, Rae had an opportunity to question these native people for days on end about the white men who had died of starvation. Only now did Rae realize, with growing horror, that they were talking about the last survivors of the Franklin expedition.

While trading for relics, and then more thoroughly afterwards, Rae asked questions with William Ouligbuck as his interpreter. The Inuit people told him that all of the kabloonas had died several years before, and the explorer had no reason to doubt this. No survivors had ever reached any HBC trading post, although Yellowknife men had been sent out to seek them with ammunition, clear instructions, and promises of reward. The newcomers explained that four winters earlier (in 1850), some Inuit families killing seals near the northern shore of a large island (which Rae now deduced was King William Island) had encountered at least forty kabloonas dragging a boat and some sledges southward.

None of these white men could speak Inuktitut, but they communicated through gestures that their ships had been crushed by ice and that they were travelling to where they hoped to hunt deer. The men looked thin and hungry, and all except the leader were hauling on the drag ropes of sledges. The leader was a tall, stout, middle-aged man who wore a telescope strapped over his shoulder. The party, obviously short of provisions, bought seal meat from the Inuit, then pitched tents and rested. The next day, these kabloonas headed east across the ice toward the mouth of a large river—a river that, Rae now recognized by its description, could only be Back's Great Fish River.

The following spring, when the Inuit visited that river to fish, they discovered about thirty corpses. They found graves on the main part of the continent (*noon-nah*) and five dead bodies on an island (*kai-ik-tak*) a long day's journey northwest of the river. Rae surmised that these references were to Ogle Point and Montreal Island. The Inuit discovered some dead bodies in tents and others under the boat, which had been overturned to form a shelter. A few other bodies lay scattered about. One of the men who had died on the island had a telescope strapped over his shoulder and a double-barrelled gun beneath him.

In one of his reports, Rae summarized what he learned with this arresting entry: "From the mutilated state of many of the bodies, and the contents of the kettles, it is evident that our wretched countrymen had been driven to the last dread alternative as a means of sustaining life."

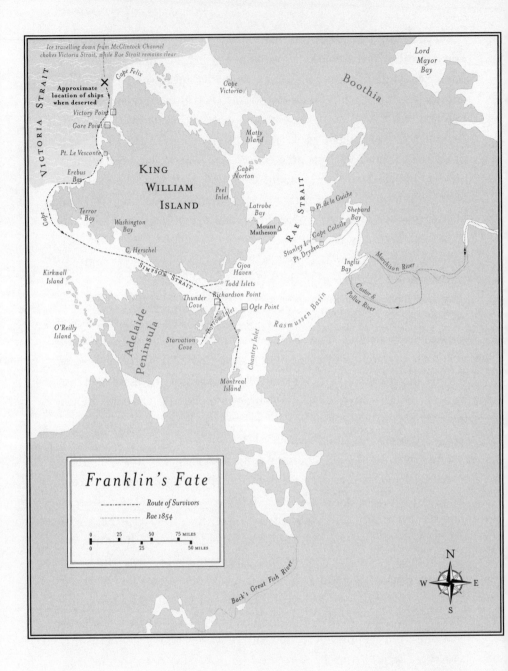

Ice travelling down from McClintock Channel
chokes Victoria Strait, while Rae Strait remains clear

Lord
Mayor
Bay

VICTORIA STRAIT

Cape Felix

✕ Approximate
location of ships
when deserted

Cape
Victoria

Boothia

Victory Point ☐
Gore Point ☐

Matty
Island

Pt. Le Vesconte ☐

KING
WILLIAM
ISLAND

Cape
Norton

Erebus
Bay

Peel
Inlet

RAE STRAIT

☐ Pt. de la Guiche

Cape

Terror
Bay

Latrobe
Bay

Shepard
Bay

Washington
Bay

Mount △
Matheson

☐ Cape Colville

Stanley I. ☐

Murchison River

C. Herschel

SIMPSON STRAIT

Pt. Dryden

Inglis
Bay

Kirkwall
Island

Gjoa
Haven

Todd Islets

Castor &
Pollux River

Thunder
Cove

Richardson Point

O'Reilly
Island

☐ Ogle Point

Rasmussen Basin

Adelaide
Peninsula

Starvation
Cove

Chantrey Inlet

Montreal
Island

Franklin's Fate

–·–·– Route of Survivors

·········· Rae 1854

0   25   50   75 MILES

0   25   50 MILES

Back's Great Fish River

N
W   E
S

None of the Inuit he questioned had seen the kabloonas alive or dead, but Rae had worked long enough in the north to appreciate the power and reliability of the native grapevine. Sitting in his tent, he conducted repeated interviews through Ouligbuck, checking the veracity of his informants against information recorded in the narratives of John Ross and Edward Parry.

The Inuit found it strange that no sledges had been found among the dead, although the boat remained. Rae pointed out that the kabloonas, having reached the mouth of the Great Fish River, would need their boat to proceed farther but might have burned the sledges for fuel. "A look of intelligence immediately lit up their faces," he wrote, "and they said that may have been so, for there had been fires." He continued,

A few of the unfortunate men must have survived until the arrival of the wild fowl (say until the end of May) as shots were heard and fresh bones and feathers of geese were noticed near the scene of the sad event. There appears to have been an abundant store of ammunition, as the gunpowder was emptied by the natives in a heap on the ground out of the kegs or cases containing it, and a quantity of shot

Rae's Franklin-expedition relics, eventually depicted in The Illustrated London News, *included a fork, several spoons, a piece of plate, and a broken compass*

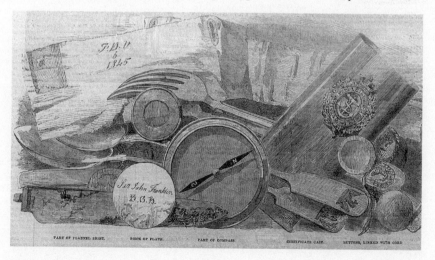

PART OF FLANNEL SHIRT.   PIECE OF PLATE.   PART OF COMPASS   CERTIFICATE CASE.   BUTTONS, LINKED WITH CORD

and ball was found below highwater mark, having probably been left on the ice close to the beach before the spring thaw commenced.

One night, having gleaned all the information he could, Rae sat in his tent sorting through the relics he had acquired. Among them were pieces of telescopes and guns, watches and compasses, all of which had been broken up. Again he counted the identifiable items, those bearing the crests and initials of officers on Franklin's two ships. These totalled fifteen. They included a gold watch, a surgeon's knife, several silver spoons and forks bearing the Franklin crest, an order of merit in the form of a star, and a small silver plate engraved "Sir John Franklin, K.C.H."

Rae studied the engraved plate by lantern light and marvelled: Franklin himself had eaten from it. The presence of this silver dish, together with the other relics, verified the Inuit story beyond doubt. The Franklin expedition had suffered a fate as terrible as the imagination could conceive.

Now Rae faced a difficult decision—perhaps the most important of his life.

He returned the silver plate to his leather bag, then stood up and stepped out the door of the tent. It was almost midnight, but it looked like evening, the sky grey and streaked with clouds. Beside the tent, Rae paced back and forth, his hands clasped behind his back. Should he return immediately to England to report what he had learned? Or should he wait here until next spring and then travel overland to see whether he could find the bodies?

Certainly with summer imminent, he could not even begin that prodigious trek for another eight or ten months. Soon the ice would begin to melt, rendering overland travel impossible. Nor did he have a boat waiting at the other end that he could then use to reach King William Island and Back's Great Fish River. And he couldn't hope to haul the boat he did have several hundred miles.

On the other hand, he had enough pemmican to last three months and enough ammunition to secure food for another winter. Most of his men were in excellent health and next season, sled dogs would be available. If he wanted to, he could conceivably wait through the winter. Should he do it?

Staring up at the scudding clouds, John Rae decided not. To the best of his knowledge, five British ships under Sir Edward Belcher and one American vessel under Elisha Kent Kane were seeking the Franklin expedition in all the wrong places. Their captains had orders to continue searching for years. Rae felt under the circumstances that he had a duty to perform: to communicate as quickly as possible the melancholy tidings he had learned, and so reduce the risk of the needless loss of more lives.

Anyway, how could Rae even dream of keeping secret such cataclysmic news? He had stumbled upon the Arctic story of the century. How could he not have felt driven to share it? On August 4, 1854, when at last the pack ice cleared, Rae sailed south out of Repulse Bay and began his long journey back to England. The explorer could not know it, but having made a career of testing himself, he was about to face the most difficult ordeal of his life.

PART TWO

THE DISCOVERY OF TRUTH

12

THE RETURN OF JOHN RAE

On October 22, 1854, after a tumultuous thirty-one-day passage from York Factory and an Atlantic crossing during which the three-masted *Prince Rupert* narrowly escaped pack ice only to run into a storm that ripped and split four of its principal sails and nearly washed away a lifeboat, the Arctic explorer Dr. John Rae, age forty-one, arrived in England. Two days before, while crossing the English Channel, the forthright but not insensitive Rae had composed a letter to the editor of *The Times*. He had obtained information and articles which proved beyond doubt that many members of Sir John Franklin's lost expedition, missing in the Arctic since 1845, had perished after five years. He had acquired several unmistakable relics, including a small silver plate engraved with Franklin's name, and promised to provide details in a subsequent account.

Blithely unaware that this letter would appear at the same time as certain shocking revelations that he had reserved for official reports, Rae concluded, "I may add that my small party wintered in snow houses comfortably enough at Repulse Bay, after some very hard work in the autumn in laying up a supply of venison and fuel. We returned to York Factory all well on the 30th August but without having completed the contemplated survey." He even added a postscript about the rough passage, noting, "I fear the season has been a most trying one for the ships in the far north."

Rae debarked in Kent at Deal, sixty miles south of London, and found a carriage waiting. Seated alone in the back, travelling through the countryside at up to fifteen miles an hour, he drew back the curtain

*In the mid-nineteenth century, the busy streets of London fairly rang
with the clatter of hooves, the cries of peddlers and the declamations of actors*

to savour the sight of the busy towns, the meadows dotted with sheep,
the countless stone walls rolling away into the wooded distance—all of
it so settled, so civilized, so unlike the white, howling barrens he had
recently left behind.

And then to enter the teeming city of two and a half million, slowly
to navigate the streets clogged with such a variety of horse-drawn
conveyances—with hansoms, hackney coaches, old stagecoaches, new
omnibuses—what a treat! At the same time, Rae could not help noticing the city's sooty, fetid smell, almost overwhelming after the crisp,
clean air of the Arctic and the biting salt wind of the Atlantic crossing.

Part of the problem, he knew, was the smoke from the thousand
belching chimneys. Still worse, two hundred open sewers flowed into
the River Thames, which provided drinking water for almost half the
populace. This lack of sanitation, the doctor was all too aware, made
London a breeding ground for diseases such as cholera, typhus, typhoid
fever, scarlet fever, smallpox, and diptheria. The average age of mortal-
ity was twenty-seven, and just fifteen years earlier, almost half the
funerals in London had marked the passing of children under age ten.

And yet Rae loved this city—the clatter of hooves, the cries of strolling peddlers selling penny dreadfuls, the pronunciamentos of travelling actors declaiming Shakespeare in crowded thoroughfares. An inveterate walker, Rae had spent whole days during previous visits wandering working-class streets teeming with urchins and lined with beer shops and gin palaces. He knew the lanes where men gambled a week's wages on cockfights and dogfights, the squares where malefactors had been pilloried or publicly hung. And he loved the city's contrasts: that not half a mile from the human pandemonium, a more orderly universe unfolded as it should, in which a better class of people strolled through parks in their finery, some of them, he had frequently noted with approval, sporting the most fashionable of beaver hats.

Rae proceeded directly to the Admiralty offices, as requested, even though it was Sunday: he was to deliver a written report directly to the First Lord of the Admiralty, Sir James Graham. He knew that his news had preceded him; Sir George Simpson had forwarded a copy of the report Rae had made to the Hudson's Bay Company on the first available ship. Clearly, he was expected. One man took his cloak and his beaver hat and another led him to a waiting room, where Sir James greeted him warmly.

Rae followed the older man into his large private office, its walls lined with books and paintings of naval scenes, its several tables cluttered with papers, maps, and charts. Smoking had recently become fashionable, and Sir James offered Rae a cigar: "Oh, that's right, you don't smoke. I've read your *Arctic Narrative*, Doctor." He moved to a liquor cabinet. "You'll take a whiskey, I hope?"

As he poured two large glasses, Sir James inquired generally about Rae's voyage.

And when both men were seated at a low table, the older man said, "So what's this about the lost navigators? You've acquired some relics, I understand."

Rae picked up his leather satchel. "Indeed, I have."

Sir James cleared the table of papers. "Let's take a look, shall we?"

From out of his leather satchel, Rae drew his handwritten report and handed it to the First Lord, saying, "I take it that you have already seen a copy of a similar document I submitted to the Hudson's Bay Company."

"I have, yes." Sir James laid the report aside. "I'll peruse this later, rest assured."

From his bag, Rae produced those items he had collected, placing them gently, one by one, on the mahogany table: the broken watches and telescopes and compasses, the surgeon's knife, the order of merit, the silver forks and spoons with the Franklin crest, and, last of all, the small silver plate engraved "Sir John Franklin, K.C.H."

John Rae as portrayed in 1854 in The Illustrated London News

Sir James examined each in turn, muttering, "Remarkable, remarkable."

He lingered over the silver plate, holding it up to the light. He blew on it and rubbed at the engraved letters with the cuff of his jacket. After a minute, he sighed and said, "There's no doubt about it, then."

"I am afraid not."

"And you acquired these where?"

"Most of them at Repulse Bay, a few at Pelly Bay. I was driving a team of dogs west when—"

"Come, Doctor!" Sir James led Rae to a larger table that was covered with a map of the Arctic. "You must demonstrate."

Using the map to trace his route, his voice a mixture of excitement and seriousness, John Rae began his tale. He described how while driving a team of dogs across Boothia, he had enountered the intelligent Inuit man whose cap-band made him wonder. He summarized the trek to Point de la Guiche, then drew on the map in pencil, sketching in the strait he had discovered that separated King William Land—"It's an island, you see"—from Boothia Peninsula. Hoping that Sir James would take the hint and speculate about the Northwest Passage, he added, "I saw nothing but young ice, there. That channel is open, I am convinced, for several months of each year."

"Mmm," the older man replied. "And the relics?"

Hiding his slight disappointment and vowing to return to the subject of geographical discovery, Rae described how, after returning to Pelly Bay, he had procured the first relics besides the cap-band, including a few of those he had just produced. How after ascertaining that the broken watches and compasses and silver spoons had come from a place where these particular Inuit people had never been before, a place far away by a great river, he promised to pay huge rewards for any further relics from that same cache. And how, back at Repulse Bay, Inuit people had begun arriving with ever more conclusive relics. "The evidence mounted and finally I knew with certainty that these items could have come from only one expedition—that of Sir John Franklin."

Rae described how as spring came on and gradually melted the ice, he sat day after day in his tent, interviewing the Inuit people with the help of William Ouligbuck, the finest translator in the North, until he had gleaned every bit of information they had.

The explorer sipped his whiskey.

"Do go on, Doctor."

In the spring of 1850, as far as Rae could deduce, Inuit hunters had encountered thirty-five or forty kabloonas dragging a boat south along the west coast of a large island. Using gestures, these white men told the Inuit that their ship or ships had been crushed by ice and that now they were travelling to where they hoped to hunt deer. They were short of provisions and, except for one officer, looked thin and ill-fed. After trading for a small seal, which was all the hunters had to spare, they proceeded on their way.

On the map, Rae indicated a spot on the west coast of King William Island: "That's where Franklin's two ships got nipped. The pack ice is impenetrable."

Sir James raised his thick eyebrows.

"Three years ago, I was in that channel," Rae said. "Just here—within fifty miles—when I sailed up the east coast of Victoria Island."

The older man shook his head and the explorer resumed. "For some reason, probably because they ran out of food, Franklin and his men abandoned their ships." He traced a line down the west coast of King William Island. "They travelled south along here—though why they didn't go east and make for Fury Beach, where the Rosses had left all those provisions, I will never understand."

"How do you know they went south?"

"Esquimaux hunters." He ran his finger south down the island and across to the continent, to Montreal Island and the mouth of Back's Great Fish River. "Some of them found bodies here."

Rae fell silent, and finally Sir James prompted him: "They found bodies?"

"Thirty-five or forty bodies." Rae hesitated again, then said, "I regret to inform you, Sir James, that the final survivors of the expedition suffered a fate as terrible as the imagination can conceive."

Sir James poured himself another glass of whiskey—the explorer had barely touched his first—and resumed his original seat by the low table now covered with relics. Joining him, Rae said, "Some of the bodies had been buried, but some lay in tents or on the ground, others under an overturned boat. One man, apparently an officer, died with a telescope strapped over his shoulder and a double-barrelled gun beneath him."

Sir James sipped his whiskey.

After another hesitation, his voice breaking, Rae added, "From the mutilated state of many of the corpses, Sir James, and the contents of the kettles, it is evident that some of our wretched countrymen had been driven to the last resource."

Sir James inhaled but maintained control of his voice: "The last resource."

"Cannibalism, Sir James. As a means of prolonging existence."

Sir James rose to his feet, moved to the window, and pulled back the curtain. For a moment he stood there, sipping whiskey, looking out at the street in silence. Finally dropping the curtain, he said, "Are you aware, Doctor Rae, that we have offered a reward of ten thousand pounds to any party who ascertains the fate of the Franklin expedition?"

"A reward? I know nothing of that."

"Ten thousand pounds, yes. To which you're clearly entitled."

"This is a quite a surprise. I have been two years away."

Straight-faced, the older man said, "You'll have no objection, then?"

"Objection?"

Sir James smiled and led the way toward the door. "Come, Doctor. We have kept the others waiting too long."

"The others, Sir James?"

"John Barrow, a man from *The Times,* one or two others."

"Is Richardson among them?"

"I'm afraid not. He lives too far south."

"The truth is, Sir James, I have been wondering about Lady Franklin. I know I must visit her, but I thought someone else might be sent to prepare the way."

"Ah, yes, Lady Franklin." The First Lord spoke without warmth or fondness. "Richardson, you think? A capital idea. His second wife was Franklin's niece, was she not?"

A front-page story appeared the next day in the mighty *Times*. It quoted not only Rae's letter to the editor, which he had intended for wide distribution, but also his far more detailed report to the Admiralty, which he had expected would remain confidential. After all, the Lords and leaders of the British Admiralty constituted one kind of audience, the general readership of *The Times* quite another.

For the Admiralty, as for the Hudson's Bay Company, Rae had described the finding of the bodies, some in tents, others under a boat. He had mentioned the officer who died with his gun. Then, still with officialdom in mind, he had written a sentence that would shock the average Victorian beyond words: "From the mutilated state of many of the corpses and the contents of the kettles, it is evident that our wretched countrymen had been driven to the last resource—cannibalism—as a means of prolonging existence."

The journalist from *The Times*, knowing a scoop when he heard one, had concluded his story with a list of the relics Rae had brought and a few closing remarks:

Dr. Rae adds that from what he could learn there is no reason to suspect that any violence had been offered to the sufferers by the natives. It seems but too evident that they had perished from hunger, aggravated by the extreme severity of the climate. Some of the corpses had been sadly mutilated, and had been stripped by those who had the misery to survive them, and who were found wrapped in two or three suits of clothes.

Decades later, the biographer Hendrick van Loon would report that his father, who lived through this period, forever remembered "the shock of horror that . . . swept across the civilized world" as news spread of Rae's report. This was the mid-nineteenth century, after all. Great Britain was the world's reigning superpower, the heart of a global empire. As a nation, it showed a keen interest in what happened around the world and an unshakable conviction of its own superiorty and invincibility.

In the autumn of 1854, when Rae arrived in London with his dreadful news, Britain was in the middle of the Crimean War. The previous January, having signed a treaty with Turkey, the Admiralty had sent warships to the Black Sea. Russia had already ignored an ultimatum to evacuate a contested area and had sent troops across the Danube River. On March 28, the war had erupted, pitting England and its allies against Russia.

Two months before, determined not to be distracted with Arctic search expeditions, the Lords of the Admiralty had declared that Sir John Franklin and his crews would be considered officially dead on March 31, 1854. Lady Jane Franklin had decried this decision as indecorous, indecent, and presumptuous in the sight of God. In protest, she had doffed her usual black widow's weeds, which she described as "the habiliments of despair," and appeared publicly in bright pink and green: "It would be acting falsehood, & a gross hypocrisy on my part, to put on mourning when I have not yet given up all hope."

After all, six ships remained in the Arctic searching for her husband.

In September 1854, however, one month before Rae reached London, Sir Edward Belcher and his men returned. Not only had Belcher discovered nothing, he had abandoned four valuable ships in the Arctic pack ice (an action for which he barely escaped court martial). That left two vessels unaccounted for: the British *Enterprise* under Captain Richard Collinson and the American *Advance* under Elisha Kent Kane.

Lady Franklin, by now an icon of the faithful, long-suffering wife, continued to call for Arctic search expeditions. She had taken an apartment not far from the Admiralty the better to conduct her relentless campaign. Indeed, her naval friends called this place "the battery."

The Admiralty, therefore, which had spent over 600,000 pounds on 55 search expeditions, had good reason not only to welcome Rae's report, but also to publish it: this finally settled the matter. The lost navigators had perished, and the Admiralty could, in good conscience, devote both money and attention to the Crimean War.

Not long after his return to London, John Rae, still wearing his full Arctic beard—an ornament that, absent from polite circles for two centuries, had only recently begun returning to fashion—paid the obligatory courtesy call on Lady Franklin. He had spoken with Sir John Richardson, with whom he had earlier travelled in search of Franklin, and did not expect a warm reception. True, Lady Franklin had sent Rae more than one flattering letter and had even sipped cherry brandy with his mother in Orkney. Her niece and constant companion, Sophia Cracroft, had described Rae's mother as "the most beautiful old lady we had ever beheld . . . and her old-fashioned courtesy is so hearty and generous."

But those had been more innocent times. Now, incensed by Rae's published report, Lady Franklin received the explorer with ominous frigidity.

White-faced and tight-lipped, a well-dressed dowager of sixty-three, Lady Franklin received Rae in her drawing room. She and her niece stood together before the fireplace. Lady Franklin did not invite the explorer to sit down.

Rae's relics, sketched for The Illustrated London News, *also included a cook's knife, a broken watch, and the original gold braid*

Coached by Sir John Richardson, Rae said, "I come only to pay my respects, Lady Franklin, and to offer my condolences. I deeply regret the death of your husband."

When Lady Franklin did not respond, he added: "You have seen the relics, I presume?'

"I have seen the relics, yes." Lady Franklin looked off into space. "Those relics are what finally convinced me that the good Sir John is dead."

"I acquired them from Esquimaux. I would—"

Lady Franklin interrupted, her voice flat and cold: "I have read your report, Doctor Rae. How *could* you? That is what I do not understand. How *could* you make such terrible allegations against my husband?"

"Madam, I have made no allegations. I did have a responsibility to report what I learned to my superiors at the Hudson's Bay Company, and also to the British Admiralty."

"That report, Doctor Rae, was shameful."

Reddening in the face, Rae said, "I did not write the report for public consumption. And I deeply regret that the Admiralty chose to publish it in full."

Lady Franklin drew herself up to her full height and hissed, "Such allegations, Doctor Rae, should never have been committed to paper in the first place."

Rae refused to be cowed. "The truth, Lady Franklin. The truth would have surfaced in any event. It could never have been suppressed. All my men knew the truth. Better it should—"

"The truth, Doctor Rae? The truth?" Two bright pink spots had appeared on her deathly white cheeks. "You speak only of what you heard from Esquimaux savages."

Controlling his emotions with difficulty, the explorer bowed from the waist. "I perceive that I have come too soon, Lady Franklin. Perhaps I—"

"The word of savages," Sophia Cracroft snorted. "Oh, you shall pay for this, Doctor Rae. For this, you shall certainly pay."

"Perhaps I should take my leave. We can pursue this conversation at a later date."

"Perhaps you *should* take your leave, Doctor Rae." Before the explorer could move, however, Lady Franklin spun on her heel and, in a rustling of crinolines, swished out of the room. Sophia Cracroft scurried after her.

If Lady Jane Franklin could not bring her husband back, she could surely salvage his place in history. With renewed intensity, she began calling for further search expeditions. She needed not only to refute Rae's horrific revelations, which threatened to taint her husband's memory, but to vindicate Franklin as the true discoverer of the Northwest Passage—even if, the previous autumn, Commander Robert McClure had begun claiming that honour for himself.

The well-connected Lady Franklin knew how to apply pressure. The Admiralty quickly realized that, the Crimean War notwithstanding, two more Arctic expeditions would be necessary: one to provide eyewitness verification of Rae's findings while seeking to acquire any remaining written records, the other to locate and relieve the missing *Enterprise*, which had now entered its fourth year in the Arctic. By far the quickest approach in both cases would be to send overland expeditions, probably in co-operation with the Hudson's Bay Company, and one of these could perhaps be led by John Rae.

Rae provided detailed recommendations for both undertakings. He specified routes, recommended individuals (including Thomas Mistegan and William Ouligbuck), and even listed boats and equipment. But he politely declined repeated requests to lead an expedition. He had had enough of Arctic trekking for the present; now forty-one years old, the veteran of four major expeditions, he yearned to marry and settle down. Sir John Richardson, his old travelling companion, wrote to the naval hydrographer, Sir Francis Beaufort, explaining that Rae's regrettable refusal was the result of "how much he suffered by his exertions in provisioning his party at Repulse Bay in the autumn of last year and the lasting rheumatism that was induced."

On November 8, 1854, word reached England that Collinson and the *Enterprise* had emerged safely from the Arctic. This meant that only one overland expedition would be necessary, to seek further evidence of the fate of Franklin. In June of 1855, the fur-trader James Anderson, one of two HBC men Rae had recommended, would lead a canoe party down Back's Great Fish River to the Arctic coast and verify Rae's report.

Meanwhile, the backlash had begun. On October 27, a *Times* editorial avoided criticizing Rae personally—except for his credulity—while targetting the Inuit: "Like all savages they are liars," it declared, and "although they are a harmless race little given to violence, they might have been tempted by the emaciation and weakness of the white men to attack them." Four days later, *The Sun* joined the assault: "The more we reflect upon the fate of the Franklin Expedition the less we are inclined to believe that this noble band of adventurers resorted to cannibalism. No—they never resorted to such horrors. . . . Cannibalism!—the gallant Sir John Franklin a cannibal—such men as Crozier, Fitzjames, Stanley, Goodsir, cannibals!"

Rae received so many letters of query and complaint, especially from those who had lost relatives on the Franklin expedition, that the HBC gave him time off to respond. Some of his critics went public. On October 30, the Reverend Edward Hornby, whose brother had sailed on the *Terror*, published a letter in *The Times*:

It appears to me that Dr. Rae has been deeply reprehensible either in not verifying the report which he received from the Esquimaux, or, if that was absolutely out of the question, in publishing the details of that report, resting, as they do, on grounds most weak and unsatisfactory. He had far better have kept silence altogether than give us a story, which, while it pains the feelings of many, must be very insufficient for all.

Victorian newspapers slandered the Esquimaux as murderous savages

Flatly refusing to credit Rae's story, Hornby raised the kinds of questions that those only slightly familiar with the Arctic would naturally ask: for example, where the Inuit can survive, what would prevent Franklin and his men from doing the same? Hornby believed that the ships had been abandoned and then plundered by Inuit people: "I would only persuade myself that I am not compelled to believe the painful details which Dr. Rae has most unwarrantably published."

Rae responded privately, answering specifics: the Inuit don't often congregate in companies of one hundred or more because the land doesn't provide enough game to support such numbers; instead, hunters range widely in small groups. Hornby repeated his assertion that Rae's grounds for alleging cannibalism were weak and unsatisfactory and that he still disbelieved them. Rae answered that Hornby's tone was harsh and unjust, and he concluded, "I could easily, and, I believe, quite as satisfactorily, have replied to the third difficulty you stated as to the first and second, but really thought it too unimportant to waste time upon it."

Clearly, the criticism was taking a toll on Rae's mood.

Privately, Arctic veterans such as Sir John Richardson, Sir John Ross, and Leopold McClintock accepted the truth of Rae's report. Publicly, the explorer stood alone. When Rae presented the final version of his report to the Royal Geographical Society in mid-November, telling the story of his entire expedition, the ailing ex-president of the Society, Sir Roderick Murchison, wrote to the executive in support of "poor Dr. Rae," expressing gratitude that he had pointed the search in the right direction. Murchison felt it important to support Rae because "so many jostling seamen" would be out to criticize him for failing to obtain first-hand evidence while suggesting that the last survivors had resorted to cannibalism.

The soon-to-be-disgraced Sir Edward Belcher, who had shamefully abandoned four ships rather than spend even a second winter in the Arctic, demanded to know why the infamous kettles had any contents at all if "our wretched countrymen had been driven to the last resource?" Over a century later, author Roderic Owen would call this fatuous remark a "pertinent observation." Owen, a descendant of and apologist for Franklin, added elsewhere that because Rae expressed no doubts about the Inuit reports, "he deserved to be pilloried; for naiveté if not for a deliberate intention to mislead. Pilloried he was."

The last sentence, at least, is true.

John Rae's harshest critics included Richard King, the surgeon and naturalist who in 1833–35 had accompanied Sir George Back down the Great Fish River. King had been lobbying to lead another Arctic expedition down that river ever since, but he had alienated and offended any potential backers with his arrogant, abrasive manner. Rae, meanwhile, had accomplished everything his bilious critic had ever dreamed of achieving. Now King joined others to criticize Rae for **being** too credulous; for not travelling to the area indicated by the Inuit to verify their story; for hurrying home to claim the reward offered for news of Franklin; and, above all, for arguing on the word of "Esquimaux savages" that men of the Royal Navy had resorted to cannibalism.

Some of these criticisms arose because Rae wrote so awkwardly. He had mastered the rules of grammar, more or less, but lacked style and flair; he had no sense of composition, of narrative. When he arrived at the point in his report when he heard vague rumours of dead sailors, Rae summarized everything he learned later at Repulse Bay, during two months of intensive cross-examination. His narrative gave the false impression that verifying the Inuit report would have been quite possible, whereas in truth he didn't have enough information to act. By the time he acquired sufficient knowledge, the looming spring thaw prevented exploration, nor did Rae possess a transportable boat or canoe to visit an island. He would have had to spend another winter at Repulse Bay while, to the best of his knowledge, half a dozen ships and several hundred men continued to risk their lives searching the wrong areas.

Other challenges arose simply because Rae had long since rejected the assumptions of his critics. Raised in Orkney and seasoned in Rupert's Land, he repudiated the prejudices of Victorian England. He drew on an unparalleled base of factual knowledge about the Arctic and so did not assume that the Inuit were inveterate liars, much less murderers. He simply did not believe that Royal Navy officers and sailors, no matter how well-educated, how devoutly Christian, were superior to all other human beings and so exempt, under extreme conditions, from normal behaviour. The Arctic had taught him otherwise.

Rae answered his critics with truth. He explained that he had sifted the story repeatedly, checking for inconsistencies through a superlative interpreter. When tested against everything he knew about scurvy and starvation, up to and including the tragic events at Pelly Banks, the terrible story rang all too true. To the assertion that he should have immediately travelled west from the Castor and Pollux River to verify the story, he explained that he hadn't at that time acquired sufficient information. Neither of the two Inuit men he had so far encountered could specify the site of the calamity, and he believed it to be a ten- or twelve-day journey to the west—a tiny area somewhere in a hummocky wasteland of yawning crevasses and ten-foot pressure ridges assailed by blizzards and blowing snow. Besides, he had doubted then that the Inuit men could be talking about the Franklin expedition, which he firmly believed—along with the vast majority of naval experts—to be lost hundreds of miles to the north.

If Sir John Franklin had run into difficulty near King William Island, surely he would have retreated not south toward the mainland, but northeast to Fury Beach on Somerset Island. There, as Franklin and his officers would certainly have known, Sir Edward Parry had abandoned the wreck of HMS *Fury* along with an immense stock of provisions. (In 1859, Leopold McClintock would find those stores still intact.) There, too, the party would have been in an area frequently visited by whaling ships. To pursue any other course would be a great mistake, one Rae simply did not believe an experienced officer would make.

When finally he did realize, with growing horror, that the Inuit were indeed describing the last survivors of the Franklin expedition, he was back at Repulse Bay. He wrote, "To have verified the report which I brought home would have been no difficult matter, but it could not possibly be done by my party in any other way than by passing another winter at Repulse Bay and making another journey over the ice and snow in the spring of 1855." By that time, if he returned instead to England, another overland expedition could be mounted with no loss of time (as, indeed, one was).

Rae pointed out later that even if he had had a boat or canoe, he couldn't have searched for further evidence in the autumn of 1854 without exposing his men to almost certain starvation. He and his men depended on their own guns for food, specifically on shooting deer during their southward migration in the autumn. If Rae had been absent searching for bodies, he could not have hunted; and the previous season, he himself had accounted for nearly half the party's game. Not only that, but to succeed in any such hypothetical expedition, he would have needed his best men with him—men who were also the next-best hunters.

In any event, by the time he knew the truth, the season was already so advanced that he and his men could not have got back to Repulse Bay until after the setting of the sea ice, and so could not have left to spread the news. Above all, Rae felt he "had a higher duty to attend to—that duty being to communicate, with as little loss of time as possible, the melancholy tidings which I had heard, and thereby save the risk of more valuable lives being lost."

Despite all this, in their introduction to Rae's *Arctic Correspondence*, J.M. Wordie and R.J. Cyriax would write, "Rae's return at this time [in 1854] has always been a matter of regret for a great chance had been lost." In fact, nobody, not even Rae, could have reached the mouth of Back's Great Fish River earlier than did the overland expedition led by James Anderson in the summer of 1855. Nothing whatever was lost by Rae's return except the services of the great explorer himself.

As a corollary to the charge of returning too soon to England, Rae's critics suggested that he had done so in order to collect the posted reward. Back in 1850, when Rae was reorganizing Fort Simpson for the Hudson's Bay Company, the Admiralty had offered 20,000 pounds to any party who found and relieved the Franklin expedition and 10,000 pounds to anyone who ascertained its fate. During the winter of 1852, which Rae spent in Britain, he probably heard this reward mentioned, but he paid scant attention and eventually forgot about it.

At that point Rae firmly believed—and stated as much in *The Times*—that he had no chance at all of learning anything about Franklin during his forthcoming expedition. He thought he was travelling to an area over 500 miles distant from that in which traces of the lost navigators would be found. Why would he register and retain the details of an irrelevant award? Later, when he realized what he had discovered, Rae would doubtless have speculated that some sort of financial reward would be forthcoming. But in fact, he dreamed mainly of being awarded a knighthood—an accolade that his friends, certainly, felt he had already earned.

Sir George Simpson, for example, before the volcano of criticism erupted, wrote of John Rae to the politician Edward Ellice, Jr.,

His long and arduous labours in the Arctic regions & this important service with which they have been closed, seem to me to entitle him to some mark of distinction at the hands of his Sovereign and I should think the public would consider a knighthood well earned & worthily bestowed. Nobody could arrange this matter so well as your father [Edward "Bear" Ellice], and if you agree in opinion with me, perhaps you will be kind enough to bring the subject under his notice.

Rae had written to the older Ellice days after his arrival in London, mentioning his conversation with the First Lord of the Admiralty: "Sir James Graham the other day mentioned that he considered I was entitled to a reward which had been promised to anyone who brought authentic tidings of Franklin's fate. I had either forgotten or never known that such was the case, and shall have no objection should it be so."

Decades later, the Franklin apologist Roderic Owen would write of Rae's explanation, "Too many things seemed to smell too strongly of fish." Subsequent authors, worried perhaps about appearing gullible, would follow Owen's lead and suggest that Rae had been lying. But Rae's most hostile critics at the time, including the anonymous author of a scurrilous pamphlet called *Arctic Rewards and their Claimants*, were quite prepared to abandon this particular criticism, which conflicted with the more damaging (and equally false) contention that Rae had failed to pursue the search for Franklin when he could and should have done so, and that he could have discovered traces of the lost expedition if only he had been willing to abandon his original geographical quest. In this version of events, which colours even the sympathetic R.L. Richards's biography of Rae, the explorer had become so obsessed with proving his original report correct about the geography of Boothia Felix—that it was a peninsula, not an island—that he refused to abandon his original geographical objectives.

On close examination and in the clear light of history, all of these allegations crumble to nonsense. They start from the premise that John Rae was a liar, if only because he asserted that men of the British navy had resorted to cannibalism: how, therefore, could he be anything else? Malicious, spiteful, invariably the product of vested interests, their intent was to discredit Rae.

If the explorer had been compelled to answer only such attacks as these—allegations and innuendoes that could be factually or logically refuted—he might eventually have seen his achievements properly recognized. He might have been universally recognized for what he was: "a man exact and truthful," in the words of Vilhjalmur Stefansson, "and in his methods of travel a generation ahead of his time."

But Rae's most devastating critics were yet to emerge.

13

ENTER CHARLES DICKENS

A t the apex of the stratified, social pyramid that was mid-Victorian England lived the Upper Ten Thousand, a leisure class of families with annual incomes of at least 10,000 pounds (in contemporary terms, well over $750,000 U.S. dollars). Many were noblemen and landowners, though recently professional and business families had begun to enter this group in greater numbers, forging links through the court and the cabinet, or else through joint financial ventures and the fashionable pursuit of horse racing.

For this upper echelon of society, the quality of life had deteriorated only slightly, if at all, from that portrayed by Jane Austen (1775–1817) in novels such as *Pride and Prejudice* and *Mansfield Park*. And it was here, among the Upper Ten Thousand, that Lady Jane Franklin had lived all her life.

Born in 1791, the daughter of a wealthy silk weaver, young Jane Griffin attended a Chelsea boarding school and emerged a compulsive journal keeper. She contrived in her twenties to hide her fierce intelligence behind a mask of conventionality. She attended glittering receptions at

The only surviving likeness of Jane Griffin / Lady Jane Franklin

court and in the mansions of Mayfair, whirling through garden parties, boat trips, balls, and summer romances. She went to Ascot and Henley on schedule and travelled around Europe, sojourning in Italy for months at a time. She flirted and danced with young Benjamin Disraeli, future prime minister of England, and conducted a long, chaste romance with Peter Mark Roget, the doctor who later created the famous thesaurus.

Articulate and ambitious, a frequenter of Royal Institute lectures, and within limits, a taker of calculated risks, Jane Griffin rejected all suitors until in 1828, at the age of thirty-seven, having prompted a proposal from a widower five years her senior—a plodding man, gloomy, bumbling, and bovine, but who, she happened to know, was to be granted a knighthood within the year—Miss Griffin scanned the horizon one last time and, seeing nobody else, seized the moment. Within six months of marrying John Franklin, Miss Jane Griffin had become Lady Jane Franklin, an appellation she felt to be far more suitable.

But now what would she do with this lumbering naval man who had made his good name in the Arctic by eating his shoes—a matter of keeping starvation at bay until Yellowknife rescuers arrived. Lady Franklin approved of her husband's appointment to a Mediterranean post, which enabled her to sojourn in Corfu, to travel in Spain, Greece, and Syria, and to become the first European lady in living memory to penetrate north of Africa (present-day Iran) as far as "the snow-white city of Tehran." Having vetoed a subsequent offer of appointment as manifestly beneath both him and herself, she entertained another, much grander proposal in 1836: would she consent to her husband becoming lieutenant-governor of Van Diemen's Land?

Although it meant running a penal colony, this appointment showed far more promise, and Lady Franklin accepted. Indeed, while living in what is now Tasmania, Lady Franklin laid claim to being the first woman to climb Mount Wellington and the first to travel overland from Melbourne to Sydney. She did her best for the colony, fostering voluntary immigration by establishing an agricultural settlement and seeking to improve living conditions for female convicts. But also she meddled in Franklin's business affairs to the point, one day, of intercepting a letter from Sir John Barrow, second secretary to the Admiralty, who was furious about some mistreatment accorded his son. Lady Franklin ordered her niece, the dutiful Sophia Cracroft, to throw the letter into the fire.

When Franklin found out, he stormed around the room, crying, "You have ruined me with my best friend! Burn a letter to me from John Barrow? No, I don't believe it! Surely you cannot be speaking the truth! Surely you never could do such a thing!"

With Sophia cowering behind her, Lady Franklin stood tall: "Yes, John, I did it. And I would do it again, too. I'm sure I did the right thing, and Sir John Barrow himself will one day be obliged to me for it."

In 1843, Sir John Franklin, derided as a victim of petticoat domination, a governor who took lessons in statecraft from his wife, was censured for incompetence and recalled from Van Diemen's Land, his successor already appointed and, indeed, on the spot before he heard a word about it.

Returned to England but not daunted, Lady Franklin learned that the Lords of the Admiralty were seeking someone to lead what would almost certainly be the most glorious Arctic expedition of them all: the one destined finally to discover the Northwest Passage. Who better to lead this triumph than her husband? Never mind that the overweight gentleman was nearing sixty years old. What better way for the good Sir John to reclaim his rightful place as a national hero? History would remember her as consort to the discoverer of the Northwest Passage.

When Lady Jane Franklin began to lobby, her husband was far down the list of non-contenders. When she finished, notwithstanding his advanced age and the declared preferences of senior Admiralty officers, Sir John Franklin was appointed to head the last great Arctic expedition. In 1845, he sailed.

And when, after two years, her husband did not reappear trailing clouds of glory, Lady Franklin recognized her obligation to mastermind the search-and-rescue operation. She augmented the Admiralty's extraordinary 20,000-pound reward for locating and assisting Sir John with 3,000 pounds of her own—the equivalent today of 150,000 pounds (U.S. $225,000). Then she began financing, both out of her own purse and by public subscription, the mounting of one disastrous search expedition after another. She purchased the ninety-ton *Prince Albert* and sent it twice to the Arctic. Then she sent the steam yacht *Isabel*. Pulling strings behind the scenes, overruling senior naval men, she saw to it that an outstanding whaling captain, William Penny, should command two government search vessels, *Lady Franklin* and *Sophia*. Yet even he found nothing.

Then John Rae arrived with his shocking report. The Admiralty ruling notwithstanding, Lady Franklin would never have accepted that her husband was dead "had not the unexpected intelligence brought by Dr. Rae in October, confirmed as it was by the relics he had obtained from the Esquimaux, convinced me ... that I should never see my dear husband again in the world, but that he had ceased to live in an earlier period than that when Dr. Rae made the acquisition of these melancholy proofs." She felt and knew herself to be a widow, she wrote, on examining the relics of her late husband, which included not just the collar and crop of his order, but a broken chronometer, a small silver plate with his name engraved upon it, and several silver spoons and forks that bore his crest.

Recovering quickly from her trauma—her husband had been gone nine years, after all—Lady Franklin turned her attention to Rae. With his recalcitrance and obstinacy, this Orkneyman, this fur-trader, was tarnishing Sir John's reputation. He was undermining her just as she was preparing to battle Robert McClure, who claimed he had discovered the Northwest Passage.

Lady Franklin launched a fierce campaign to discredit the upstart explorer. She denigrated and reviled Rae to her friends and relations, among them numerous knights, lords, and leading politicians. Then, having encountered some resistance—Rae was not without achievement, after all—she hit upon an especially devious stratagem: she would enlist the aid of the most influential writer of the age. In November 1854, less than one month after Rae arrived back in England, Lady Jane Franklin invited a writer to her home for the first time—a writer named Charles Dickens.

*

Born one year before John Rae, the son of a navy clerk who had fallen on hard times, Dickens had long since established himself as England's most popular author. Already his published works included *Oliver Twist*, *A Christmas Carol*, *David Copperfield*, and *Bleak House*. Dickens was profoundly a man of his times. Of all Victorian writers, he was the one most committed to social reform, especially to improving the lot of the poor. His was the voice of the people, raised to an unparalleled eloquence.

Charles Dickens used his eloquence and influence in a masterful attempt to repudiate the notion of cannibalism among the final survivors of the Franklin expedition

Yet like many of his contemporaries, Dickens was prone to an obtuse and irrational racism. In *Bleak House*, which he completed mere months before Rae returned to London, he wrote of a member of a visible minority, "He is not softened by distance and unfamiliarity; he is not a genuine foreign-grown savage; he is the ordinary home-made article. Dirty, ugly, disagreeable to all the senses, in body a common creature of the common streets, only in soul a heathen."

In 1857, when British newspapers would be awash in wildly exaggerated reports of atrocities committed by rebellious Hindus during the "Indian mutiny," Dickens would advocate not justice or even retribution, but genocide. "I wish I were commander-in-chief in India," he would write. "I should do my utmost to exterminate the Race upon whom the stain of the late cruelties rested."

Since 1850, the prolific Dickens had also been publishing a popular weekly magazine called *Household Words*. That journal, Lady Franklin realized, would provide the perfect venue for a devastating repudiation of John Rae—and, not incidentally, a complete vindication of her late husband.

Lady Franklin had long since mastered the use of flattery to achieve her ends. A few years before, when she hoped Rae might discover Franklin in the Arctic, she had written him an almost fawning letter. Now she and Sophia Cracroft—an attractive woman who had twice spurned marriage proposals from Franklin's second-in-command, the Irishman Francis Crozier—turned their wiles on the most influential writer of the age.

Dickens, owing in large part to his own childhood, was a socially ambitious man, one for whom recognition by the likes of Lady Franklin would mean much. On November 19, 1854, in response to a written invitation, he called at 60 Pall Mall, a fashionable address just north of St. James's Park. The drawing room scene is not hard to imagine: the finest sherry, the ladies in their crinolined dresses, one of them perhaps playing piano, Dickens himself at his eloquent best.

Before he arrived, the overworked author had scarcely glanced at John Rae's report on the Franklin expedition. But he had no trouble agreeing with Lady Jane Franklin that it was a scandalous piece of work: the very idea of crediting allegations made by Esquimaux savages! The morning after he visited Lady Franklin, Dickens wrote to one W.H. Willis, "It has occurred to me that I am rather strong on Voyages and Cannibalism, and might do an interesting little paper for the next No. on that part of Dr. Rae's report, taking the arguments against its probabilities. Can you get me a newspaper cutting containing his report? If not, will you have it copied for me and sent up to Tavistock House straight away?"

Charles Dickens's "little paper" evolved into a two-part proclamation of faith. Entitled "The Lost Arctic Voyagers," it became the apogee of the criticism levelled against Rae. Part one of the essay appeared December 2, 1854, as a lead article in *Household Words*. Where Lady Franklin had raged that cannibalism should never even have been mentioned in writing, Dickens acknowledges that Rae had a responsibility to report what he had heard. He slams the Admiralty, however, for publishing the unedited report in *The Times* without considering its effects. Where other critics had charged that Rae had been remiss in not immediately travelling to the specified area to verify the allegations and claimed that he had hurried home to collect the reward, Dickens dismisses the allegation, exonerating Rae personally but attacking his conclusions. John Rae had established that Sir John Franklin and his party were no more, Dickens writes,

[but] there is no reason whatever to believe that any of its members prolonged their existence by the dreadful expedient of eating the bodies of their dead companions. Quite apart from the very loose and unreliable nature of the Esquimaux representations... we believe we shall show that close analogy and the mass of experience are decidedly against the reception of any such statements, and that it is in the highest degree improbable that such men as the officers and crews of the two lost ships would, or could, in any extremity of hunger, alleviate the pains of starvation by this horrible means.

Before elaborating, Dicken makes a point of exonerating Rae. Noting his reputation as a skilful, intrepid, and experienced Arctic traveller as well as his "manly, conscientious and modest personal character," Dickens concedes Rae's right to defend his opinions. He dismisses the suggestion that the explorer was motivated to return by greed and accepts that he did so to prevent "the useless hazard of valuable lives. . . . With these remarks we can release Dr. Rae from this inquiry, proud of him as an Englishman, and happy in his safe return home to well-earned rest."

Dickens then quotes the most challenging paragraph from Rae's report, which refers to the mutilated corpses and the contents of the kettles and which concludes "that our wretched countrymen had been driven to the last resource—cannibalism—as a means of prolonging existence." He proposes to refute this suggestion both by analogy and "on broad general grounds, quite apart from the improbabilities and incoherencies of the Esquimaux testimony; which is itself given, at the very best, at second-hand. More than this, we presume it to have been given at second-hand through an interpreter; and he was, in all probability, imperfectly acquainted with the language he translated to the white man."

Dickens elaborates on the difficulties of translation, argues that a lack of fuel would have precluded cooking "the contents of the kettles," and suggests that bears, wolves, or foxes might have mutilated the bodies. What is more, scurvy would not only cause dreadful disfigurement and woeful mutilation, but also "annihilate the desire to eat (especially to eat flesh of any kind)." Where does all this lead? To the assertion of a suspicion of murder:

[Nobody can rationally affirm] that this sad remnant of Franklin's gallant band were not set upon and slain by the Esquimaux themselves. It is impossible to form an estimate of the character of any race of savages, from their deferential behaviour to the white man while he is strong. The mistake has been made again and again; and the moment the white man has appeared in the new aspect of being weaker than the savage, the savage has changed and sprung upon him. . . . We believe every savage to be in his heart covetous, treacherous, and cruel; and we have yet to learn what knowledge the white man—lost, houseless, shipless; apparently forgotten by his race; plainly famine-stricken, weak, frozen, helpless, and dying—has of the gentleness of the Esquimaux nature.

Having suggested that the Inuit murdered the starving sailors and concocted a story to hide their guilt, Dickens unveils his analogy. He writes of "a little band of British naval officers, educated and trained exactly like the officers of this ill-fated expedition" who suffered life-threatening hardship in roughly the same region of the Arctic. He is referring to Franklin's first expedition, and after revealing this, he quotes extensively from Sir John's *Narrative of a Journey to the Shores of the Polar Sea in 1819–22*, describing this saga of heroic endurance as "one of the most explicit and enthralling in the whole literature of Voyage and Travel."

Though starving to death, the men of the Royal Navy didn't even conceive of cannibalism until an Iroquois man named Michel shot one of them dead as he sat by the fire. Having realized that Michel had become a predator, "Sir John Richardson, nobly assuming the responsibility he would not allow a man of commoner station to bear, shot this devil through the head—to the infinite joy of all the generations of readers who will honour him in his admirable narrative of that transaction." Dickens quotes Richardson's final judgement on Michel: "His principles,

During his expedition of 1819–21, John Franklin and his surviving men were ultimately rescued by natives

unsupported by a belief in the divine truths of Christianity, were unable to withstand the pressure of severe distress."

Dickens probably did not not know that on at least one occasion (October 11, 1821), Richardson and another navy man, John Hepburn, ate human flesh with the Iroquois Michel—though possibly unaware. C. Stuart Houston, who later edited Richardson's journal from that expedition, wrote, "We shall never know whether Richardson ate the flesh of one of the *voyageurs* knowingly or unknowingly. But eat it he did."

In part two of his extended argument, a less compelling piece than part one, Dickens tests "the Esquimaux kettle stories" against some of the most famous cases of hunger and exposure on record. He summarizes the sufferings and conduct of men driven to the verge of starvation, highlighting eight or nine instances in which they resisted turning to "the last resource." These include shipwrecked sailors from such vessels as the *Centaur*, the *Pandora*, the *Juno*, the *Peggy*, the *Thomas*, and the *Medusa*. To strengthen the credibility of his argument, Dickens sets out four other cases that did involve cannibalism and argues, unconvincingly, that these reflected particular circumstances.

At the heart of Dickens's argument lies a profound racism:

The word of a savage is not to be taken for [cannibalism]; firstly because he is a liar; secondly because he is a boaster; thirdly because he talks figuratively; fourthly because he is given to a superstitious notion that when he tells you he has an enemy in his stomach you will logically credit him for having his enemy's valour in his heart. Even the sight of cooked and dissevered human bodies among this or that tatoo'd tribe, is not proof. Such appropriate offerings to their barbarous, wide-mouthed, goggle-eyed gods, savages have been often seen and known to make.

After once more invoking the Christian judgment of Richardson, whose second wife was Franklin's niece, Dickens brings his argument to a crescendo:

In weighing the probabilities and improbabilities of the "last resource," the fore-most question is—not the nature of the extremity but the nature of the men. We submit that the memory of the lost Arctic voyagers is placed, by reason and experience, high above the taint of this so easily-allowed connection; and that the noble conduct and example of such men, and of their own great leader himself, under similar endurances, belies it, and outweighs by the weight of the whole universe the chatter of a gross handful of uncivilised people, with a domesticity of blood and blubber. . . . Therefore, teach no one to shudder without reason, at the history of their end. Therefore, confide with their own firmness, in their fortitude, their lofty sense of duty, their courage, and their religion.

Dickens's two-part essay was a tour de force, eloquent and heart-rending, the kind of work that only a literary genius could have produced. It was also, as subsequent revelations would prove, a master-piece of obfuscation, self-deception, and almost wilful blindness—though that didn't help John Rae.

Having his report assailed and his conclusions attacked by England's most influential author, who had immense literary resources at his command, took a heavy toll on Rae. On Christmas Eve, 1854, shortly after Dickens published his devastating screed, Rae debarked in Kirk-wall, Orkney, during a heavy rainstorm and grew furious when the carriage he had booked arrived a few minutes late. Refusing to take it, he set out in a temper—and in the pouring rain—along the dark, wind-ing road to Stromness and ended up hiking the fourteen miles to his mother's house, catching a bad cold in the process.

By then, Rae had already written his reply to Dickens. In it, he gives the impression, according to English author Francis Spufford, of a man who had sidestepped a whole tranche of contemporary British feeling, perhaps as a matter of temperament, perhaps because he had worked too long across the ocean: "He was aware (he could hardly fail to be) of the powerful sentiments attending on the [cannibalism controversy], and that, since he did not precisely share them, he possessed no quick and sensitive grasp on public reaction. He was also crucially bad with words, the medium in which exploration was created for the public as much as in real, polar actions."

The explorer's reply is studded with observations and frank judgements certain to offend and infuriate Royal Navy personnel, among others. First, Rae defends William Ouligbuck as the finest of all Inuit interpreters. He argues that the information he received was reliable precisely *because* it had been delivered second-hand by people who feared and disliked its originators and who would have welcomed an opportunity to reveal wrongdoing. He explains that for fuel to heat kettles, the last survivors would have used wood from sledges, kegs, and cases, and he mentions that wild animals rarely touch a dead human body.

At considerable cost to himself, Rae stoutly defends the Inuit. Against the shameful libel that they murdered the last survivors, he cites instances of their generosity, truthfulness, and reliability. Sir John Ross, for example, wintered three years in Prince Regent's Inlet near the same tribe of accused Inuit, and though his men travelled in various directions, "yet no violence was offered to them, although there was an immense advantage to be gained by the savages in obtaining possession of the vessels and their contents." In 1846–47, after wintering at Repulse Bay, Rae had sent men in all directions, "yet no violence was offered, although we were surrounded by native families, among whom there were at least thirty men. By murdering us they would have put themselves in possession of boats and a quantity of cutlery of great value to them." During that same expedition, while snowshoeing alone, unarmed and carrying a box of valuable astronomical instruments on his back, Rae encountered four Inuit men armed with spears, bows, and arrows. He greeted them and travelled on. The previous spring, Rae and his seven men had remained in constant communication with a party of Inuit four times their number who made no attempt to harm them, though "by getting possession of our boat, its masts and oars, and the remainder of our property, they would have been independent for years."

Turning to the question of character, Rae observes, "I have had some opportunities of studying Esquimaux character; and, from what I have seen, I consider them superior to all the tribes of red men in America. In their domestic relationship, they show a bright example to the most civilised people. They are dutiful sons and daughters, kind brothers and sisters, and most affectionate parents."

Rae notes that this opinion is shared by most Hudson's Bay Company officials, as well as by Moravian missionaries and residents of Danish settlements on the west shores of Greenland. Furthermore, although Inuit were sexually accommodating to many explorers, often in exchange for trinkets, Rae adds that,

during the two winters I passed at Repulse Bay, I had men with me who had been in all parts of the Hudson's Bay Company territories. These men assured me that they had never seen Indians so decorous, obliging, unobtrusive, orderly, and friendly, as the Esquimaux. Oh! some one may remark, perhaps they had some private reason for this. Now, my men had not any "private reason" for saying so. I firmly believe, and can almost positively assert, that no case of improper intercourse took place between them and the natives of Repulse Bay during the two seasons I remained there—which is more, I suspect, than most of the commanders of parties to the Arctic Sea can truthfully affirm. . . .

Much stress is laid on the moral character and the admirable discipline of the crews of Sir John Franklin's ships. What their state of discipline may have been I cannot say, but their conduct at the very last British port they entered [Stromness] was not such as to make those who knew it consider them very deserving of the high eulogium passed upon them in *Household Words*. Nor can we say that the men, in extreme cases of privation, would maintain that state of subordination so requisite in all cases, but more especially during danger and difficulty.

Rae concludes his rebuttal by noting that his opinions remained unchanged:

That twenty or twenty-five Esquimaux could, for two months together, continue to repeat the same story without variation in any material point, and adhere firmly to it, in spite of all sorts of cross-questioning, is to me the clearest proof that the information they gave me was founded on fact. That the "white men" were not murdered by the natives, but that they died of starvation, is, to my mind, equally beyond a doubt.

Rae's rejoinder appeared in *Household Words* in two parts on December 23 and 30, 1854. It could easily have run in a single issue, but Dickens cleverly divided it so as to reduce its impact and to insert a long description of an Inuit attack on Franklin's expedition of 1819–22—an attack that took place two thousand miles away among completely different Inuit who believed white interlopers to be unfriendly because they regularly supplied guns to their Loucheux enemies.

The imaginative Dickens later co-authored and enthusiastically performed in *The Frozen Deep*, a play celebrating the Arctic heroism of British explorers. But he offered no further commentary in *Household Words* except to publish early in 1855, to his credit, John Rae's complete, unabridged report to the Hudson's Bay Company, datelined York Factory, Sept. 1, 1854. In so doing, Dickens anticipated the interest of posterity:

We do not feel justified in omitting or condensing any part of [the report]; believing, as we do, that it is a very unsatisfactory document on which to found such strong conclusions as it takes for granted. The preoccupation of the public mind has dismissed this subject easily for the present; but, we assume its great interest, and the serious doubts we have of its having been convincingly set at rest, to be absolutely certain to revive.

In this, the literary giant was prescient. In 1990, British novelist and biographer Peter Ackroyd would characterize Dickens's two-part essay as a strange work that "throws more light on his own excitable and anxious state of mind than upon the ostensible subject of his concern." Ackroyd mentions Dickens's attack on the "savage," or non-white, races, alludes to his horror of cannibalism, and summarizes his long essay as "in the end no more than a litany to the virtue and hardihood of the white explorer."

Ackroyd then makes a revealing error. He writes, "This story can be completed with the news that, in 1986, the corpses of some members of that same Franklin expedition were found preserved in permafrost. And Dickens was right, after all: they appear to have died of tuberculosis and starvation."

Unfortunately for Ackroyd, those corpses, exhumed by a Canadian forensic anthropologist, Owen Beattie, were of three men who died during the Franklin expedition's initial phase, long before the final act of the tragedy began. His literary genius notwithstanding, Charles Dickens was wrong. Forensic science has put this beyond dispute: John Rae was right.

14

THE WRATH
OF LADY FRANKLIN

W hy did Victorian England react so furiously against John Rae? His revelations were certainly unpleasant, even shocking. But more importantly, in an age of European, and especially British, imperialism, they undermined the deepest foundations of the colonial enterprise: the unshakeable conviction of absolute superiority. By virtue of this perceived superiority, the Victorians, like other Europeans, felt justified in seizing lands and subjugating peoples in India, Africa, the West Indies, and many other parts of the world. Even late Victorians felt threatened by the notion that all human beings share an essential similarity, as James George Frazer would discover when he advanced the idea in *The Golden Bough* in 1890 and saw his work dismissed as neither safe nor proper.

While the cannibalism controversy swirled through journals and newspapers, a geographical tempest erupted that revealed the extent of the reaction against Rae. Captain John Washington, the newly appointed naval hydrographer, produced an Arctic map with a note on it that attributed Rae's charting of Victoria Island to Captain Richard Collinson, who had sailed along the coast two years later in HMS *Enterprise.*

Rae immediately called upon the mapmaker at his Admiralty office, protesting that the note was both erroneous and unfair to explorers who had acted on behalf of the Hudson's Bay Company. William Dease and Thomas Simpson had mapped roughly 120 miles of the island's coast in 1839. Twelve years later, Rae himself had charted another 570 miles. Over one year after that, Collinson had surveyed the coast in far less detail, travelling only 10 miles farther north.

Rae had already explained all this in response to a query from Washington's predecessor, Sir Francis Beaufort. In spite of this, the note on this map suggested that Collinson had been the first to survey the entire coast of Victoria Island, with "the inner bays and lakes being adapted from Dr. Rae's survey." The hydrographer was crediting 700 miles of Arctic coast surveyed by HBC expeditions to a naval officer who had visited the same area much later and done a survey far less detailed.

Determined to set the record straight, the explorer asked, "Did my survey contain any significant errors?"

Tight-lipped, the hydrographer admitted, "The outer points agree with those of Captain Collinson."

"In that case, Sir," said Rae, "I think you should correct this note."

The hydrographer sniffed and replied, "The note cannot and will not be changed."

Rae indicated the map on the desk between them. "In fact, Captain, this map has been copied without significant alteration from my own chart, which was published two years ago by William Arrowsmith. Captain Washington, you leave me no choice." Rising to leave, Rae continued: "If you have not that objectionable note removed in a week—I give you a week to think it over—the whole disgraceful proceeding will be published in *The Times*."

The captain looked aghast. "You would do that to the British Admiralty?"

"It was perhaps not good manners," Rae admitted later, "but I fairly laughed to his face."

Before distributing the Arctic map further, the hydrographer had the erroneous note pasted over. Nonetheless, the next edition of the map contained a note that was only marginally improved. It wrongly attributed most of the Victoria Island coast to Dease and Simpson, while falsely asserting that Collinson had "passed and repassed" the coast in 1851, the same year as John Rae.

Later, in his unpublished memoirs, Rae observed that these notes were without precedent, and that Collinson had also passed and repassed coastline originally explored by Franklin and Richardson. To make that claim against those surveys, however,

would have been robbing Peter to pay Paul, for they were the work of officers of her majesty's navy. But to claim or falsify the explorations of the Hudson's Bay Company's people, there need be no scruples, therefore the first note inserted conveyed to anyone not conversant with the subject the utterly erroneous impression that the commander of the *Enterprise* was the first explorer of about seven hundred English miles of coast line to which he had not the shadow of a claim. The second note, which still remains on the charts, is about equally erroneous for it credits Dease and Simpson with the whole survey, whereas they did little more than one sixth of it.

Rae added that he did not believe Collinson, "the gallant captain of HMS *Enterprise*," took any part in advancing these false claims. Clearly, the explorer had become *persona non grata* in certain rich and powerful circles.

At the same time, however, the woman who had been stoking the flames of this animosity found herself reconsidering John Rae's report. Lady Jane Franklin had accepted that her husband was dead, but she had not abandoned her deepest ambition: to see him glorified as the discoverer of the Northwest Passage.

Did Rae's story not suggest that, before dying, Franklin might have discovered this elusive waterway? If so, perhaps her husband had left written records. Perhaps he could yet be hailed as a hero—and herself, by extension, a heroine. This glorification could never happen, of course, while allegations of cannibalism sullied Sir John's good name—allegations put forward by the detestable Doctor Rae. The matter grew increasingly complex. At one point, Lady Franklin responded to a lawyer's request by copying most of a letter Rae had sent her (a letter which today is nowhere to be found); she wrote that the part she had omitted did not bear on the question at hand, "and I cannot copy nor allow to be copied details of horror, the very existence of which is more than doubtful, and which ought never to have been published or even recorded."

Early in 1855, when Rae officially applied for the Admiralty reward for ascertaining the fate of the lost expedition, Lady Franklin refocused her campaign against him. Any reward payment would undermine her efforts to convince the Admiralty to finance yet another search expedition, one that would perhaps restore Franklin to heroic stature.

She began lobbying to delay the payment of any monies to Rae, and she had clearly lost none of her abilities. The Admiralty buckled and decided to delay payment until it received the results of the Hudson's Bay Company's overland search expedition. The HBC itself, which Rae had championed so valiantly for so long, gave in to the flood tide of anti-Rae sentiment, declaring that the chief factor's regular pay should also be kept in abeyance until the British government decided whether he would receive the reward.

Shocked by this mistreatment, Rae protested. No logical connection existed between his regular remuneration and any possible reward for discovering the fate of Franklin. Besides, the fur-traders William Dease and Thomas Simpson, having explored the Arctic for three summers and two winters, had been awarded a government pension of 100 pounds a year for life. By comparison, Rae had spent eight summers and four winters surveying the North and had seen more of the Arctic coast of North America than any man living. As expedition leader, he had individually traced as much new coastline as Dease and Simpson jointly, the main difference being that he had done so largely on snowshoes, hauling supplies, while they had mostly voyaged in boats—relatively easy work. Rae had saved the Company huge sums of money by living off the land, serving as sole commanding officer and single-handedly shooting more than one-third of all game. Several hundred naval men, recently returned from the Arctic, had received double salary, and Rae alone faced this humiliating and extremely disagreeable situation.

The HBC, though not easily persuaded, eventually did pay up.

*

In the summer of 1855, acting on Rae's plan, fur-trade veteran James Anderson led a canoe expedition down Back's Great Fish River to Chantrey Inlet on the Arctic coast. There, from a group of Inuit, Anderson obtained a few more relics of the Franklin expedition. Having failed to secure an interpreter, however, he was unable to gather detailed information. He did confirm that much of the tragedy had occurred across Simpson Strait on King William Island, which was unreachable by canoe. This information eventually enabled Leopold McClintock to travel directly to the correct area.

Confused rumours would surface in 1857 and again in 1890: first, that some survivors of the Franklin expedition had been living on the mainland as late as 1855, and second, that one of Anderson's men (the Ojibwa Paulet Papanakies) had spotted two masts at a great distance and didn't disclose this for fear of lengthening the canoe expedition beyond safe limits. The first rumour derives recognizably from a garbled report about Anderson's own party, while the second remains an enigma—at least one of Franklin's ships had long since sunk to the bottom, and no traces of either ship have ever been found.

Anderson's relics confirmed Rae's original discovery of the expedition's fate, though not to the satisfaction of Lady Franklin and her allies. On January 22, 1856, the Admiralty announced that within three months, it would make a judgement about the reward. Claimants included not only John Rae, but also several naval officers who had served on search expeditions, the whaler William Penny, and the obnoxious Richard King, who wrote, "I alone have for many years pointed out the banks of the Great Fish River as the place where Franklin could be found."

Rae's claim remained the only serious one.

Toward the end of January, Lady Franklin and the explorer met again. Rae probably initiated the meeting after consulting Sir John Richardson, in hopes of mitigating the dowager's implacable opposition to him. As Francis Spufford has noted, "With Sophia Cracroft at her side as a go-between, and when occasion required as a mouthpiece for her displeasure, she could blight or accelerate careers, bestow or withhold the sanction of her reputation. No other nineteenth-century woman raised the cash for three polar expeditions, or had her say over the appointment of captains and lieutenants."

Rae informed Lady Franklin confidentially that, in Canada, in co-operation with his expatriate brothers, he had ordered a schooner built. He would use any reward money he received to mount yet another Arctic expedition, during which he would certainly resume the search for relics of the Franklin expedition, if only to secure confirmation of his report. Lady Franklin responded that she still intended to publicly oppose his claim to the reward money. After the meeting, she wrote, "Dr. Rae has cut off his odious beard but looks still very hairy and disagreeable."

In April 1856, Lady Franklin went public. She sent the Admiralty a long, closely argued letter, clearly the product of more than one well-educated mind, observing that the reward had been designed to go "to any party or parties who in the judgement of the Board of the Admiralty should by virtue of his or their efforts first succeed in ascertaining the fate of [the Franklin] expedition." The letter argues that the fate of the crews of the *Erebus* and *Terror* had not been ascertained and that Rae had not "by his efforts" ascertained it; that giving the reward

The Erebus *and the* Terror *locked in ice:*
Lady Franklin argued that the fate of the crews had not been determined

would not only deny it to those who would, in future, rightly earn it, but would also create a check or block "to any further efforts for ascertaining the fate of the expedition, and appears to counteract the humane intention of the House of Commons in voting a large sum of money for that purpose."

This epistle also contains the well-known passage that paved the way for further exploration:

What secrets may be hidden within those wrecked or stranded ships we know not—what may be buried in the graves of our unhappy countrymen or in caches not yet discovered we have yet to learn. The bodies and the graves which we were told of have not been found; the books [journals] said to be in the hands of the Esquimaux have not been recovered, and thus left in ignorance and darkness with so little obtained and so much yet to learn, can it be said and is it fitting to pronounce that the fate of the expedition is ascertained?

Lady Franklin notes that James Anderson believed that a vessel should be sent to explore King William Island, then she observes, "Dr. Rae declares himself favourable, at this moment, to further search, were it only, as he has assured me, to secure for his statements that confirmation which he anticipates." If Rae himself recognized the need for confirmation, she implies, how then could he be said to have ascertained the fate of the expedition?

This careful letter constituted only one volley in Lady Franklin's well-organized campaign. Early in April 1856, two anonymous pamphlets appeared. The first, entitled *The Great Arctic Mystery*, argues that Rae did *not* ascertain the expedition's fate and repeats the familiar criticism that he turned back prematurely. Admitting that "Dr. Rae has great merit as an enterprising and able Arctic explorer," the writer declares that "we do most earnestly and solemnly protest against" his receiving the reward. To this, Rae wrote a response to the Admiralty in which he quotes from field notes he wrote at Pelly Bay on April 21, 1854—notes that make it clear that he did not at that time have enough information to conduct a search.

The second pamphlet, *Arctic Rewards and their Claimants*, elaborates similar arguments in even more inflammatory language, its ludicrous claims revealing the old familiar prejudices against both the Inuit and the Hudson's Bay Company. It suggests that Rae turned back early for good reason:

[He chose not to trust himself] and his small party among savages, who may have ill-treated, robbed, murdered, and who perhaps still hold among them some solitary individual of the strong party which Sir John Franklin despatched to the Fish River, doubtless in order to send home the history of his dire necessity. To the same feeling, which is to be considered as by no means derogatory to their courage, may be imputed the subsequent hasty advance and retreat of Mr. Anderson upon the Fish River, and the extreme unwillingness of the Hudson's Bay people to winter at the mouth of the river, infested as it is by Esquimaux.

The authors of this racist diatribe accept that Rae "may not have known of the reward: we can readily believe this, or he would have acted otherwise." The explorer was damned if he knew and damned if he didn't. Rae wrote to Sir John Richardson, observing,

These things produce *now* little effect upon me, for in the whole of my Arctic journey (I allude to the last one) no other motive influenced me than to do what was right. Yet when acting for the best of motives my actions have been so distorted, my reports so garbled, that it would be absurd to publish a reply, particularly as the author or authors (although they may be guessed at) are not known.

Rae also mentioned that he had recently left the service of the Hudson's Bay Company, although he had been asked repeatedly to reconsider: "It appears from some words which fell from the Secretary the other day that there was some notion that I might take Sir George Simpson's place when he gave up visiting the north. It is needless to say how unfit I would be for such a situation even if I had the ambition to think of aspiring to it."

Because Rae had sought the monetary reward once he learned of it, Lady Franklin and her wealthy friends sought to portray him as grasping and greedy. Yet judgement (and money) had waited first on a report from the Anderson expedition and then on one from Collinson, even though Collinson had already sent a report from Bering Strait and there was no chance that he would bring any news of Franklin. On May 21, 1856, having waited one month beyond the promised three, Rae wrote hoping that their lordships would not keep him waiting much longer "on a matter which the multiplicity of other affairs of infinitely more importance may have caused them to overlook."

Finally, on June 19, the Admiralty notified Rae (and the HBC) that he would receive the reward. The explorer had already proposed that the Company distribute one-fifth of the total (2,000 pounds) among his men. Those men who had remained with Rae at Repulse Bay received as much as 260 pounds each, while those he had sent back from Chester-field Inlet collected lesser amounts. Rae himself received 8,000 pounds, the equivalent today of 400,000 pounds, or roughly U.S. $600,000. He had acquired enough money to live comfortably for the rest of his days.

Lady Franklin bought the Fox, *shown here wintering in the ice pack*

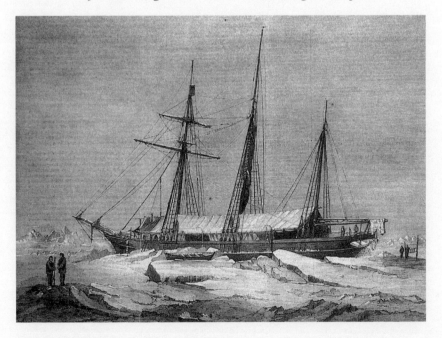

By this time, the Admiralty had spent over 600,000 pounds on searching for Franklin (in today's money, 30 million pounds or approximately U.S. $45 million!). Lady Franklin had argued that rewarding Rae would undermine search efforts, but now she proceeded with plans to launch yet another expedition. In addition to a contribution of her own, she again secured monies, not this time from the British government, but by public subscription. She bought the *Fox*, a small, manoeuvrable steam yacht of 177 tons and, in April 1857, offered the command to Francis Leopold McClintock, who had captained one of the four ships (HMS *Intrepid*) abandoned by Sir Edward Belcher in 1854.

McClintock sailed on July 2, 1857. On the voyage out, he called at several settlements in Greenland to acquire dogs and an Inuit sledge-driver. In mid-August, just off the coast of Greenland in Melville Bay, he got locked into pack ice. Over the winter, he drifted back through Davis Strait. Released in April 1858 and advancing through Lancaster Sound, McClintock visited Beechey Island, the site of the three graves from early in the Franklin expedition, and then headed south down Peel Sound. Blocked by ice, he sailed back around Somerset Island and then south down Prince Regent Inlet to the eastern end of Bellot Strait, where, frozen in ice, he wintered.

In the spring of 1859, McClintock divided his men into sledge parties. He himself travelled south down Boothia Peninsula, completing the mapping of the Arctic coast, and then along the east coast of King William Island. He circled the island clockwise, finding an abandoned boat and several skeletons on the southwest coast, as well as clothing, hardware, and scientific equipment. He also purchased a few identifiable relics (gold chains, buttons, and knives) from the Inuit of Boothia Peninsula and heard stories confirming Rae's report.

Meanwhile, his second-in-command, Lieutenant William R. Hobson, proceeded down the west coast of King William Island. At Victory Point, in a large cairn, he found the only written record that survived the Franklin expedition: a brief note scrawled by senior officers. It declared "all well" in May 1847, although the *Erebus* and *Terror* were beset by ice. A subsequent addition revealed that Sir John Franklin died less than one month later, on June 11, 1847, and that the

A fanciful depiction, from The Illustrated London News,
of men opening the Victory Point cairn that contained the Franklin note

following year, with nine officers and fifteen crewmen already dead and no reason given, the surviving sailors had started trekking south, making for the mouth of Back's Great Fish River.

That was it, the sum total of information, but for Lady Jane Franklin, it would be enough. McClintock sailed home and made all the right noises. Instead of reiterating the reports of cannibalism, he emphasized Franklin's "virtual completion" of the Northwest Passage. As well, he vindicated Sir John personally. The captain had died before his crew abandoned ship: he, at least, could have been no cannibal. Finally, McClintock confirmed Rae's information about the route along which the survivors had travelled.

Lady Franklin hailed McClintock as a hero. Victorian England followed her lead, and subsequent historians did the same. Even the authors of the introduction to Rae's *Arctic Correspondence*, published in 1951, would write, "The private search expedition organised by Lady Franklin and commanded by McClintock succeeded in 1859 in ascertaining more fully the proceedings and ultimate fate of the missing officers and men. McClintock, not Rae, has ever since been acknowledged as the real discoverer of the fate of the Franklin expedition."

Acknowledged by whom? The co-authors of that introduction, J. M. Wordie and Richard J. Cyriax, were both notable scholars. But today we understand that even the most learned and scrupulous among us proceed from biases and preconceptions. Wordie was president of the Royal Geographical Society, which lionized McClintock and eventually displayed an ambiguous attitude, shall we say, toward John Rae. Cyriax is best known for his 1939 book *Sir John Franklin's Last Arctic Expedition*, which is dedicated "to the memory of those whose deeds are herein recorded."

With Lady Franklin's enthusiastic support, McClintock became an admiral in the Royal Navy. He received not only the knighthood that forever eluded John Rae, but the freedom of the city of London, several honorary degrees, the patron's gold medal from the Royal Geographical Society, and a monetary reward of 5,000 pounds. Lady Franklin presented him with a silver model of the *Fox*, which he proudly kept under a glass case in his drawing room. Most significant of all, she had his name inscribed on the memorial to her dead husband at Westminster Abbey.

Lady Jane Franklin had begun her revenge.

15

RESTORING THE FATE

I n 1875, when the marble bust of Sir John Franklin was placed in the august sanctuary of Westminster Abbey complete with a eulogistic epitaph by poet laureate Alfred Lord Tennyson (who also happened to be Sir John's nephew by marriage), it included a second chiseled homage: "Here also is commemorated Admiral Sir Leopold McClintock / Discoverer of the Fate of Franklin in 1859." The doughty seamen had found what many believed to be his rightful place in history.

His lionization began immediately upon his return from the Arctic. On October 11, 1859, less than one month after he arrived home, the influential Sir John Richardson, until now divided in his loyalties, turned his back on John Rae. Richardson wrote to Lady Franklin lauding the greater authority of McClintock's self-censored reports because they were based on the testimony of eyewitnesses: "The intelligence procured by Dr. Rae was less reliable, as coming from a tribe who had seen neither the wrecks nor the crews themselves, alive or

Encouraged by Lady Jane Franklin, Leopold McClintock began claiming that he had determined the fate of the lost expedition

dead, but had got their information and the European articles they possessed through an intervening party. Some of their reports therefore are to be regarded merely as the habitual exaggerations of a rude people in repeating a story."

By the following spring, encouraged by Lady Franklin and her coterie, McClintock was claiming that he had ascertained the fate of the Franklin expedition—a notion that prompted a terse exchange with the cartographer William Arrowsmith, who asserted Rae's prior claim. In March 1860, McClintock wrote to Rae complaining of Arrowsmith's tone.

In his response from London, Rae entered into a protracted, somewhat testy correspondence, originating the argument elaborated here in the light of subsequent history: that McClintock merely confirmed and clarified Rae's findings and that, in future, other searchers would shed additional light on the fate of the Franklin expedition.

It is very generally allowed that the information brought home by me in 1854, together with the numerous relics bearing the crests and initials of fourteen of the officers of the *Erebus* and *Terror*, were sufficient evidence that a large portion of both Franklin's ships had died of disease and starvation in the neighborhood of the Back River and King William's Land on or previous to 1850, and that these were the last survivors of the party. I was told also that the ship or ships had been destroyed by ice.

Your information does not contradict that brought by me in any important fact, and proves the correctness of the Esquimaux intelligence even in regard to the route followed by the unfortunate people on their way to the Back River.

You leave 102 persons out of 129 unaccounted for, except through information similar to that from which mine was obtained—*my* interpreter was perfectly acquainted with the dialect and language of the Esquimaux of Repulse Bay, many of whom I had known in 1846–47, and had always found with a few exceptions honest and truthful.

There are other more minute particulars that I might dwell upon, but the great fact that a large portion of Franklin's party died of starvation and (leaving little doubt as to the fate of the remainder) at a certain locality which I named correctly on or before 1850, was communicated by me in 1854....

W. Arrowsmith showed me your note to him, after perusing which I scarcely think his note to you can be called intemperate.

I write in perfect good feeling, as I hope people may do in a matter of opinion on a subject where there always will be *two* sides of the question, perhaps *three*, were another expedition to go out and find the journals of some of the latest survivors.

From Dublin, addressing his letter "My dear Rae," McClintock replied:

I quite agree with *all* you state as to the information and relics brought home by you in /54; they afforded circumstantial evidence as to the fate of a large party, probably the last survivors of Franklin's crews; and the impression was strong as to the sad fate of the whole.

But positive proof was wanting, therefore in /55 Anderson was sent out by the government, but he was unable to do more than confirm your locality of Montreal Island. In /59 I confirmed more of your report and found such further traces and records as have cleared up the fate of the whole expedition. Now it is evident that as these traces were unknown to the natives themselves, no information respecting them could have reached you; therefore these skeletons, records, several cairns and a boat, besides articles innumerable, are my discovery.

Also, by having been able to judge of their equipment from specimens seen, of their state of health, and of the absence of game upon the coast they travelled, I have shown that they could not possibly have reached beyond Montreal Island and must have all perished....

This should not be confused with the information you received respecting those who died upon the mainland. All native information whether obtained by you or I must be limited to the SW shoreline of King William Island, since they have not visited the NW coast. But you will see that I have managed my work as to be independent of their testimony altogether.

My object in the *Fox* was to examine the whole of the unexplored area between the Barrow Strait beaches and Anderson and I did so. Had your information as to locality been conclusive this great labour would have been unnecessary. Now in spite of these additional and important facts, Arrowsmith does me the injustice of giving you credit for the *whole*, and simply mentioned me as having "fully confirmed" you, and talks of "the first intelligence of the Fate" as if anything could be *discovered twice.*

To this, Rae responded:

I must confess that your able arguments do not in any material point alter my opinions, no more than any thing I could say would be likely to alter yours. Your information although of course fuller than that obtained by me does not account for 102 persons or about ¾ of Franklin's party, except through Esquimaux testimony which you say you managed to be "wholly independent of."

The exchange continued, wending into details of less relevance, neither contributor fully recognizing that Rae had already presented the decisive argument.

Since the mid-nineteenth century, countless investigators, among them fur-traders, sailors, and scientists of many nationalities, have added detail and nuance to John Rae's original findings. In a 1991 tour de force called *Unravelling the Franklin Mystery*, Canadian historian David C. Woodman summed up succinctly, "For one hundred and forty years the account of the tragedy given to Rae by In-nook-poo-zhee-jook and See-u-ti-chu has been accepted and endorsed. As we shall see, it was a remarkably accurate recital of events. But it was not the whole story."

In the 1860s, the eccentric Charles Francis Hall of Cincinnati, Ohio, became obsessed with the idea that some of Franklin's men had found permanent refuge among the Inuit. Financed by New York–based Henry Grinnell (who had earlier sponsored Elisha Kent Kane), Hall abandoned his family to spend several years in the Arctic seeking survivors. Based mostly at Repulse Bay and supplied by whaling ships, he gathered much suspect material. But finally, in 1869, guided by Inuit to the west coast of King William Island, Hall found numerous

Franklin relics and also, despite the snow, uncovered near James Ross Point a complete skeleton that later proved to be that of Lt. Henry Le Vesconte of the *Erebus*.

Hall's main contribution, however, lies in the eyewitness accounts he gathered during that visit. These stories remain the most complete source of the Inuit version of what happened to the Franklin expedition. They include horrific tales whose details are so vivid as to be utterly convincing, including references to cuts of human meat that would facilitate boiling in pots and kettles: "One man's body when found by the Innuits flesh all on & not mutilated except the hands sawed off at the wrists—the rest a great many had their flesh cut off as if some one or other had cut it off to eat."

Other entries spoke of numerous bodies found in a tent at Terror Bay on the west coast of King William Island. One described a woman using a heavy sharp stone to dig into the ice and retrieve a watch from the body of a corpse: "[The woman] could never forget the dreadful, fearful feelings she had all the time while engaged doing this; for, besides the tent being filled with frozen corpses—some entire and others mutilated by some of the starving companions, who had cut off much of the flesh with their knives and hatchets and eaten it— this man who had the watch she sought seemed to her to have been the last that died, and his face was just as though he was only asleep."

Hall multiplied these gruesome examples, recording tales of finding bones that had been severed with a saw and of skulls with holes in them through which brains had been removed "to prolong the lives of the living." Hall also met

In the 1860s, Charles Francis Hall turned up horrifically detailed eyewitness accounts that supported John Rae's reports of cannibalism

In-nook-poo-zhe-jook, Rae's first informant, who explored King William Island after McClintock's visit and at Erebus Bay found not only a pillaged boat, but a second boat, untouched, about one thousand yards away. Here he also discovered "one whole skeleton with clothes on—this with flesh all on but dried, as well as a big pile of skeleton bones near the fire place & skulls among them." Bones had been broken up for their marrow, and some long boots that came up as high as the knees contained "cooked human flesh—that is human flesh that had been boiled."

Drawing on his predecessors, Hall formulated the "standard reconstruction," according to which the party of thirty or forty men who travelled east along the south coast of King William Island were the last survivors of all those who had abandoned ship in 1847 and landed at Victory Point. From there, they marched south en masse and reached the Todd Islets off the south coast of King William Island. When the ice broke up, they sailed across Simpson Strait to the mainland, where most of them died.

In 1879, another American, Lieutenant Frederick Schwatka of the Third United States Calvary, located and named Starvation Cove on the mainland. Schwatka and a newspaper man, Henry Gilder, spent a summer exploring from the mouth of the Back River to Cape Felix on the northwest coast of King William Island, discovering much that would in winter have been covered by snow. William Ouligbuck accompanied them, and Gilder would affirm, as Rae had asserted, not only that Ouligbuck spoke all the Inuktitut dialects fluently, but that he "spoke the [English] language like a native—that is to say, like an uneducated native."

Schwatka failed to find any records or documents. But on the west coast of King William Island, he did discover remains and a complete skeleton—that of Lt. John Irving of the *Terror*—buried four miles from Victory Point, where the main party had apparently landed after abandoning ship. This body provided the first concrete evidence that the standard reconstruction, to which Schwatka subscribed, did not tell the whole story, though he failed to recognize that.

Schwatka interviewed Inuit people who had met retreating white

In 1880, Frederick Schwatka, here showing an Illustrated London News
to interested Inuit, was hailed as having determined the fate of Franklin

men. He heard tales of Inuit people entering an abandoned ship and
accidentally sinking it by cutting a hole in the side, and he heard stories
of papers being distributed among children, buried in sand, and blown
away by the wind. He also gathered complete accounts from several
Inuit people of their discoveries at Starvation Cove, where thirty or
forty members of the expedition perished, and of the presence of many
skeletons at Terror Bay. Gilder's florid newspaper articles about this
expedition, including one that appeared in the *New York Herald* on

October 29, 1880, included headlines such as "Franklin's Fate Determined"—as if, at last, an American lieutenant had done the job.

The twentieth century brought still more clarification. In 1923, a Danish anthropologist, Knud Rasmussen, not only collected additional stories, but found bones and skulls at Starvation Point: "There, exactly where the Eskimos had indicated, we found a number of human bones that were undoubtedly the mortal remains of members of the Franklin expedition; some pieces of cloth at that same place showed that they were of white men." Rasmussen gathered the bones, built a cairn over them, and hoisted two flags at half-mast, the Danish and the English: "Thus without very many words we did them the last honours."

Subsequent discoveries, such as those of remains found fifteen miles west of Starvation Cove in 1926 and 1936, suggested that instead of marching south in a single body, the survivors had split into smaller groups. In 1931, a Hudson's Bay Company trader, William "Paddy" Gibson, found the remains of four skeletons on one of the Todd Islets near Gjoa Haven; on an islet in Douglas Bay on the south coast of King William Island, he found the remains of seven men and buried them beneath a large stone cairn.

Half a century later, a forensic anthropologist, Owen Beattie, discovered and analyzed some skeletal remains from the mainland. They showed evidence of scurvy and such high levels of lead as to suggest lead poisoning. In 1984 and 1986, Beattie excavated three early-expedition graves at Beechey Island, where bodies had been buried in permafrost. His most significant discovery, as described in his book *Frozen in Time*, was that the three men had indeed suffered from lead poisoning, although it had not killed them. Beattie speculated that lead poisoning, contracted from the lead solder used to seal cans of preserved food, affected the entire expedition. Symptoms of lead poisoning include anorexia, weakness, fatigue, anemia, paranoia, and irritability, matching Inuit tales of disoriented survivors.

Historian David Woodman remains skeptical that lead poisoning played a major role in what happened. He challenged the standard reconstruction in his 1991 book *Unravelling the Franklin Mystery*, arguing mainly from Inuit testimony that the note found during McClintock's expedition indicated only what the surviving sailors intended to do, not what they did. He contends that in 1848, with Franklin dead, Captain Francis Crozier set out with the bulk of the remaining men to hunt near the mouth of Back's Great Fish River, 900 miles away, but that this party reversed itself and retreated to the ice-locked vessels. Woodman argues, further, that the last large group of men didn't abandon ship until after the winter of 1849–50; that in 1851, some Inuit hunters met this party, weak and starving, slogging south; and that these were the men later described to John Rae. Woodman also contends that a smaller group of men wintered with the Inuit, started south for the coast in 1852, and perished along the way.

In the mid-1990s, archaeologist Margaret Bertulli and physical anthropologist Anne Keenleyside investigated a grisly discovery in Erebus Bay on the west coast of King William Island. They catalogued more than 200 identifiable artifacts—nails, buttons, combs, clay pipes, wire gauze from snow goggles—and analyzed more than 400 bones, the remains of at least eight men. They not only found high lead levels, supporting Beattie's hypothesis of lead poisoning, but also, using an electron microscope, discovered cut marks on ninety-two bones—marks easily distinguished from animal tooth marks and even marks made by stone tools, occurring "in a pattern consistent with intentional disarticulation." Translation? The survivors dismembered the bodies and carved away the flesh.

This forensic examination, as British author Roland Huntford observed in *The New York Times Book Review*, proves beyond doubt that starvation reduced the Franklin expedition to cannibalism and, in turn, "vindicates Dr. John Rae of the Hudson's Bay Company, who, through contact with the Eskimos in 1854, uncovered the first traces of the expedition, including reports of cannibalism. He has been reviled, or ignored, for his pains by apologists for Franklin ever since."

The quest continues. In *Ice Blink*, published in 2000, American author Scott Cookman argues that botulism wreaked more damage—and killed far more men—than lead poisoning. Undoubtedly, both took a toll.

With the advantage of hindsight, we can see that McClintock, who remained oblivious, or perhaps impervious, to evidence of cannibalism, can hardly be said to have discovered the fate of Franklin. In fact, as Woodman observes, "the vague stories he collected were essentially uninteresting to the British public. They added detail to Rae's account, and confirmed it, but presented little that was new."

McClintock—or rather his second-in-command, Lt. William R. Hobson—did discover the only written document that has yet been salvaged from the expedition. But Anderson's 1855 journey to the mouth of Back's Great Fish River had already narrowed the search, and he would not have accomplished that if Rae had not returned with the original information.

Admiral Sir Leopold McClintock certainly deserves recognition as one of the investigators who added detail and nuance to Rae's discovery. Nonetheless, it was Rae who correctly reported in 1854 that all members of the Franklin expedition were dead, Rae who revealed where many of them died and indicated where others had probably perished, and Rae who divulged the least welcome, yet somehow most significant, truth of all: that some of the final survivors had resorted to cannibalism.

The fate of the Franklin expedition will never be known in every detail. Explorers and researchers who visit King William Island may yet find another message in a cairn, though this is unlikely. Eventually, someone will almost certainly discover the wreckage of at least one of Franklin's ships, and that discoverer will add his or her name to the ever-growing list of those who have clarified the fate of Franklin.

The first name on that list, however, will forever remain that of John Rae. The maverick Rae, not the deferential McClintock, brought England the first authentic tidings of the ruination of the Franklin expedition. Lady Jane Franklin to the contrary, John Rae, not Leopold McClintock, deserves to be commemorated at Westminster Abbey as the discoverer of the fate of Franklin.

Yet even that would right only half the historical wrong.

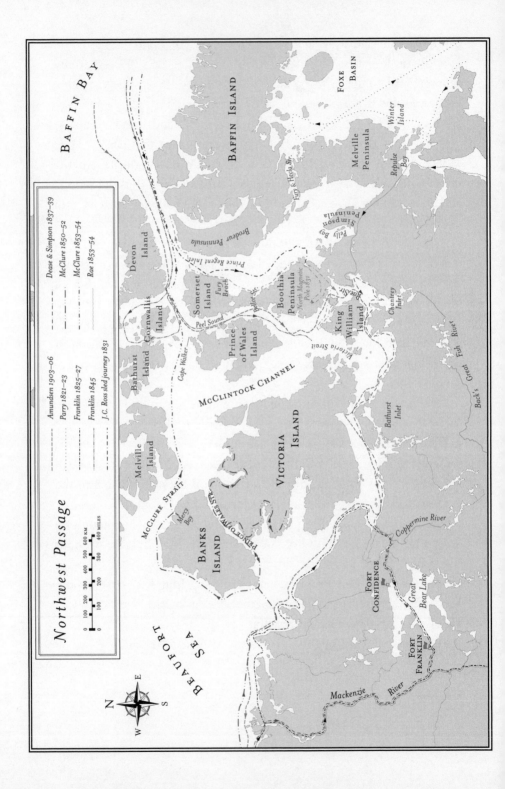

Northwest Passage

BAFFIN BAY

BAFFIN ISLAND

FOXE BASIN

Winter Island

Melville Peninsula

Repulse Bay

Simpson Peninsula

Pelly Bay

Broder Peninsula

Prince Regent Inlet

Fury & Hecla Str.

Fury Beach

Somerset Island

Boothia Peninsula

North Magnetic Pole 1831

Back Str.

Chantrey Inlet

Devon Island

Cornwallis Island

Peel Sound

Bellot Str.

King William Island

Back's Great Fish River

Bathurst Island

Prince of Wales Island

Victoria Strait

Bathurst Inlet

Cape Walker

McCLINTOCK CHANNEL

VICTORIA ISLAND

Melville Island

McCLURE STRAIT

Mercy Bay

BANKS ISLAND

PRINCE OF WALES STRAIT

Coppermine River

FORT CONFIDENCE

Great Bear Lake

FORT FRANKLIN

BEAUFORT SEA

Mackenzie River

Legend

Amundsen 1903–06

Parry 1821–23

Franklin 1825–27

Franklin 1845

J. C. Ross sled journey 1831

Dease & Simpson 1837–39

McClure 1850–52

McClure 1853–54

Rae 1853–54

Scale

0 100 200 300 400 500 600 KM

0 100 200 300 400 MILES

N E S W

16

AWAKENING TO THE PASSAGE

T he discovery of the Northwest Passage involved the work of countless European explorers, many of whom relied heavily on native people. And yet, as historian Leslie H. Neatby writes, "Posterity has not hesitated to endorse the judgment of [Captain Leopold] McClintock that 'to Franklin must be assigned the earliest discovery of the North West Passage': in truth the old seaman not only won the honour, but richly deserved it." While he lost a great many men, Franklin did chart nearly 1,850 miles of Arctic coastline and so "put a roof on the map of Canada." Neatby sums up by suggesting that "for daring and sheer achievement Franklin stands alone; and succeeding generations have rewarded him by associating his name pre-eminently with the Passage."

The verdict of generations, then, has been for Sir John Franklin—at least through the twentieth century. But how well does that verdict stand contemporary scrutiny? Sir John died aboard his stranded vessel off the coast of King William Island in Victoria Strait—an impenetrable, ice-choked channel that challenges even today's icebreakers. Subsequently, in a bid to survive, some of his men—walking skeletons—dragged boats south along the west coast of the island. A few of them crossed Simpson Strait and reached the North American continent before dying of scurvy and starvation. Somehow, we're told in the memorable words of Sir John Richardson, these poor devils "forged the last link with their lives."

Sir John Franklin was celebrated through the twentieth century as the discoverer of the Northwest Passage

But where exactly? In this vicinity, no Passage exists. Victoria Strait, perennially jammed by pack ice pushing south down McClintock Channel, remains forever impenetrable to sailing ships. Grand monuments and official histories to the contrary, Sir John Franklin discovered no Northwest Passage, and the same holds true for the last survivors of his starving, scurvy-ridden crew.

The explorer who completed the discovery of the only Northwest Passage navigable by nineteenth-century ships was the nearly forgotten John Rae. He did it during his final Arctic expedition when he determined that a channel (Rae Strait) separated "King William Land" from Boothia Peninsula. In Rae Strait, he found the final link in the Passage. He could not prove it, having no ship at his command. But he told Leopold McClintock, who relayed the message to Roald Amundsen, who finally did prove it by sailing through it in 1903–06.

How then did Sir John Franklin, and not Rae, come to be celebrated as the discoverer of the Northwest Passage? The answer is both intricate and revealing of the forces that shape the historical record. In *The Myth of the Explorer: The Press, Sensationalism and Geographical Discovery*, American scholar Beau Riffenburgh writes,

Historians and geographers have agreed that what is perceived to exist or happen is equally as important as what actually exists or happens. This was particularly true of the images created of exploration and the explorers themselves, because they could be designed for the consumption of select audiences—geographical societies, financial supporters, scientists or the general public—bearing in mind little other than the benefit to the press and the explorers.

John Rae offers an early example, Riffenburgh flatly declares, "of an explorer shunned for presenting facts with which the establishment, the public or the press were not pleased. Unlike almost every other major contemporary British explorer—Parry, both Rosses, Franklin, Back, Richardson, McClure and McClintock—Rae was neither knighted nor accepted into the circle of national heroes."

To render John Rae invisible by ignoring his achievements was only half the outrage. To understand the other half, we must turn again to Lady Jane Franklin and her supporters, among them Sir John Richardson.

In September 1859, as we have seen, McClintock returned to England with a one-page document that confirmed where Franklin's ships had become trapped in ice: off the northwest coast of King William Island. The next month, Richardson wrote to Lady Franklin not only about the fate of her husband, but also about the Northwest Passage:

On the strength of the first intelligence of the loss of the ships brought by Dr. Rae, I formally wrote a letter to *The Times*, claiming for the survivors of the crews of the *Erebus* and *Terror* priority in the discovery of a North-West Passage, a portion of which, though a small one, was obstructed by ice. This may be done on still stronger grounds, and the passage may be said to have been traced by open water through Victoria Strait by the conjoined efforts of several parties. For Dr. Rae in his boat passed to the northward of the position of the *Erebus* and *Terror* when first beset, and Captain Collinson traced the coast line some miles beyond Rae.

Richardson, aware of the geographical niceties involved, was suggesting that Victoria Strait (Franklin's supposed "Passage") had been proven navigable. On sober second thought, he wisely abandoned this proposition as untenable and settled instead for his celebrated metaphor, according to which starving men forged a non-existent link with their lives.

Who then was to be hailed as discoverer of the Passage? Ever since

1854, when John Rae had returned with proof of her husband's death, Lady Jane Franklin, backed by allies such as Richardson, had been devoting her energies to answering that question. In 1855, the House of Commons appointed a committee to enquire into Northwest Passage awards. Claims were advanced not just for Franklin, but also for Robert McClure, who had recently returned from the Arctic after "walking" on ice over an apparent passage, and for James Clark Ross, John Ross, William Dease and Thomas Simpson, George Back, Richard King, and John Rae.

After due deliberation, the committee awarded McClure 10,000 pounds (including 5,000 for his men) and a knighthood, for "having been the first to perform the actual passage over water." This judgement represented a last-minute, all-too-convenient change in the rules of the game, however, because like Franklin, McClure had found no Northwest Passage navigable by sailing ships.

In August 1850, arriving from the Pacific Ocean, McClure had sailed HMS *Investigator* through Bering Strait into Arctic waters. Having passed the Mackenzie River, he abandoned the coastline and struck north between Victoria Island and Banks Island into the Prince of Wales Strait, whose east end is blocked year-round by pack ice drifting slowly south from the permanent polar ice cap. Halted and forced to winter over in the strait, McClure sledged in October to the northeast coast of Banks Island. Looking out across an ice-choked channel sixty-five miles wide (now called McClure Strait), he saw Melville Island, which Edward Parry had discovered in 1819, and decided he was viewing the Northwest Passage.

Robert McClure, after being rescued from his ice-locked ship, received both a monetary reward and a knighthood

The following spring, after again failing to penetrate the Prince of Wales Strait, McClure sailed west and then north around Banks Island, only to become trapped in the pack ice at Mercy Bay on the northeast coast. In 1853, with his ship still beset, his men began to die of scurvy. McClure, demonstrating a pathological passion to "complete" a Northwest Passage at any cost, conceived a sinister plan to rid himself of his thirty sickest men. Claiming it was the only way to save their lives, he proposed to send them south and east in two sledge parties. They would embark, radically undersupplied, on a journey to almost certain death. The following spring—with the remaining men, the healthiest—McClure hoped either to free the *Investigator* and sail through the supposed passage or to make his own escape.

In April 1853, mere days before he acted on this plan, a searcher from H M S *Resolute*, trapped sixty miles away, chanced upon the *Investigator*. McClure and his men trekked across the impassable ice to the *Resolute*, which had entered Arctic waters from the Atlantic. Johann Miertsching, a Moravian interpreter, described the scene:

Two sick men were lashed into each of the four sledges; others, utterly without strength, were supported by comrades who still preserved a little vigour; others again held onto and leaned on the sledges, and these were drawn by men so unsteady on their feet that every five minutes they would fall and be unable to rise without the help of their comrades, the captain, or one of the officers.

McClure, who had abandoned the *Investigator* under protest, and contrived to destroy most of the journals his officers had kept, later argued that sledging across the pack ice to the *Resolute* constituted a "completion" of the Northwest Passage. And he found fellow officers to support him: Sherard Osborn, for example, wrote a book called *Robert McClure's Discovery of the Northwest Passage*—a work that Lady Franklin did not soon forgive.

Yet Lady Franklin, aware of the tenuousness of her own claim on behalf of her husband, could hardly argue that McClure had found no navigable Northwest Passage because he had been forced to abandon his ice-locked ship to walk across the frozen sea.

Instead, she accepted the "walk-a-passage" argument as legitimate. She then introduced the notion that several Northwest Passages existed and claimed, though she lacked proof, that her husband had discovered his Passage first:

It would ill become me, and it is indeed far from my wish, to attempt to question the claims of Captain M'Clure to every honour his country may think proper to award him. That enterprising officer is not less the discoverer of a North-West Passage, or, in other words, of one of the links which was wanted to connect the main channels of navigation already ascertained by previous explorers, because the Erebus and Terror under my husband had previously, though unknown to Captain M'Clure, discovered another and more navigable passage. That passage, in fact, which, if ships ever attempt to push their way from one ocean to the other, will assuredly be the one adopted.

In this last assertion she was bluffing and blatantly wrong, but it did not matter. The House of Commons Committee accepted McClure's claim. The only alternative would have been to admit that none of the so-called Passages put forward, including both Franklin's and McClure's, satisfied the original condition of being navigable. To acknowledge that reality would have meant admitting that England had failed in its quest—or at least had not yet succeeded. Instead, money and knighthood went to Robert McClure, a graceless individual who flatly refused to share the reward either with his immediate superior, Richard Collinson, or with his rescuer, Henry Kellett.

John Rae, writing to Richardson from Orkney in August 1855, could only express disbelief:

I agree perfectly with you in thinking that McClure has been most lucky in the decision of the Arctic committee. The late Sir Edward Parry and his crew were awarded 5000 pounds [for sailing west beyond a certain latitude], of which Parry got only 1000, whereas McClure gets half. As to what was said . . . in the House about McClure's claims and the award of the 10,000 for discovering the NW Passage, it was all balderdash and could only go down with those who knew nothing of the subject.

Lady Franklin was less stoic. She had already fitted out three search expeditions largely at her own expense, sending out ships in 1850, 1851, and 1852. When the Admiralty turned down her request to borrow yet another ship, she raised money through public subscriptions and bought the 177-ton *Fox*. This was the ship, refitted to handle ice and provisioned for twenty-eight months, in which Captain Leopold McClintock steamed out of Aberdeen harbour early in July 1857.

His return in 1859 with a document indicating that Franklin's men had walked *their* Northwest Passage in 1848—six years before McClure walked his—gave Lady Franklin and her allies new ammunition. McClintock, who owed the blossoming of his career to Lady Franklin, published reports and a book about his expedition in which he revived the case for Franklin's claim.

Not surprisingly, this initiative met resistance. In January 1860, for example, William Johnson of King's College, Cambridge, strongly dissented in a letter published in *The Athenaeum*. Johnson attacked McClintock for crediting Franklin with work done by others, notably William Dease and Thomas Simpson, and alluded in passing to a fundamental, though inconvenient, truth: "As if you could prove a passage to be navigable except by sailing—not the greater portion of it, but the whole of it."

Unfortunately, Johnson made enough questionable assertions—claiming that Alexander Mackenzie, for example, deserved credit for elaborating the Passage—that Franklin supporters were able to effectively rebut him. McClintock himself suggested that the good Sir John might have learned before he died in 1847 that some of his men had walked across the ice and effected a passage:

But we do know for certain that in the following year [1848] the discovery was completed, in the same manner that Sir Robert McClure completed his discovery of another passage nearly 400 miles further to the north-west in 1851 [*sic*], namely, by walking over the frozen sea. Indeed, public opinion did not even require it to be walked over, but rightly awarded to McClure the discovery under date the 26th of October 1850, when he first sighted Melville Island.

Robert McClure, having arrived from the Pacific, had sighted a distant landmark originally visited from the Atlantic. This, apparently, now constituted the discovery of a Northwest Passage, though between McClure's vantage point and the barely visible Melville Island lay sixty-five miles of impassable ice. The question of navigability, decidedly inconvenient to Franklin's claim, had been quietly set aside. McClintock's assertion, however, that sighting a passage is rightly all that is required lends inadvertent support to John Rae's real discovery of 1854. When Rae gazed out over the young ice of Rae Strait—and, indeed, walked north upon that ice—he correctly identified the only Northwest Passage navigable by ships of the time.

Blithely unaware of the irony, McClintock himself testified to this reality in the book he published about his voyage:

Had Sir John Franklin known that a channel existed eastward of King William Land (so named by Sir John Ross), I do not think he would have risked the besetment of his ships in such very heavy ice to the westward of it; but had he attempted the northwest passage by the eastern route, he would probably have carried his ships safely through to Behring's Straits. But Franklin was furnished with charts which indicated no passage to the eastward of King William's Land, and made that land (since discovered by Rae to be an island) a peninsula attached to the continent of North America; and he consequently had but one course open to him, and that the one he adopted.

In the discussion that unfolded in the leading periodicals, the complexities of Arctic geography, presented without maps, easily defeated most readers. They were invited to accept the guidance of those experts who supported Lady Jane Franklin in her claim, among them Sir John Barrow, Sir Francis Beaufort, Sir John Richardson, Sir Roderick Murchison, John Washington (the hydrographer), Richard Collinson, Leopold McClintock, and the Americans Elisha Kent Kane and Henry Grinnell. Beaufort summarized the consensus: "Let due honours and rewards be showered on the heads of those who have nobly toiled in deciphering the puzzling Arctic labyrinth, and who have each contributed to their hard-earned quota; but let the name of

Discoverer of the North-West Passage be forever linked to that of Sir John Franklin."

Later historians, such as Leslie H. Neatby, supported the Franklin claim in full knowledge that he had failed to discover a navigable passage: "The true Passage lies to the left of Cape Felix [at the top of King William Island]," Neatby wrote, "through Ross and Rae Straits, for, once in Simpson Strait, the navigator can hope for reasonable plain sailing along the continental shore to Alaska. The key, then, to the navigable North West Passage lay in the well-concealed waters which separated King William Island from the Boothia Peninsula."

Neatby, an important interpreter of exploration history through the 1960s and 1970s, reiterated McClintock's opinion that sailing ships could make the Passage only "by passing to the left of Cape Felix, using King William Island as a shield against polar ice pressing in from the north-west. Hence James Ross's error in closing the life-saving corridor between Boothia Isthmus and the island had the disastrous effect of diverting the Franklin expedition to the right into the ice-choked channel which it ought, at all costs, to have avoided."

James Ross had marked that bay on the map "with the conjectural dotted line, expressing belief only, not positive assertion that land existed where he showed it." But his uncle, John Ross, closed the line in naming "Poctes Bay," even though the bay "was no bay but the open strait afterwards discovered and named by John Rae."

Until recently, then, Arctic experts remained untroubled by what, to the contemporary reader, stands forth as an egregious contradiction: they would freely acknowledge that Rae Strait constituted the final link in the only Northwest Passage navigable by nineteenth-century ships; they would admit that, judging from the evidence, Franklin went nowhere near Rae Strait; yet at the same time, they would assert that Franklin should be recognized as the discoverer of the Northwest Passage.

Recent writers have addressed this scholarly embarrassment only obliquely. In *Unravelling the Franklin Mystery*, a model of creative analysis, David C. Woodman attempts to resolve the contradiction in Franklin's favour. He speculates that Sir John might have tried and failed to sail at least one ship down Rae Strait. Lacking convincing evidence, he suggests that while beset in Victoria Strait, Franklin might have sent a sledge party to explore the east coast of King William Island—a party that would then have discovered Rae Strait. These propositions constitute the weakest, most conjectural sections of the book. In any case, a discovery uncommunicated and unverified remains no discovery at all.

Two British authors take a harder line than Woodman. In *The Last Place on Earth*, a classic real-life adventure first published in 1979, Roland Huntford tells the story of the race to the South Pole in the early twentieth century. While demonstrating the vast superiority as an explorer of the Norwegian Roald Amundsen over the English icon Robert Falcon Scott, Huntford hails John Rae as Amundsen's mentor and mentions Franklin as "a man who, looked at in the cold light of history, is one of the great bunglers of polar exploration."

Eighteen years later, in an award-winning book called *I May Be Some Time: Ice and the English Imagination*, Francis Spufford elaborated on Huntford:

Rae and Franklin, Amundsen and Scott; somehow the same pair of contrasted types seem to recur over and over, the laconic competent explorer versus the catastrophe-prone legend who nonetheless holds the lien on public sympathy, because he thinks of himself as the public thinks of him. Their pairing is permanent in polar history, like Don Quixote and Sancho Panza.

Huntford draws attention to the "English device of explaining away material inferiority by inventing some factitious ideal . . . part of the moralistic approach that has bedevilled English public life." Spufford

Roald Amundsen vindicated John Rae as the true discoverer when he sailed through Rae Strait

illustrates this specifically, showing how Lady Jane Franklin, having admitted that her husband was dead, contrived not only to vindicate him as an explorer, but to turn him into a national hero. He argues that, using her status as an icon of fidelity, she achieved Franklin's apotheosis by acting in the domestic sphere, setting out deliberately to shape the collective memory of Arctic events. Franklin satisfied the English taste for martyrdom, for pairing bodily loss with spiritual gain and conquest with abegnation. Discovering the Northwest Passage was "carefully redefined as an impalpable goal that did not require one to return alive, or to pass on the news to the world." Navigability, obviously, no longer figured: discovering the Passage had become a moral enterprise, not a geographical one.

Spufford observes that Lady Franklin even had the foresight to delay the constructing of memorials to her husband. Why? Because she didn't want them celebrating Franklin in ambiguous terms (that is, in anything short of panegyric). In Westminster Abbey, Britain's national shrine, the marble relief of Franklin—completed in 1875, shortly after Lady Franklin's death, but according to her instructions—features a tribute by Alfred Lord Tennyson, Franklin's nephew-in-law, which flatly declares Sir John "the discoverer of the North West Passage." Not far away, at Waterloo Place, a larger-than-life statue does the same. This monument also lists the names of those who died on Franklin's final expedition and includes Richardson's vivid but empty pronunciamento that they "forged the last link with their lives."

Lady Jane Franklin orchestrated the beatification of her dead husband. This historic fraud would matter less than it does if it had not been perpetrated at the expense of another man, the explorer who really did discover the final link in the Northwest Passage. Half a century would elapse before Roald Amundsen would vindicate John Rae. In 1903–06, when Amundsen became the first to navigate the Passage, he did so by sailing a small forty-seven-ton ship called the *Gjøa* through the channel Rae had discovered in 1854. While en route, Amundsen raised a sentimental toast to Franklin, whose published narratives had inspired him as a boy. Later he acknowledged that many expeditions seeking Franklin "did good work; but the expeditions of Admiral Sir Richard Collinson and Dr. John Rae, especially, were the most important steps towards the final achievement of the navigation of the North West Passage."

Of Collinson, who followed Rae in exploring the coast of Victoria Island, Amundsen wrote,

He guided his great, heavy vessel into waters that hardly afforded sufficient room for the tiny *Gjøa*. But, better still, he brought her safely home. His recompense for the heroism shown was, however, but scant. His second in command, Sir Robert McClure, who had to abandon his vessel, the *Investigator*, in Mercy Bay, on the north-east coast of Banks Land, and who was then helped home by others, received all the honour, and one-half of the promised reward went to him and his

Amundsen, who emulated Rae's meticulous preparedness,
conquered the Passage in the forty-seven-ton Gjøa

men as discoverers of the North West Passage.... McClure had proved that it was impracticable to make the passage by the route he tried. To Collinson belonged the still greater merit of pointing out a really practicable way for vessels—as far as he reached.

As for Rae, Amundsen explicitly credited him with having discovered the final link in the Passage: "He deserves great credit for his exploration of North Eastern America. His work was of incalculable value to the *Gjøa* expedition. He discovered Rae Strait which separates King William Land from the mainland. In all probability through this strait is the only navigable route for the voyage round the north coast of America. This is the only passage which is free from destructive pack ice."

History has proven Amundsen correct. In 1940, when the Canadian schooner *St. Roch* became the second vessel to navigate the Passage and the first to do it from west to east, Captain Henry Larsen succeeded by travelling through Rae Strait. In 1944, Larsen managed to return by McClure's more northerly route, but he relied almost entirely on twentieth-century technology in the form of a three-hundred-horsepower diesel engine. The *Gjøa*, by comparison, drew auxiliary power from a thirteen-horsepower engine, while Franklin's *Erebus* had boasted a fifteen-ton steam engine.

Since those days, technology has changed the nature of Arctic exploration. In 1960, a nuclear-powered submarine, the USS *Sea Dragon*, became the first vessel to glide through the deep-water channel beneath the ice of McClure Strait (it could just as easily have sailed beneath the permanent polar ice pack). Nine years later, a 155,000-ton supertanker, the *Manhattan*, which was able to draw on steam turbines producing 42,000 horsepower, was halted several times while battering away at the pack ice of McClure Strait. Eventually, and with the help of icebreakers, it made the passage through Prince of Wales Strait.

Since Amundsen, all vessels lacking twentieth-century engine power have followed essentially the same route. In 1977, when Willy de Roos became the first solo yachtsman to sail the Northwest Passage, he took his forty-three-foot steel ketch, the *Williwaw*, through Rae Strait.

In 1986, when Jeff MacInnis and Mike Beedell sailed the Passage (at least from Inuvik to Pond Inlet off Lancaster Sound) in an eighteen-foot catamaran, *Perception*, they took Rae Strait. Examples are becoming more numerous, but they all reiterate the same message: no vessel lacking twentieth-century power has ever navigated the Northwest Passage without sailing through Rae Strait.

Within the next few decades, global warming and the damming of freshwater rivers flowing into the Arctic (which increases the corrosion of ice by salt water) may dramatically reduce both the depth and the extent of the northern ice pack. This might open channels and passages which remain, even today, impenetrable to any surface vessels except nuclear-powered icebreakers. None of these changes will alter the truth of discovery, however. The man who discovered the final link in the only Northwest Passage navigable by ships of the nineteenth century was the same man who determined the fate of the Franklin expedition: John Rae.

17

THE
CONSUMMATE TRAVELLER

I n 1856, John Rae began to organize yet another Arctic expedition. Having resigned from the Hudson's Bay Company in April after twenty-three years of service, he meant to conduct this one on his own. Seven years earlier, while wintering at Fort Confidence, Rae had envisaged conquering the Northwest Passage. The most feasible plan, he had suggested then, would be to start from an HBC fort in two strong, square-rigged vessels of seventy to one hundred tons, "built so as to draw little water, with much rake in the stem so as not to strike hard on the ice, and with rounded sides so as to be raised up by the ice if squeezed. These would be manned by eight or ten men each."

With his Hamilton-based brothers, Rae had begun to build a schooner along these lines—a ship that, after taking him to the Arctic, would ply the Great Lakes as a commercial vessel. Now, having finally received the Admiralty reward for ascertaining the fate of Franklin, Rae invested one-quarter of his total (2,000 pounds, the equivalent today of roughly fifty times that, or U.S. $150,000) in finishing this schooner, called the *Iceberg*. He proposed to make his Fort Confidence dream, or something like it, a reality. His stated objective was to complete the survey of the Arctic coastline of North America—an action that would entail, not coincidentally, sailing through Rae Strait and so "completing" the Passage. Rae also proposed, more as an excuse than as a rationale, to co-operate with the forthcoming Franklin search expedition. He traded best wishes with its leader, Leopold McClintock, who wrote

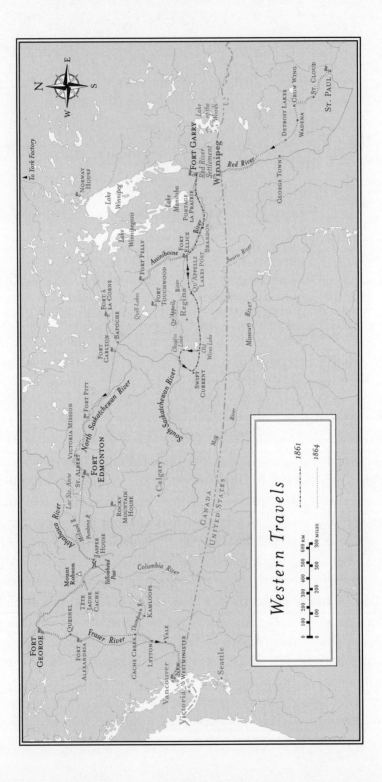

Western Travels

1861 — ⋅ — ⋅ — ⋅ —
1864 ⋅⋅⋅⋅⋅⋅⋅⋅⋅⋅⋅⋅

0   100   200   300   400   500   600 KM
0   100   200   300 MILES

of Rae's intention to sail the Passage: "Nothing would give me greater pleasure than hearing of your safe transit through the unexplored area and your arrival at San Francisco, nor do I think it at all improbable."

Rae hoped to sail north in 1857, but the Railway Shipyard in Hamilton completed the vessel too late in the year. Rather than let his investment sit idle, Rae agreed with his brothers to put the eighty-ton schooner into service earlier than planned. In mid-August, while carrying coal from Cleveland to Kingston, Ontario, the *Iceberg* went down in a storm. Reluctantly, Rae abandoned his quest to sail the Northwest Passage.

But once a traveller, always a traveller. Between 1858 and 1865, while putting behind him the devastating cannibalism controversy, the resilient Rae undertook several major journeys. One of these adventures would enable him to demonstrate yet again, almost despite himself, his effortless superiority—indeed, his peerlessness—as a rough-country traveller.

Between 1857 and 1859, Rae made his home in Hamilton, where his brothers Richard and Thomas had developed a meat-packing business. He lived at the same address as Thomas and practised some medicine, but the Arctic remained an obsession: on at least one occasion, he was seen rambling the streets in Inuit garb, shouting commands to imaginary husky dogs. A Hamiltonian named Julian Arnold captured something of the explorer's eccentricity: "He has a curious way of mingling in his conversation memories, abrupt and epigrammatical, of the adventures which he had survived among the snows and blizzards of the Arctic circle. Often he would ejaculate strange words of Eskimo origin or suddenly cry commands to a leash of huskies, the reins of which he imagined were in his hands."

These idiosyncrasies notwithstanding, Rae served as vice-president of the Hamilton Association for the Advancement of Literature, Science and Art when it was founded in 1857, and as president the following year. While in Hamilton, he also acted as an advisor to the Palliser Expedition, which mapped much of the Canadian West (now southern Saskatchewan and Alberta).

In the autumn of 1858, Rae travelled with Edward "Bear" Ellice, now seventy-seven years old, through Canada and the United States.

From Toronto, the two went by rail through Detroit, Chicago, and Milwaukee to La Crosse, Wisconsin, and then by steamer to St. Paul, Minnesota, where they joined Sir George Simpson. After a week in Minnesota, the three men journeyed down the Mississippi to Galena and then to St. Louis, Cincinnati, and Philadelphia. In Washington, D.C., they met President James Buchanan before returning to Toronto through New York, having travelled in all more than 4,580 miles.

While living in Hamilton in 1858, John Rae sat for a portrait by Stephen Pearce

The following January, the forty-five-year-old Rae hiked forty miles in seven hours to give a paper about icebergs at the Canadian Institute in Toronto. He dined and then performed without showing any sign of fatigue.

A few months later, Rae travelled west on a hunting trip with Sir George Simpson, James Carnegie (earl of Southesk), and the artist Paul Kane, whose paintings of native people and western landscapes would soon make him famous. From Hamilton, Rae travelled by train to Chicago (a booming city of 120,000), then caught a steamer up the Mississippi. He overtook the rest of the hunting party north of St. Paul, Minnesota. Rae had indicated that he would travel at least to Fort Garry, though he would not have come this far without hoping to continue westward to hunt buffalo and grizzly bears.

The party followed the Crow Wing Trail west across the plains, then went north along the swollen Red River, with Sir George rattling along in a cart. Rae rode a handsome, well-bred Vermont and shared a tent with Carnegie. From time to time, Rae went ahead with the guide, James McKay—a good-looking, bearded man who dressed Red River–style in a blue-hooded frock-coat, red-and-black flannel shirt, leather moccasins, and striped, homemade trousers—and hunted prairie fowls, ducks, and plovers, greatly improving an otherwise mediocre diet.

One night, a violent thunderstorm erupted. In pitch darkness, Carnegie awoke in a pool of water. He lit a guttering candle and found that his side of the tent had been completely flooded. His companion, Rae, remained sound asleep on higher ground, the water threatening only his feet and ankles. While Carnegie tossed and turned and tried to keep dry, the prescient explorer slept quietly until morning, when the gradually rising water finally woke him.

Fort Garry had grown into a small, scattered town divided by the Red River. Scottish, English, and half-breed settlers occupied the river's western bank, while French Canadians, Métis, and First Nations people lived on the eastern. Both sides were well-served by places of worship. With Carnegie, Rae visited the Roman Catholic nunnery, where the Sisters of Charity wore dark-blue, white-dotted petticoats over close-fitting gowns of fawn-coloured cotton, black poke-bonnets, and the ubiquitous moccasins. Here they heard a student recital. On Sunday, both attended the imposing St. John's Anglican Cathedral, where the sober, deliberate service recalled their native Scotland.

Rae helped organize the hunting party, which required horses and vehicles, weapons and provisions. The men filled three two-wheeled Red River carts and a four-wheeled wagon with baggage: tents and oilcloth squares, blankets, clothes and personal effects, bales of tea and sugar, sacks of flour and rice, biscuits, jam, eggs, dried tongues, some excellent "plug" tobacco for Carnegie and his men, and a ninety-pound roll of coarser twist for trading purposes. It formed quite a contrast with Rae's Arctic expeditions. The stores also included a copper box of rifle powder, kegs of common powder, bullets, shot, caps, a variety of axes, hammers and saws, a canteen, a portable table, a campstool, and cooking utensils.

Having supervised these preparations, John Rae suddenly said goodbye to his fellow travellers and headed back to Upper Canada. Carnegie writes nothing about this defection. But having received letters from Hamilton, Rae had grown agitated. He explained that urgent business matters required his immediate attention, which was no doubt partly true. Almost certainly, however, Rae was summoned east by an affair of the heart: the peerless explorer had fallen in love.

Over the years, while pursuing one northern adventure after another, John Rae had made no secret of his yearning to take a wife. A few months before this, while attending a service in a Toronto cathedral, he had met a charming young woman named Catherine (Kate) Jane Alicia Thompson. Kate had won a medal for her skilful lace-making at an exhibition in New York. She, too, lived in Hamilton. And Rae had begun to court her.

Details are scarce, but it appears that Kate's father—Major George Ash Thompson, originally of Ardkill, County Londonderry, and Munechrone, Country Tyrone, in northern Ireland—had only now, in Rae's absence, discovered the seriousness of the relationship. And Major Thompson found reason to disapprove loudly. The retired major, bewhiskered, increasingly red in the face, stood huffing and puffing in his crowded sitting room, the place stuffed to confusion with furniture and bric-a-brac, while his wife and his third child stared fixedly at their needlework.

What, then? Was the major expected to stand by and complacently watch while his youngest daughter married an explorer who had famously gone native? An explorer who, like the deplorable Simpson himself—with whom, at this very moment, Rae was hunting—had probably taken not one, but two or three country wives? And scattered half a dozen bairns around Rupert's Land into the bargain? In all likelihood, John Rae already had a wife. Such a marriage would never do!

In tears, ignoring her father's shouted threats to come back, the strong-willed Kate raced upstairs to her bedroom, slamming the door behind her and locking it. She wept uncontrollably on her bed, then composed herself, sat down at her desk, and wrote a letter to John Rae, mailing it to Rupert's Land by express. She did not believe her father's accusations for an instant. But how was she to respond?

This is the letter that, received at Fort Garry, would have caused Rae to abandon the hunting party and go storming back across the country. True, Rae was forty-six years old, Kate Thompson only twenty-one. But his bitter, protracted battle with Lady Franklin and her allies had affected him in many ways, and one of them had been to reinforce his natural disdain for conventional morality and its keepers. John Rae meant to follow his heart.

By the time Rae arrived in Hamilton, Kate's mother had induced Major Thompson to at least make inquiries. Ultimately, the major would consult James Hargrave, formerly chief factor at York Factory, now living in Sault Ste. Marie. This old friend of Rae's would assure the concerned father that the explorer was free of encumbrances: he had taken no country wife, fathered no illegitimate children.

In January 1860, the strong-willed Catherine (Kate) Jane Alicia Thompson married John Rae

The major capitulated with as much grace as he could muster. But John Rae never forgave him. In January 1860, after marrying in Toronto, he and Kate sailed immediately for Great Britain, ostensibly to enjoy an extended honeymoon. From this time forward, however, although they would shuttle back and forth between England and Orkney, they would never again live in Canada.

In 1860, after exchanging testy letters with Leopold McClintock, the indefatigable Rae became involved in a surveying expedition that took him to Greenland. The Atlantic Telegraph Company (ATC) wanted to run a telegraph cable from Britain to North America. Using short sea crossings, it would link northern Scotland, Orkney, Shetland, the Faroe Islands, Iceland, Greenland, and finally Labrador in North America. The ATC, which was affiliated with the HBC, hired Rae to undertake the land portion of the survey.

In August, after surveying the Faroe Islands, Rae boarded the *Fox*—the same steam yacht McClintock had used for his famous voyage—and, doubling as ship's surgeon, sailed to the east coast of Iceland. With two men, he crossed that country on horseback. He identified no insuperable difficulties, reboarded the *Fox* in Reykjavik, and sailed on to Greenland. There, in late October after a stormy voyage, he and another man journeyed up a fjord in a whaleboat rowed by Inuit women. After hiking across a glacier for sixteen miles, they encountered a heavy snowstorm and turned back. Finding their boat frozen in, they sheltered in an abandoned farmhouse for four days before a sledge party from the ship arrived to rescue them.

Rae made a great impression on the local Inuit, according to Vihljalmur Stefansson, who visited Coronation Gulf decades later. They told stories, for example, of Rae attending a ball in Julianshaab, where, though happily married, he kicked up his heels, enthusiastically dancing reels and polkas with the Inuit women who had rowed his boat.

The explorer returned to London for the winter, but in the summer of 1861, he led a hunting expedition into western Canada. Having left Kate in Hamilton to visit her family, he travelled west with two wealthy young Englishmen, Henry Chaplin and Sir Frederick Johnstone. In June, Rae left Fort Garry with ten people, twenty-two horses, two spring wagons, and three Red River carts. He led this party up the Assiniboine and Qu'Appelle rivers and then became the first European to chart Old Wives Lake and Chaplin Lake, located in the rolling grasslands southwest of present-day Regina. He travelled north up the west side of Chaplin Lake to the Saskatchewan River (a route identified by John Hudson and C. Stuart Houston), camping in a deep ravine where the riverbanks rose five or six hundred feet above the stream. Having successfully hunted buffalo, antelope, and wapiti (a kind of deer), Rae hoped to go north in search of grizzly bears but turned back east in the rolling Vermilion Hills when he learned that the natives ahead, the Young Dogs, were not welcoming visitors.

In 1863, Captain John Palliser incorporated Rae's charts of this territory into a map that accompanied a report of his own expedition. Later, in a report to the Royal Geographical Society, Rae praised the fertility of the rolling, tree-dotted lands he had traversed but noted the lack of a ready market for produce. As well, he stressed that the local native people opposed European settlement of their lands: "There is one mode, it is true, by which the Indians might be got rid of but one which, I believe, no Englishman or Canadian would dream of adopting, even to promote so great an object as the colonization of the Saskatchewan Valley." In offering this anti-colonialist opinion, Rae was elaborating a view he had already expressed to a select government committee studying the HBC charter. Asked whether the HBC opposed colonization, Rae answered, "I should fancy so: it never proposed to be a colonizing Company."

In 1864, under mounting pressure from settlers at Red River, the Hudson's Bay Company undertook to construct a telegraph line over two thousand miles to the Pacific coast, crossing the rolling grasslands and the towering Rocky Mountains. Who best to survey the proposed route? When, at home in London, John Rae informed his wife that he had been invited to lead another major expedition, the outspoken Kate must have protested vociferously: she did not wish to be abandoned to her family in Hamilton yet again. Instead, Rae brought the spirited twenty-five-year-old with him for the first part of the journey.

The story unfolds in letters Rae wrote to Thomas Fraser, the HBC's London secretary. On May 7, 1864, Rae and his wife left Liverpool on the steamer *Persia*. They reached New York twelve days later, collected expense monies, then took a train north to Montreal. There, Rae consulted engineers about the telephone poles required: kinds of timber, length and circumference, number per mile. On May 23, with Kate and an assistant named A.W. Schwieger, a respected civil engineer, Rae left Montreal by train, travelling through Toronto, Detroit, and Chicago to La Crosse, Wisconsin, on the Upper Mississippi. From there, the party travelled upriver by sternwheeler to St. Paul, Minnesota, where Rae bought horses. These he sent ahead to Crow Wing, about 125 miles north, together with two wagons and two Red River carts. Rae, Kate, and Schwieger followed by stagecoach.

On June 8, 1864, Rae led a cavalcade of horses, wagons, and carts west from Crow Wing, through Wadena and the Detroit Lakes, then north

Red River carts leaving Fort Garry, 1863:
one year later, Rae led a slightly smaller entourage west out of this stone fort

along the Red River. In this normally verdant valley, grass fires and grasshoppers had created drought-like conditions that threatened the horses, so Rae pushed harder than he would have liked, especially with Kate along. He reached Fort Garry, usually ten days' journey, in a single week. While Schwieger analyzed road and bridge requirements, Rae calculated that the 417-mile stretch from St. Cloud to Fort Garry would require 9,908 telephone poles.

Rae spent a week at Fort Garry, which had become home to a number of the men he had led into the Arctic. "These fine fellows," he wrote, "were just as eager as ever to make another voyage of 800 or 900 miles along a rugged coast in small boats, to work hard all autumn to get food to keep them alive and to scrape together a little fuel to boil their kettle." He replaced the horses with hardier stock and hired six men: three to travel as far as the Rockies and then return with Schwieger, three to accompany him all the way to the Pacific coast.

Responding to a request, Rae also met with sixty Salteaux people at the courthouse. Led by Panaasay, "The Orator," they sought information about the purpose of this survey through their lands. Rae told them he had no authority to make a treaty, but he argued that a telegraph line would do no harm and would earn them an annual stipend—and better the British than the Big Knives (Americans) from the south. The Orator responded with a long speech, and the meeting ended with Chief Factor William MacTavish distributing provisions, ammunition, and tobacco. The Salteaux would prove to be correct: projects like this one would eventually lead to their dispossession.

At Fort Garry, where the journey promised to grow more rugged and dangerous, Rae parted company with the adventurous Kate. She travelled north by the usual route to York Factory, sailing across Lake Winnipeg to Norway House and then canoeing up the Nelson River with a group of HBC men. On September 20, she left for England on the Company's *Ocean Nymph* and arrived in London one month later.

Meanwhile, John Rae travelled west.

Late in August 1864, two months out of Fort Garry, having finished preparations to canoe down the Fraser River, one of the most turbulent waterways in the Canadian Rockies—indeed in all of North America—and while encamped at Tête Jaune Cache near Jasper House, Rae climbed a forested mountain to the treeline, where at this season, snow halted further progress, and looked out on the most spectacular mountain vista he would ever see.

Gazing around from 7,170 feet above sea level, Rae estimated that some of the surrounding snow-covered peaks, dazzling white in the midday sunshine, projected another 4,000 feet into the sky. To the west and north, he could see the lush rainforest of the Robson River Valley and, as if rolling into that valley in slow motion, the gravelly, glacial ice flats that over the decades had moved down the mountains and through the passes.

Again and again, Rae found his gaze drawn back to Mount Robson, so named after an 1820s fur-trader, but which the Shuswap Indians called *Yah-hai-has-kun* or "mountain of the spiral road to heaven." The previous year, while travelling this way with Walter Cheadle, the novice explorer William Fitzwilliam had written the first detailed description of this landmark:

Immediately behind us, a giant among giants, and immeasurably supreme, rose Robson's Peak. This magnificent mountain is of conical form, glacier-clothed and rugged. When we first caught sight of it, a shroud of mist partially enveloped the summit, but this presently rolled away, and we saw its upper portion dimmed by a necklace of light, feathery clouds, beyond which its pointed apex of ice, glittering in the morning sun, shot up far into the blue heaven above.

At 12,970 feet, Mount Robson is easily the highest mountain in the Canadian Rockies. Indeed, it presents the tallest, most visually overwhelming rock face in North America, its snow-capped peak looming 9,740 feet above its base; its nearest rival, Pike's Peak in Colorado, reaches 7,212 feet. Mount Robson also stands more than 1,730 feet higher than the next highest peak in the area, Resplendent Mountain, and John Rae, lacking the verbal skills even of Fitzwilliam, could only silently feel that he was looking at one of the natural wonders of the Western world.

On the ground around him, Rae had noticed *Andromeda tetragona*, the plant he had used for fuel while wintering at Repulse Bay, and also several other hardy familiars, most of which had attained roughly the same size as they did along the Arctic Circle on the west side of Hudson Bay. Seating himself with his back against a well-positioned rock, Rae munched pemmican while scratching notes in his journal.

During the past two months, he had passed through a remarkable variety of landscape. From Fort Garry, Rae had led seven men, one wagon, three Red River carts, and fourteen horses westward through rolling grasslands and along fertile river valleys. After covering the sixty miles to Portage La Prairie in three days, Rae had led the party along the Assiniboine River west to Fort Ellice and then north to Fort Pelly. Along the way, he noticed sturdy oaks, elms, and ashes, and then numerous bluffs of poplar (aspen) and several stands of pine, all of which would serve well as telegraph poles. Exploring north of the Assiniboine, he encountered a stretch of burned timber and stunted poplar that urged him back to the valley.

At Fort Pelly, surrounded by woods rich in spruce (pine) and larch, Rae had admired the fertile black loam, the luxuriant vegetation, the flourishing crops of barley and potatoes. Just twenty miles to the west, the woods thinned out then dwindled to scrubby baldness, and the stretch from Touchwood Hills to Fort Carlton proved to be the worst yet, with little timber except a few small poplars and willows, many of them burnt. Water was scarce and the soil nothing but a layer of dirt over a bed of gravel, mud, and clay: "I am at a loss to say where poles could be most easily obtained for this part of the route."

The route from Fort Carlton to Fort Pitt was nearly as desolate, offering only a few groves of spruce along the North Saskatchewan River. At Fort Pitt, Rae divided the party in two. His assistant, Schwieger, led four men with wagons and carts along the well-travelled south bank of the North Saskatchewan River, while Rae crossed over and, with two men and pack horses, followed the north bank. On July 28, both parties reached Fort Edmonton, which impressed Rae with its thick, beautiful grasses, flowering plants, and thickly matted wild peas, as well as its rolling fields of wheat, barley, and potatoes.

Knowing that rougher country lay ahead, Rae traded for and bought additional horses, bringing the total to twenty. He then sent Schwieger west with carts and wagons. After waiting a day for a returning chief factor who failed to arrive, Rae rode after Schwieger. At St. Albert, he stopped to visit a three-year-old Catholic mission established by Father Lacombe, not yet a legend, who received him most hospitably and "seems remarkably well fitted for the work he is employed upon."

Travelling through rolling farmland, Rae caught up with Schwieger at Lac Ste. Anne. Directly ahead, with the Rockies looming jagged and white on the horizon, the trail grew rougher. As planned, Rae left the wagon and carts and redistributed the supplies among the pack saddles. On August 3, accompanied initially by several Métis and Iroquois families who were travelling west to their winter quarters, Rae set out along a rough, crooked trail through a forest, the mountains looming ever nearer. Now passing through lake country, Rae crossed the Pembina River, observing that the Norway or red pine would make good telephone poles. Then came the foothills, low-lying mountains covered by evergreens beyond which rocky peaks beckoned.

Two days into the Rockies, with snow-covered peaks jutting high above the treeline, the Métis and Iroquois families left for their winter quarters, leaving with Rae a Métis guide named Paulette Finlay. One

Traversing the Rockies meant
guiding pack horses through some of
the roughest country in North America

night during a violent thunderstorm, lightning struck a tree fifty yards from the tents, astonishing Rae by splintering it into shreds.

The party reached the Athabasca River, followed it southwest for two days, and stopped for lunch almost directly opposite Jasper House, which was not large enough to merit a visit. Rae proceeded along the Miette River, where the valley was steep, the twisting path narrow and covered in deadfalls from a recent forest fire. The men had to lift and drag charred stumps from across the dirt trail so that the horses could proceed.

In mid-August, with the air thinner than any he had ever known, Rae used the Yellowhead Pass to traverse the Great Divide, the mountainous ridge that separates areas drained by rivers flowing east and west toward opposite sides of the continent. Now the trail wound steeply downhill through fallen timber, and the men had to use picks, crowbars, and shovels. On the evening of August 22, still surrounded by towering mountains, Rae reached Tête Jaune Cache at the confluence of the Fraser and McLennan rivers. This last stretch of country provided no shortage of timber, the potential dangers to a telegraph wire being, instead, fire and falling trees.

Travelling now grew dangerous, and Rae prepared to divide the party. From here, Schwieger, the Métis guide, and two other men would take most of the horses back through the Yellowhead Pass. Once out of the Rockies, they would make their way home, exploring an alternative route. John Rae, nearly fifty-one, proposed to canoe guideless down the Fraser River, known for its canyons, gorges, and whitewater rapids. He set the men to work building the frame for a deerskin canoe. They had almost finished when some Shuswap people, camped nearby, offered to trade two long, narrow dugout canoes, hollowed from poplar logs, for fifteen made beaver. Rae closed the deal with an equivalent offer: one blanket, some ammunition, and some tobacco.

To Thomas Fraser, after describing the mountainous, forested country as favourable for a telegraph line but abominable for travelling, Rae reported that, except for a few miles, he had walked all the way from Lac Ste. Anne, often going ahead to hunt partridge with a view to improving the pemmican diet: "When there have been rain or heavy dew I got soaked quite through from the long grass and willows, but then I soon walked myself dry again if the sun came out or got before the fire when we stopped for dinner or to encamp. I have not been in such good working condition for some years."

That he had written the day before. Today, Rae had climbed this mountain to the snowline. Now, taking one last, long look at Mount Robson from this height, he began his descent to the forested tent camp on the banks of the Fraser River.

The next morning, with four men and two dugouts, and after saying goodbye to his assistant, Rae set about canoeing north down the twisting Fraser River toward Fort George (now Prince George). Three days out, encountering some serious rapids, Rae made two short portages. On August 31, he ran a long, dangerous stretch of white water, where several people had drowned in recent years. That afternoon, he arrived at Fort George, whose houses, he wrote, were in a "wretched state, there being no other windows but parchment, and the look of the place is a disgrace to the Company."

From this unimpressive post, Rae sent three of his four men back to Tête Jaune Cache, where he had left five horses to carry them back over the Rockies to Fort Garry. He now faced the toughest stretch of the Fraser River—a one-hundred-mile run south through dangerous rapids. Rae hired a native guide and, in a single day, made the descent almost without stopping. He found Quesnel to be a village of about one hundred houses crowded with over a thousand mercenary dreamers drawn there by the Cariboo Gold Rush. Rae stayed at the principal hotel, the Occidental, pronouncing the meals good but the prices high.

Discharging the native guide, Rae paddled down the Fraser with a single companion to Fort Alexandria and the new Cariboo Road, built to accommodate the Gold Rush. Here, Rae hired three horses and, with two men, spent almost two weeks exploring the surrounding mountains and valleys. Then he rode a horse south to Yale along the winding, cliff-hugging Cariboo Road, the steep banks falling away to deep gorges through which the Fraser River roared. He noted that "the construction [of the road] in many places must have required great skill and perseverance."

From Yale, where at last the Fraser grows wide and tame, Rae took a sternwheeler to New Westminster on the Pacific coast. He then travelled by side-paddle steamer to Victoria on Vancouver Island, arriving September 28. He gave a lecture on the Yellowhead route, then caught a steamer to Panama, crossed the isthmus by train, and continued to England by steamer, arriving not long after his wife.

The Hudson's Bay Company never did build a telegraph line along the route Rae explored. The Western Union Telegraph Company acted first, running a line north from San Francisco that reached both New Westminster and Quesnel in 1865. Six years later, the Northwestern Telegraph Company ran a line from Minnesota to Fort Garry. And when, in 1876, the telegraph line finally crossed the Canadian prairies, it diverged from Rae's route, running north of it as far as the South Saskatchewan River and then south of it to Edmonton.

This journey of Rae's received little publicity until recently, when Canadian historian William Barr described it in *Manitoba History*. The expedition provides an enlightening comparison with the well-known expedition along roughly the same route undertaken the year before by William Fitzwilliam, Viscount Milton, and Walter B. Cheadle. A narrative, *Cheadle's Journal of a Trip across Canada, 1862–1863*, was republished in 1971. Barr was the first to make the comparison:

Rae, the consummate traveller, described his workmanlike trip—a journey that involved no serious mishaps or accidents—in a straight-forward, matter-of-fact manner. There were no dramatic accidents or even incidents, and certainly nothing remotely comparable to Milton and Cheadle's nightmare journey from Tête Jaune Cache south to Kamloops during which the entire party came close to starving. In short, Rae's journey was precisely what one would have expected of him. And, as one would also expect of him, he maintained his reputation as a traveler *sans pareil.*

Barr notes that, travelling with wagons and Red River carts, Rae covered the 825 miles from Fort Garry to Fort Edmonton in thirty-four days, including stops, for an average daily distance of 25 miles. He travelled the section from Lac Ste. Anne to Tête Jaune Cache almost entirely on foot at a rate of 20 miles a day. Finally, he travelled 290 miles down the Fraser River from Tête Jaune Cache to Fort Alexandria by canoe in eight days, including a rest day at Quesnel.

Rae made hard travel look easy. In western Canada, as in the Arctic, to compare his elegant successes with the gawky failures of others is to see the truth in stark relief: as a rough-country traveller, John Rae had no peers.

18

RETURN TO ORKNEY

A larger-than-life sculpture of John Rae sprawled under a buffalo hide, wearing Inuit mukluks, with an open book and a musket by his side, lies in St. Magnus Cathedral in Kirkwall, the capital of Orkney. In the leafy churchyard behind the twelfth-century cathedral, beneath a weather-beaten white headstone, the explorer's remains are buried. This is where Rae's wife of over thirty years brought his body for burial after he died in London at age seventy-nine, acknowledging the importance of his connection to the rugged island world in which

The Rae memorial in St. Magnus Cathedral, Kirkwall

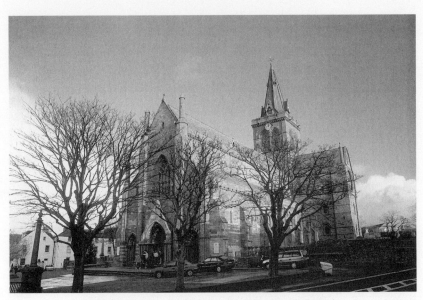

John Rae's gravesite lies behind St. Magnus Cathedral,
which houses the memorial to the explorer

he felt most at home. The Portland stone monument, unveiled in December 1895, was financed by citizen donations. A bold-face inscription reads: "John Rae, M.D., L.L.D., F.R.S., F.R.G.S. / Arctic Explorer / Intrepid discoverer of the fate of Sir John Franklin's last expedition / Born 1813–died 1893 / Expeditions: 1846–7, 1848–9, 1851–2; 1853–4. Erected by public subscription, 1895."

In addition to this memorial, a contemporary visitor to Orkney can find several sites of importance to John Rae. The most significant is the Hall of Clestrain, the three-storey stone manor house in which the explorer-to-be was born and raised. Built in 1769, and standing alone in a sheep field, this classic laird's house has fallen into disrepair, although a local group bent on restoring the mansion has managed to get it classified as a Grade A heritage site, one of only three in Orkney. From the top floor, one can look out across the choppy waters of Hoy Sound, where the tide reaches twelve knots, and see the skerries of Clestrain, the low-lying, offshore rocks that taught Rae to be a wary navigator.

Across the sound, roughly three miles away, one can discern the harbour of Stromness, where as boys, Rae and his brothers would race their two-masted yawl, the *Brenda*, against pilot boats. In Stromness itself, a plaque marks the site of Login's Well: "There watered here the Hudson Bay Co's Ships 1670–1892." Here, in 1845, before setting out to seek the Northwest Passage, Sir John Franklin took on fresh water as sailors had done since Viking times and as they continued doing—mainly on behalf of the Hudson's Bay Company—into the late nineteenth century.

In Stromness, down by the harbour, visitors can find relics of Rae at the Stromness Museum and at the Piers Arts Centre, once the headquarters of the Hudson's Bay Company. Among these are his octant, his double-barreled shotgun, and an inflatable Halkett boat that he received too late to use on his final Arctic expedition. Not far away, a sign marks the site of The Haven, formerly a three-storey house where Rae's mother lived after his father died and where Rae stayed many times. Next door, at the home of his sister Marion and her doctor-husband, John Hamilton, Lady Franklin and Sophia Cracroft once dined with Rae's mother.

On the outskirts of town, on a windblown hill in the old Stromness "kirkyard" behind the stone ruins of a church, are the gravesites of Rae's parents: "John Rae Esquire of Wyre Isle / Died: 20 Oct. 1834 age 62"; and Margaret Campbell Rae, who died February 11, 1855: "She was a friend of the poor / and an enemy to no one."

Fifteen miles east of Stromness along a winding, two-lane highway lies the Orkney capital of Kirkwall. On the outskirts of town, down a rutted dirt road that runs through some woods, sits Berstane House—now an imposing, if somewhat rundown, rooming house. A century and a half ago, this stone mansion facing east over the Bay of Berstane was the heart of a thriving waterfront estate that included a greenhouse, a gardener's house, separate lodgings for servants, a long driveway, and a dock where visitors could come and go by boat. In the mid-1860s, John Rae and his wife lived here for two years. For many summers, even after he settled in London, Rae would go shooting a few miles away at Westhill in Rendall parish, where he bought 160 acres of rolling terrain.

In a way, the consummate traveller never left his native land.

In the mid-1860s, Berstane House was the heart of a waterfront estate

In 1865, after being based for five years mostly in London, John Rae and his wife, Kate, decided to settle in Orkney. For two years, they rented Berstane House on the outskirts of Kirkwall from the wealthy Balfour family. They regularly attended Sunday services at St. Magnus Cathedral, usually arriving by coach, Rae beaver-hatted or sporting a kilt and Kate in her crinolined finery.

Far from the wilds of the Arctic, where he had foraged for edible weeds or for evil-tasting *tripe de roche* and had been glad when he could boil either over a small fire, Rae sat down every evening to a table graced with white linen, to be waited upon by a woman servant wearing a bonnet who ladled out tasty vegetable soup, piled his plate with venison and fowl, and spooned out as much gravy as he desired. Later, instead of crawling beneath a single, fetid blanket or deerskin in a freezing igloo, there to huddle in the dark with a pair of stinking male companions while a blizzard raged outside, Rae would climb the narrow stairs to the bedroom he shared with his darling wife, the adorable and enthusiastic Kate, and tumble her into a featherbed for the night.

Rae had hoped to have children and raise them in Orkney. But when none arrived, he began to rethink his life. In nearby Westhill, he could pursue his passion for hunting each summer. At Christmas and New Year's, he and Kate could witness the spectacle of The Ba, a tradition that continues today. The Ba is an annual doubleheader of street football in which two teams of one hundred men each, the Uppies and the Doonies, battle for hours to drive a leather ball either up Kirkwall's main street and over a stone wall or else all the way down it and into the harbour, the reckless melee having no other rules. The Raes also enjoyed dinner parties with a small circle of friends.

But Kate in particular felt the lack of a wider circle and of contact with people her own age. She also felt confined, hedged about: having grown up in the open spaces of North America, she experienced island life as restricting. Nor did Orkney provide much in the way of intellectual stimulation.

In February 1866, Rae gave an extemporaneous talk about Arctic exploration to the Young Men's Literary Association of Kirkwall, but where would he find his next local audience? In April, he travelled south to the University of Edinburgh to receive an honorary doctor of laws, recognition that gave him immense pleasure. That occasion, with its bustle and conviviality, also reminded him of what he had been missing. During the early 1860s, whenever he found himself in London, Rae had attended meetings of the Royal Geographical Society. He enjoyed the teeming life of the metropolis, thriving above all on the thrust and parry of debate with men who shared his passion for the Arctic, if not all his opinions about it.

Not that he enjoyed every aspect of London.

The previous August, Rae had received a typically nasty letter from Sophia Cracroft. Since 1854, Cracroft and Lady Franklin had never ceased denigrating Rae to anyone who would listen. In 1859, for example, after hearing vague rumours, later discredited, about possible survivors of the Franklin expedition, Cracroft had written to Sir Roderick Murchison. She asked him

not to place this information in the hands of Mr. Shaw, of whose mischieveous partisanship with Dr. Rae we have just had a fresh instance. He seems to make it his [business] to help Dr. Rae out of the dilemma in which his own shortcomings have placed him.... If Dr. Rae were to hear of the story today, we should have a letter in tomorrow's *Times* which would overthrow the whole in the opinion of his supporters, though it is quite impossible he should know anything about it.

In her 1865 letter, Cracroft wrote that she had intercepted an anonymous communication addressed to Lady Franklin, which she suspected had been sent by Rae himself. Yet only the explorer's reply to Cracroft survives. Rae states flatly that he sent no such letter. He denies ever speaking disrespectfully of Sir John Franklin, allowing that he might have said Franklin "was not well fitted for a long and difficult foot journey over a rough country, not being a good walker," and that, as Lady Franklin herself admitted, Sir John Richardson had saved Franklin's life. Rae then goes on the offensive, suggesting that Cracroft might recall that

her ladyship asked me more than once to perform a somewhat confidential duty, namely to have her signature removed from a subscription list to which she had put down a considerable sum (which had not then been paid if it is now) to aid in fitting out an Expedition to search for Sir John Franklin, and urged as a plea that the Expedition had returned unsuccessful.

Is it usual for Lady Franklin to employ men she despises in such affairs, or is it because the [illegible: contribution?] was the reverse of generous or liberal that she employed or tried to employ the services of a person she thought meanly of?

As regards the relics to which you allude, they were purchased from the Esquimaux and not given to me by them.... I made no secret of having these relics, nor of how they were obtained, and thousands of persons have seen them before and after dinner. A thief does not generally act in this way....

For my own part I am not conscious of any unfair dealing towards Lady Franklin and I am perfectly indifferent to the use you make of the letter that has so strangely come into your hands. I fancy I am somewhat timid and easily alarmed, but in this instance I am not "afraid," but I would have been "ashamed" had I been guilty of the action you have imputed to me.

By 1869, his permanent feud with Lady Franklin notwithstanding,

Rae had not only moved to London, but had also bought a house on a corner lot (with doors situated at both #2 and #4 Addison Gardens) in Kensington, an upper-middle-class neighbourhood that, for Rae, was an easy walk to the Royal Geographical Society. In that house, with Kate, he would spend the rest of his life.

During the 1850s and 1860s, while adventuring, Rae published three major articles about geographic exploration in the *Journal of the Royal Geographic Society*. The first treated his journey from Great Bear Lake to Wollaston Land in 1851; the second, his explorations along the south and east coast of Victoria Island that same year; the third, his final Arctic expedition, "with information respecting Sir John Franklin's missing party." Rae also published an article about the birds and mammals of North America with the Linnean Society, and the eminent botanist J.D. Hooker contributed a list of the seventy-nine Arctic plants the explorer had collected.

During the next two decades, while sporadically practising medicine in London, Rae amassed over 200 artifacts of First Nations and Inuit peoples and presented and published more than a dozen additional articles about the Arctic, its inhabitants, and its natural history. He treated everything from snowhuts, sledges, and sledge journeys to glacier motion, the formation of icebergs, and the characteristics of the native tribes around Hudson Bay. He referred to the Inuit as "my friends the Eskimos" and celebrated snow goggles, the retractable, segmented harpoon, and the architecture of the igloo as products of "scientific skill" rather than mere "ingenuity," so recognizing, some-what controversially, the magnitude of achievement involved in adapting to the hostile Arctic environment.

His audiences included the Physical Society of London, the Anthropological Institute, the Ethnological Society, the Royal Institution, the Society of Arts, the Linnean Society, and, most prestigious of all, the British Association for the Advancement of Science. Having presented papers at British Association meetings in Cheltenham in 1856 and in Oxford in 1860, Rae did the same in Edinburgh in 1871, in Dublin in 1878, in Aberdeen in 1885, and in Birmingham in 1886. He also served on an Association committee to study "permanently frozen soil," or permafrost. In addition, between 1871 and 1888, Rae contributed more than forty letters to *Nature* magazine, touching on the wanderings of the Inuit, the sound of the aurora borealis, the buoyancy of bodies in water, intelligence in animals, duck diving, the migration of the wagtail, and "unconscious bias in walking."

Throughout these years, Rae expressed strong opinions, embroiling himself in numerous controversies and at least one major battle. In 1872, having been elected to the council of the Royal Geographical Society, Rae joined its Arctic committee to consider plans for an expedition to the North Pole (this was eventually the Nares Expedition). He attended one meeting and, when plans for a large-scale, naval-style undertaking carried the day, promptly resigned.

The Admiralty hydrographer, G.H. Richards, had blithely observed that he did not know of any private expedition that succeeded, except for Leopold McClintock's. Rae, the most cost-efficient explorer who ever lived, wrote to him sharply:

[Such opinions, expressed by any ordinary individual,] would have been simply laughed at by those who knew anything of the subject, but coming from an Admiral . . . they carried a certain amount of weight to which they were not otherwise entitled. It would be very easy to show that a number of private Arctic expeditions with which no naval officer was in any way connected did as much good work in accuracy of surveying and in distances travelled *in proportion to the number of men employed and money spent* as any purely Admiralty or Government expedition that ever went to the Arctic Sea.

The officially sanctioned polar expedition, led by Sir George Nares sailing in HMS *Alert*, left in 1875. But the debate continued, shifting to technological grounds. Rae criticized the sledges and snowshoes adopted, and he also contended that the explorers should have used Inuit-style snowhuts instead of tents. In 1877, when Nares addressed the Royal Geographical Society, Rae entered into a heated debate with both him and the hydrographer, disputing their easy generalizations about sea ice, the rate of drift down the Greenland coast, and areas of open water in the frozen sea.

Subsequently, in an article called "Practical Hints for Arctic Travelling," Rae summarized his views on sledges, diet, and travelling methods and ridiculed Nares's contention that men couldn't haul sledges while wearing snowshoes, observing that "the gallant knight knows nothing about it, probably never having in his life seen a sledge so-hauled, yet he gives his opinion with as much confidence as if he had great experience."

Rae argued that future expeditions should use not Royal Navy men, but men experienced in snowshoe walking, sledge travelling, and setting nets under ice. They might be recruited in

The Alert, *captained by Sir George Nares, beset by ice in Kennedy Channel*

Winnipeg among the half-breeds, "who are as fine fellows as a person could wish for for such work." Rejecting the vaunted need for naval discipline, Rae observed that "no men could have been more obedient than the men of various nationalities I had on three occasions under me; the cheerfulness with which they did an immense deal of hard work would have surprised most people and this, too, without a word of bad language or an oath that could have offended the most delicate lady!"

So much for the Nares expedition and its lessons.

In the 1880s, having become a fellow of the Royal Society, Rae participated in the public debate about the commercial development of a sea route through Hudson Strait. Proponents advocated transporting prairie grain by train to a Hudson Bay port and then by sea to Britain. They claimed that Hudson Strait remained navigable for steamships from mid-June through October. Rae, who had voyaged through that strait three times and been turned back by ice in 1833, presented papers disputing this assertion. He argued that given the transcontinental railway, the Hudson Bay sea route could not compare with the route through the Great Lakes and the St. Lawrence seaway—a contention that remains true even today.

Rae visited Canada for the last time in 1882. In Montreal, as an invited guest of the American Association for the Advancement of Science, he presented a paper on Arctic exploration in North America. He and Kate visited relatives in Hamilton and travelled to Winnipeg, where Rae spoke to the Manitoba Historical and Scientific Society on "Arctic Regions and the Hudson Bay Route." The couple then took a train west to Regina to the end of the Canadian Pacific Railway tracks (the "last spike" would not be driven until three years later).

In 1891, at age seventy-seven, Rae resumed his old battle for justice, publishing two letters in the journal of the American Geographical Society. The first dealt with British Admiralty charts: four decades after the fact, the latest versions attributed his Victoria Island survey to Richard Collinson. Rae had recently visited the current hydrographer, a Captain Wharton, to request "that the six hundred miles of survey of which I have for such a very long period been dishonestly dispossessed should be restored to me." Wharton had agreed, he reported, to "rectify the injury that had been done, as far as was in his power."

John Rae, pictured later in life with some of the Franklin relics he purchased, never stopped fighting to correct the historical record

In his last published letter, Rae criticized a biography of Sir John Franklin by A.H. Markham. He cited numerous factual errors and noted, most importantly, that his own survey of the west coast of Melville Peninsula had been attributed to Sir Edward Parry. His need to correct the historical record remained as strong as ever, and he asked that his letter be published "in the interests of truth and the correction of the history of Arctic exploration, to say nothing about a sense of common justice to myself." Later, an obituary would note that "the feeling which grew upon him to a painful extent as he became older that his brilliant explorations were not adequately recognised and acknowledged on Admiralty charts, somewhat embittered his later years."

Yet, in these later years, Rae also enjoyed great happiness. Throughout the 1860s and 1870s, he often took part in an annual shooting competition, first with the Orkney Artillery Volunteers, later with the London Scottish Regiment. The oldest private in the volunteer force of 200,000 men—he had refused a commission as too much trouble—Rae remained almost fanatically fit. At age seventy-three, he decided to attend the Easter Monday review at Dover. When he informed Kate that he intended to walk to the train station in central London, she implored him to take a coach. Rae replied that if he was not fit to walk, he was not fit to attend the review.

He rose at three in the morning, donned his uniform, and downed coffee, bread and butter. At 3:30, he departed with rifle, haversack, and water bottle. Rae arrived at the train station, four miles away, fifty-four minutes later. After a train ride of two hours and forty minutes, he spent ten hours at exercises—walking, running, firing blank cartridges, climbing fences, struggling through brambles, and winding up with a march past. He returned to London by train and caught a coach home, arriving at 9:30 p.m., fresh enough to assert that he would have walked from the station had it not been for the thought of keeping Kate sitting up.

Almost every summer during these later years, Rae returned to Orkney to sail and shoot. One observer would later declare, "Those of us who saw him on his annual visits to Orkney even when he was close on his allotted span can never forget his striking figure, his indomitable expression, and how, shouldering his fowling piece, he strode along at a pace which left young men far behind." In 1888, Rae could still walk twenty or twenty-five miles a day, do his drills, and teach shooting. At some point, however, he may have felt chest pains, because doctors warned him against straining his heart. In August 1890, he insisted on "sticking to volunteering, the most healthful and pleasant amusement I have"—though toward the end of that year, at seventy-seven, he resigned from the London Scottish Regiment.

Starting in the 1880s, Rae suffered occasionally from gout, a metabolic disturbance that causes a painful inflammation of the joints, especially of the feet and hands. In 1890, he spent ten days in bed with bronchitis, but he didn't take seriously ill until April 1893, when at age seventy-nine he began to suffer from influenza and lung congestion. Early in July, he improved and contemplated a visit to the sea. But he relapsed and, on July 22, 1893, John Rae died of an aneurysm.

The Royal Geographical Society published a grudging obituary:

It is easy to understand that Dr. Rae's views as to the equipment of expeditions in Arctic travel would differ in many respects, rightly or wrongly, from those who advocated the costly naval expeditions then in vogue. He could point to instances of his own superior success and to the disaster that befell the survivors of the Franklin expedition, as they toiled with a miscellaneous collection of heavy articles. Putting forward his views, as he did, with point and insistence, his remarks were, as a rule, somewhat unwelcome to the naval authorities.

Kate Rae, having been married to John Rae for thirty-three years, would live comfortably for another twenty-six years and pass away in Chislehurst, Kent. She would spend more than a decade trying without success to organize Rae's memoirs into publishable form, the end result being the palimpsest now held at the Scott Polar Research Institute. In private correspondence, she would angrily assert even fourteen years after her husband's death that Leopold McClintock had cheated Rae of recognition, noting that he had visited Rae repeatedly to discuss Franklin's whereabouts and had then found remains precisely where Rae stipulated, but had "never acknowledged in any even slight reference what he owed to the lead" her husband had given him.

Now, in 1893, after a short service at St. John the Baptist Church, Kate and her sister Emily Skeffington Thompson, who had lived with the married couple, transported the explorer's body to Orkney for burial. During the return journey to London, on a train rattling south through Scotland, Kate began a long letter to her Canadian niece, Jessie Hamilton, a letter that she would finish only after arriving home. She wrote that Rae had left no instructions regarding a final resting place, but that she had resolved to take his body to his beloved Orkney, for she knew both from long-ago conversations and from recent reminiscences that this was what he would have wished.

Kate Rae transported her husband's remains from London to Orkney for burial

On the Thursday morning he sent me out on a message for him. I was only away about twenty minutes. I had not been out for a long time and I was a little surprised when he asked me to go myself and get him a postal order to send his subscription to the Kirkwall Sailing Club (his last subscription). You can imagine how I flew there and back, and when I came back I ran up to him and I said, "well, darling, was I not quick?" and he held out his hand to me and said "well, I don't know, it seemed a long time" and we both laughed. . . . & he said, "will you be about now?" & I said, "yes darling, I am going to sit beside you," then he said, "I will go to sleep," and he went to sleep holding my hand. That is the way he nearly always slept with his hand in mine, and I wrote so little because I could not bear to be away from his side. . . .

. . . He said he was feeling better and had no pain, and he went to sleep and had a nice sleep, and he seemed so much better, but I saw him looking up intently, and I said darling, what are you looking at, and he said in a whisper, "Oh, Katie, the beautiful music, the beautiful music," I am sure now it was the heavenly music he heard. . . .

. . . Got back yesterday morning. . . . It is so dreadfully sad here, it is hard to keep up, every turn reminds us of his dear bright presence. Everywhere his pictures smile at us. I am writing at the little table in his room where there is an unfinished letter I began to you on the 19th, but never could go on with, for he was always calling me back to his side, either with his voice or his dear loving eyes, of a morning when I was doing my hair he would always turn himself so that he could watch me, and I would often get up and go over to him, all these memories are my dearest treasures. But I must go on with that Saturday morning. . . .

. . . He was getting weaker and weaker and the last words I heard him say were, "oh my darling wife, it is all over, my darling wife, my darling wife," over and over again, his beautiful eyes were gazing into mine, and I went on speaking to him for I was certain from his expression he could hear, and every now and then I moistened his dear lips, with cold water, and though he could not speak he would press mine and Emily's hand as she prayed. The doctors and the nurse said they never saw a more peaceful death but at 7 o'clock he drew his last gentle breath, just as our little clock chimed 7, dearest Jessie, it was not death it was life, his beautiful spirit passed away in the light he loved, there was such a glorious sunset, everyone remarked it, but I could look only at him, I could not believe he had gone, and if those two doctors had not been there I could not have believed he would not speak to me again.

I sat beside him all night, dearest Emily and the nurse wanted to sit with me for they wouldn't go to bed till it was morning, but I wanted to be alone with him. There was such a noble look on his beautiful features, I would have given anything if I could have had him painted, none of his photographs, none of his pictures are half so beautiful as he was in this illness, and his eyes were glorious, you will not think me silly. Everyone who saw him towards the end of his illness said the same. The doctors were to say when they saw him so bright and full of life, your husband is a marvellous man. You could not believe he was leaving us. . . .

AN ARCTIC HOMAGE

At twenty minutes past midnight near the top of the world, as across the High Arctic daylight dwindled to dusk, three men guided a motorboat carefully through the shallows of a hard-to-find bay on the west coast of an obscure peninsula. Fifty yards from shore, the twenty-foot boat ran aground and the three voyagers—Louie Kamookak, Cameron Treleaven, and myself—pulled on rubber boots, clambered over the side, and dragged the vessel farther onto the reef before burying two anchors in the sand.

As dusk yielded to twilight at around half past one in the morning, we finished lugging our equipment and supplies on shore and, on the rocky, treeless ground, pitched a floorless, handmade canvas tent, securing it with stones. Knowing that the sun would rise above the horizon in just two hours, we unrolled our sleeping bags and crawled into them, hoping to fall asleep quickly.

We had left Gjoa Haven, an Inuit hamlet of about nine hundred people, immediately after supper but had stopped to explore the eastern coast of King William Island. At 9:45 p.m., we had regained the boat and, while a stiff north wind created whitecaps and spray billowed over the canopy of the vessel, thumped our way fifteen miles across Rae Strait.

We had come to this desolate spot, rarely visited except by Inuit hunting parties, to celebrate the Arctic adventurer whom Vilhjalmur Stefansson had hailed as the most challenging figure in the history of nineteenth-century exploration. We had come to honour John Rae. With us we had brought a plaque of weather-resistant, anodized aluminum that we had screwed to a slab of Honduran mahogany and whose inscription begins, "This plaque marks the spot where Arctic explorer John Rae (1813–93) discovered the final link in the Northwest Passage."

Our late-twentieth-century campsite sat by the strait through which Roald Amundsen had sailed in 1903 as the first explorer to navigate the Northwest Passage. And somewhere in this vicinity, facing the strait that would later bear his name, John Rae, in 1854, had built a stone cairn. Our objective was to find this cairn and, during this last summer of the twentieth century—and indeed the millennium—mark the spot where he had fit the final piece into a centuries-old puzzle.

For Treleaven and Kamookak, experienced northern travellers, the outing was a break from exploring sites pertaining mainly to the last disastrous expedition of Sir John Franklin. For me, our quest constituted a gesture epitomizing everything I felt driven to say about Rae, an explorer victimized by powerful contemporaries and shamefully wronged by history.

As I lay in the tent in my sleeping bag, I found myself marvelling anew at the injustice that had brought me to these rocky shores. Building on the work of explorers who had gone before him, and aided only by a motley few outsiders—First Nations and Inuit, fellow Orcadians, Métis, and Scottish half-breeds—John Rae had solved the two great mysteries of nineteenth-century Arctic exploration, discovering both the fate of the Franklin expedition and the final link in the Northwest Passage. Yet his enemies, Lady Jane Franklin chief among them, had contrived to steal the credit for both accomplishments.

Endowed with almost superhuman physicality, rightly hailed as "a genius of Arctic travel," Rae had remained extraordinarily open to learning from the native peoples of North America—a post-colonial figure in a colonial age even before he became embroiled in controversy. Between 1846 and 1854, he led four major Arctic expeditions, travelling more than 23,000 miles. The chief hunter of every one, Rae surveyed 1,751 miles of unexplored territory, including 1,538 miles of northern coastline. A cost-efficient marvel of stamina, resilience, and resourcefulness, he trekked 6,504 miles in the Arctic alone, mostly on snowshoes, and travelled another 6,634 miles in canoes and small boats.

Back in England, as Stefansson later observed, Rae was criticized for doing his own menial work and for living "like a savage—in snow houses and so forth. This behaviour did not seem cricket to the British public ... the object of polar exploration was to explore properly and not to evade the hazards of the game through the vulgar subterfuge of going native."

When prevarication might have kept a coveted knighthood within reach, Rae stood by his principles, refusing to recant, refusing to sell out the Inuit peoples. And so this peerless figure became the only major British explorer of the age never to receive a knighthood. No wonder I felt driven—not only to experience Rae's Arctic, as I had visited his native Orkney, but also to mark the site of his greatest achievement, a miracle of sagacity, perseverance, and endurance that had been lost to official history.

Anyone who lives in Calgary, Alberta, and develops a serious interest in the Arctic will sooner or later encounter antiquarian Cameron Treleaven, owner of Aquila Books and, not incidentally, one of the finest collections of Arctic books and paraphernalia in North America. As it happens, he has also done some exploring with an Inuit friend who lives in Gjoa Haven, the settlement nearest Rae Strait.

When I told Treleaven that I proposed to visit and mark the site of John Rae's historic discovery, he suggested that we turn the venture into a three-man expedition. Instead of building an easily destroyed cairn, why not erect a commemorative plaque? Treleaven contacted Kamookak. We juggled schedules and spent a few hundred dollars to create a memorial that incorporated not just my 250-word text, but also an image of Rae in native clothing.

From Calgary, near the Rockies, Treleaven and I drove north to Edmonton and then flew still farther north to Yellowknife in the Northwest Territories (a small city at roughly the same latitude as Anchorage, Alaska). The next day, we flew two and a half hours northeast to Gjoa Haven, named after the *Gjøa*, in which Amundsen completed his celebrated passage. Located roughly eight hundred miles above the treeline, this scattering of one-storey frame houses in a landscape of rocks and boulders, moss, lichen, and stunted shrubs, overlooks a bay that the Norwegian explorer, relieved to find a winter shelter, pronounced "the most beautiful little harbour in the world."

Louie Kamookak met us at the airstrip. Proudly Inuit, he remains proud as well that one of his grandfathers was William "Paddy" Gibson of the Hudson's Bay Company. In the 1930s, Gibson not only discovered and buried the remains of several Franklin sailors, but also wrote expertly about the lost expedition.

Kamookak heads a family of six, supervises the maintenance of local housing, pursues a keen interest in Arctic exploration, and is immersed in two scholarly projects: one involving Inuit place names, the other, traditional oral stories. Before Treleaven and I left the Arctic, we would watch Kamookak harvest Arctic char from his nets and see him down a caribou at 120 yards with a single rifle shot through the heart— and then carry the carcass on his back for almost half a mile. But all that came later.

Today, visitors to Gjoa Haven usually stay at the barn-like Amundsen Hotel, where a shared room costs over two hundred dollars per person per night. Luckier than most, Treleaven and I would spend our last two nights in the Arctic in a one-room cabin Kamookak had built four miles out of town and our first two at the home of one of his friends.

One evening, we travelled by motorboat fifteen miles west to the Todd Islets. Kamookak showed us the site his grandfather had established: a scattering of white bones on the ground, with a few larger bones protruding from beneath the earth. These remains lay along a known route of retreat and had not been locked in permafrost. To me, they could reveal nothing new. Besides, I had come for John Rae.

The following night, after Kamookak finished work, we roared west across the whitecaps of Schwatka Bay, then headed north up the east coast of King William Island to a high plateau that the Inuit call Avak. Easily the most visible landmark in the area, John Rae saw it from across the channel and, thinking of an HBC director, named it "Matheson," which remains the official name.

After hiking to the top of this plateau—notable for its panoramic view and the strewn debris of a dismantled Dew Line station—we regained the boat and set out east across Rae Strait. During the thumping, exhilarating ride across waters so cold that a swimmer would not survive ten minutes, and in which hitting a floating log would mean almost certain death, I scribbled in my notebook, "Incredible to think that I should find not one but two fellow madmen to join me in this lunatic quest."

Once we had established our camp on the coast of Boothia Peninsula, our first objective was to find the cairn that Rae built. Fortunately, the explorer not only described the place where he created the marker, but also noted its geographical co-ordinates. Both Treleaven and Kamookak carried Global Positioning System receivers that drew on globe-girdling satellites to specify locations and distances. John Rae, of course, had been forced to rely on less sophisticated equipment. Because he was meticulous, his latitude reading, I believed, would be fairly precise. But in the mid-1800s, the portable technology to provide accurate longitude readings had yet to be perfected. Indeed, when I checked the map, Rae's longitude put the cairn far inland, which did not match his description of having travelled north along the coast.

Even so, we headed inland that first morning, roughly northeast, with a view to reaching Rae's designated point and then heading west along the correct latitude so that we could not possibly miss the cairn. Under a limitless blue sky, we hiked for hour after hour across treeless, rock-strewn tundra, slogging through marshes, scrambling over ridges, and occasionally spotting caribou in the distance. A couple of times, we sighted landmarks that resembled grandiose cairns on the horizon, but they always proved to be giant rocks.

At about three o'clock in the afternoon, when we arrived at a broad inlet we had hoped to ford, we discovered that at best this would mean wading fifty yards through freezing, fast-flowing, groin-deep water while sinking in rock-filled mud to our knees. Treleaven insisted that we could do it, and maybe he was right. Kamookak wryly observed, "It's too much work, this Rae stuff." He and I voted to add a couple of miles to our hike, so instead of fording, we all three walked around.

At 4:30 p.m., we again approached Rae's latitude, only now we were hiking north along the coast, the three of us strung out eighty yards apart, scouring the landscape. As we approached the tip of the peninsula that Rae had named Point de la Guiche, Kamookak, who was travelling along a ridge, found what looked like the remains of a cairn. Instead of hollering, he simply placed his GPS receiver on the capstone, sat down, and waited for Treleaven and me to join him.

The cairn itself had been dismantled but was still clearly recognizable as a human creation, even with its stones covered in yellow and black lichen. Nor was it the kind of cairn, Kamookak explained, that hunters would build to cache game: the builder of this cairn had placed big rocks in the centre on top of smaller ones, a practice that would crush fresh meat. It was the only man-made structure for miles. And the GPS told us that although the longitude of this spot differed from Rae's by three minutes and thirty-six seconds, the latitude agreed within a few yards. This was indeed Rae's cairn.

Standing in the wind with open water visible to the west, the northwest, and the northeast, I could see the scene as it had unfolded in the wintry snowscape of early May 1854. A resolute man of forty-one, Rae had led his small party across ice and rough country for over 320 miles, man-hauling sledges through blizzards, gale-force winds, and temperatures as low as −62 degrees Fahrenheit. All of the men suffered from snow-blindness, and one froze two toes. Only Rae and his two hardiest men—the Inuit William Ouligbuck, Jr., and the Cree Thomas Mistegan—reached this spot on the west coast of Boothia Peninsula.

Louie Kamookak examines the remains of the cairn John Rae built

From here, Rae sent Mistegan northward across the ice beyond rocky and windswept Point de la Guiche to see what he could see. He put Ouligbuck to work building an igloo in which all three of them would later rest and recuperate. Kamookak, himself an expert igloo builder, said that the Inuit man would have built the snowhut on the small lake directly behind the windy ridge on which we stood, because such a ridge causes drifting and so creates the best snow for cutting blocks.

Rae himself, after using his sextant to take readings, would have set about building the cairn before us—the cairn that marked his discovery of the final link in the Northwest Passage. Half a century would elapse before Amundsen would vindicate that achievement, and by then the Orcadian explorer would be a decade dead.

We spent half an hour exploring the boulder-strewn tip of the peninsula, as doubtless Rae himself had done, before starting back to camp. We arrived at 9:45 p.m. with the sun still high in the sky. All told, we had hiked through rugged country for twelve hours and covered roughly twenty miles—a minuscule distance by John Rae's standards, but far enough to get the idea.

The next morning, we faced the challenge of the plaque. Rae's cairn lay just five miles north of our camp. While returning the previous evening, we had stumbled, miserable and soaking wet, through bog and muskeg. Detouring around that stretch would mean a round trip of roughly twelve miles—not a great distance compared with our first day. Now, however, we had a plaque to transport—a plaque that, screwed to a waist-high stand that Kamookak had constructed of welded steel, weighed an unwieldy thirty-five pounds or more.

My fellow explorers would not even hear of using the motorboat to shorten the trek and, grudgingly, I admitted they were right: if we could not hope to emulate the consummate traveller, who on snowshoes had hauled a sledge most of the way from Repulse Bay, we could at least pay homage to the spirit of his achievement by lugging the memorial plaque overland. Kamookak created a sling out of a sweatshirt and proposed that we carry the awkward creation "traditional Inuit style."

While Treleaven and I packed last-minute items into our daypacks, Kamookak set off across the tundra at a pace I considered unsustainable

—wrongly, as it turned out. He had covered half a mile by the time we two stragglers departed, and we expected that he would pause to rest; but after half an hour, he showed no sign even of slowing. Treleaven and I maintained a rigorous pace, but Kamookak, gliding effortlessly over the land, increased his lead. Then the realization hit: he was testing us. Like a champion bicycle racer making a bid to leave the pack, Kamookak was threatening to become the only one of us to actually carry the Rae memorial to its destination.

I work out five times a week and consider myself physically fit, but Treleaven runs fifty miles a week, plays squash well enough to compete nationally, and makes a habit of scrambling up peaks in the Rockies. I felt that he, better than I, could do what had to be done. As I lengthened my stride, Treleaven, carrying a twenty-five pound daypack, broke into a vigorous jog. After fifteen or twenty minutes of

Author Ken McGoogan prepares to lug the
plaque north along Rae Strait

non-stop running, he caught Kamookak on a ridge, foiling his friend's mischievous bid for solitary glory. The two of them rested and, when I caught up, Kamookak said, "You thought I was going to put the memorial in the wrong place?"

"Not exactly," I replied.

But Treleaven and I carried it the rest of the way.

A few yards south of the remains of the cairn, we jammed the stand into the ground and piled boulders around it. Then we toasted John Rae and his men with a bottle of dry red wine. We took some photos, and we created instant collectors' items by signing books and other objects.

Kamookak, having waited for this moment, stood and read the plaque out loud:

HOMAGE TO JOHN RAE

This plaque marks the spot where Arctic explorer John Rae (1813–93) discovered the final link in the Northwest Passage. In the spring of 1854, acting on behalf of the Hudson's Bay Company, and after wintering in Repulse Bay, Rae led four men across Boothia Peninsula bent on completing the mapping of the northern coast of North America. By delineating the coastline between two accessible points—the mouth of the Castor and Pollux River and Bellot Strait—the intrepid Rae meant to establish or invalidate the existence of a navigable Northwest Passage.

Hauling sledges through gale-force winds, blowing snow and bitter cold, the Orcadian Rae and his two hardiest men—the Inuit William Ouligbuck, Jr., and the Cree Thomas Mistegan—reached the mouth of the Castor and Pollux River, which Europeans had attained from the Pacific Ocean. Rae then led the way northwest along the coast of Boothia towards what was still called "King William Land." On May 6, 1854, the party arrived at this promontory (Point de la Guiche: latitude 68 57 52, longitude 94 32 58) and built a snowhut and a cairn.

Standing here, looking out over a channel covered by "young ice," Rae realized that "King William Land" was an island. The channel before him, which joined known points accessible by sailing ship, constituted the missing link in the Northwest Passage. In 1903–06, when the Norwegian Roald Amundsen became the first European to navigate the Northwest Passage, he did it by sailing through Rae Strait.

At the bottom of the plaque, Kamookak discovered our three names in large italics. He let out a whoop and said, "That's the first time I've noticed. I waited until now to read the inscription."

In response, I proposed yet another toast: "To a consummate traveller, a man wronged by history and vindicated at this place. To the greatest Arctic explorer of them all. Gentlemen, to John Rae!"

We all drank and then, looking out over Rae Strait in the sunshine, we savoured the notion that we had created a memorial that could endure the High Arctic climate for half a century or more. And even if some destructive soul were to remove the plaque, our modest accomplishment would remain: we had become the first to commemorate John Rae's greatest achievement at its location. Nobody could take that away from us.

The sun stood high in the sky and showed no sign of waning, but we looked at each other and knew that it was time. We shouldered our daypacks and clustered around the memorial, reluctant to leave. I said, "John Rae was here."

Treleaven said, "Of that there is no doubt."

Kamookak grinned, and turned, and led the way south.

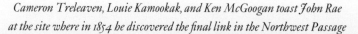

Cameron Treleaven, Louie Kamookak, and Ken McGoogan toast John Rae at the site where in 1854 he discovered the final link in the Northwest Passage

BIBLIOGRAPHY

Ackroyd, Peter. *Dickens*. London: Sinclair-Stevenson, 1990.

Amundsen, Roald. *The North West Passage*, 2 vols. London: Archibald Constable, 1908.

Anonymous. *Arctic Rewards and Their Claimants*. London, 1856.

Ballantyne, R.M. *Hudson Bay; or Everyday Life in the Wilds of North America*. London: Thomas Nelson, 1910.

Barr, William, ed. *Searching for Franklin: The Land Arctic Searching Expedition*. London: Hakluyt Society, 1999.

Beattie, Owen, and John Geiger. *Unlocking the Secrets of the Franklin Expedition*. Saskatoon: Western Producer Prairie Books, 1987.

Berton, Pierre. *The Arctic Grail: The Quest for the North-West Passage and the North Pole, 1818–1909*. Toronto: McClelland & Stewart, 1988.

Brannan, Robert Louis, ed. *Under the Management of Mr. Charles Dickens: His Production of 'The Frozen Deep.'* Ithaca, New York: Cornell University Press, 1966.

Bunyan, Ian, Jenni Calder, Dale Idiens, and Bryce Wilson. *No Ordinary Journey: John Rae, Arctic Explorer, 1813–1893*. Edinburgh: National Museums of Scotland, 1993.

Carnegie, James, Earl of Southesk. *Saskatchewan and the Rocky Mountains*. Edinburgh: Edmiston & Douglas, 1875.

Cookman, Scott. *Ice Blink: The Tragic Fate of Sir John Franklin's Lost Expedition*. New York: John Wiley, 2000.

Cyriax, R.J. *Sir John Franklin's Last Arctic Expedition*. London: Methuen, 1939.

Davis, Richard C., ed. *Lobsticks and Stone Cairns: Human Landmarks in the Arctic.* Calgary: University of Calgary Press, 1996.

Delgado, James. *Across the Top of the World: The Quest for the Northwest Passage.* Vancouver: Douglas & McIntyre, 1999.

De Roos, Willy. *North West Passage.* London: International Marine Publishing, 1979.

Dickens, Charles. "The Lost Arctic Voyagers." *Household Words,* December 2 / 9, 1854, 361–65.

Fleming, Fergus. *Barrow's Boys: The Original Extreme Adventurers.* New York: Atlantic Monthly Press, 1998.

Francis, Daniel. *Discovery of the North: The Exploration of Canada's Arctic.* Edmonton: Hurtig Publishers, 1986.

Franklin, John. *Narrative of a Journey to the Shores of the Polar Seas in the Years 1819–1822.* London: John Murray, 1823.

Friesen, Gerald. *The Canadian Prairies: A History.* Toronto: University of Toronto Press, 1984.

Galbraith, J.S. *The Little Emperor.* Toronto: Macmillan, 1976.

Hall, Charles Francis. *Arctic Researches and Life Among the Esquimaux.* New York: Harper & Brothers, 1865.

Holland, Clive. *Arctic Exploration and Development, c. 500 B.C. to 1915: An Encyclopedia.* New York: Garland Publishing, 1994.

Hooper, William H. *Ten Months among the Tents of the Tuski.* London: John Murray, 1853.

Houston, C. Stuart, ed. *Arctic Ordeal: The Journal of John Richardson, Surgeon-Naturalist with Franklin, 1820–1822.* Montreal and Kingston: McGill-Queen's University Press, 1984.

Huck, Barbara. *Exploring the Fur Trade Routes of North America.* Winnipeg: Heartland, 1999.

Huntford, Roland. *The Last Place on Earth / Scott and Amundsen revised.* New York: Random House, 1979.

Inwood, Stephen. *A History of London.* London: Macmillan, 1998.

Johnson, Robert E. *Sir John Richardson.* London: Taylor & Francis, 1976.

Keenleyside, Anne, Margaret Bertulli, and Henry C. Fricke. "The Final Days of the Franklin Expedition: New Skeletal Evidence." *Arctic* 50, no. 1 (March 1997): 36–46.

Lopez, Barry. *Arctic Dreams: Imagination and Desire in a Northern Landscape.* New York: Charles Scribner's Sons, 1986.

MacLeod, Margaret A., ed. *The Letters of Letitia Hargrave.* London: Champlain Society, 1947.

McClintock, Sir F.L. *The Voyage of the Fox into the Arctic Seas.* London: John Murray, 1860.

Markham, Sir A.H. *Life of Sir John Franklin.* London: George Phillip & Son, 1891.

Morton, A.S. *Sir George Simpson: Overseas Governor of the Hudson's Bay Company.* Toronto: J.M. Dent, 1944.

Mowat, Farley. *Ordeal By Ice.* Toronto: McClelland & Stewart, 1960.

Nalodny, Sten. *The Discovery of Slowness.* New York: Viking/Penguin, 1987.

Neatby, Leslie H. *Conquest of the Last Frontier.* Athens: Ohio University Press, 1966.

————. *In Quest of the Northwest Passage.* Toronto: Longmans, Green and Co., 1958.

————. *Search for Franklin.* New York: Walker, 1970.

Newman, Peter C. *Company of Adventurers.* Toronto: Penguin/Viking, 1985.

————. *Empire of the Bay: An Illustrated History of the Hudson's Bay Company.* Toronto: Viking/Madison, 1989.

Osborn, Sherard. *The Career, Last Voyage and Fate of Sir John Franklin.* Edinburgh: William Blackwood & Sons, 1865.

————, ed. *The Discovery of the North-West Passage by H.M.S. Investigator.* London: Longman, Brown, Green, Longmans, & Roberts, 1856.

Owen, Roderick. *The Fate of Franklin.* London: Hutchinson, 1978.

Pullen, H.F. *The Pullen Expedition in Search of Sir John Franklin.* Toronto: Arctic History Press, 1979.

Rae, John. *Dr. John Rae's Autobiography.* Unpublished manuscript, Scott Polar Research Institute (Ms. 787/1).

————. *Narrative of an Exploration to the Shores of the Arctic Sea in 1846 and 1847.* London: T. & W. Boone, 1850.

————. "The Lost Arctic Voyagers." *Household Words,* December 23, 1854.

————. "Dr. Rae's Report." *Household Words,* December 30, 1854.

————. "Sir John Franklin and His Crews." *Household Words,* January 6, 1855.

Rawnsley, Willingham Franklin. *The Life, Diaries and Correspondence of Jane Lady Franklin, 1792–1875.* London: Erskine MacDonald, 1923.

Rich, E. E., ed. *John Rae's Correspendence with the Hudson's Bay Company on Arctic Exploration.* London: Hudson's Bay Record Society, 1958.

Richards, R.L. *Dr. John Rae.* Whitby: Caedmon of Whitby, 1985.

Richardson, Sir John. *Arctic Searching Expedition: Journal of a Boat Journey through Prince Rupert's Land and the Arctic Sea in Search of the Discovery Ships under the command of Sir John Franklin.* London: Longman, Brown, Green and Longmans, 1851.

Riffenburgh, Beau. *The Myth of the Explorer: The Press, Sensationalism, and Geographical Discovery.* London: Belhaven Press, 1993.

Savours, Ann. *The Search for the North West Passage.* London: Chatham Publishing, 1999.

Seaman, L.C.B. *Life in Victorian London.* London: Batsford, 1973.

Simpson, Alexander. *The Life and Travels of Thomas Simpson, The Arctic Discoverer.* London: Richard Bentley, 1845.

Smith, D. Murray. *Arctic expeditions from British and foreign shores.* Southampton: Charles H. Calvert, 1877.

Spufford, Francis. *I May Be Some Time: Ice and the English Imagination.* London: Faber and Faber, 1996.

Stefansson, Vilhjalmur. *My Life with the Eskimos.* New York: Macmillan, 1913.

————. *Unsolved Mysteries of the Arctic.* New York: Macmillan, 1939.

Stenson, Fred. *The Trade.* Vancouver: Douglas & McIntyre, 2000.

Struzik, Edward. *Northwest Passage.* Toronto: Key Porter, 1990.

Tames, Richard. *Victorian London.* London: Batsford, 1984.

Trevelyan, G.M. *English Social History: A Survey of Six Centuries, Chaucer to Queen Victoria.* Harmondsworth: Penguin, 1967

Van Kirk, Sylvia. *Many Tender Ties: Women in Fur-Trade Society in Western Canda, 1670–1870.* Winnipeg: Watson & Dwyer, 1981.

Wiebe, Rudy. *A Discovery of Strangers.* Toronto: Vintage, 1994.

Wilkinson, Douglas. *Arctic Fever.* Toronto: Clarke Irwin, 1971.

Wilson, John. *North with Franklin: The Lost Journals of James Fitzjames.* Markham, ON: Fitzhenry & Whiteside, 1999.

Woodman, David C. *Unravelling the Franklin Mystery: Inuit Testimony.* Monteal and Kingston: McGill-Queen's University Press, 1991.

Woodward, Frances J. *Portrait of Jane: A Life of Lady Franklin.* London: Hodder and Stoughton, 1951.

UNPUBLISHED MANUSCRIPTS AND PAPERS AT:
Aquila Books / Cameron Treleaven
Hudson's Bay Company Archives
National Museums of Scotland
National Maritime Museum
Orkney Public Library
Public Records Office
Royal Geographical Society
Scott Polar Research Institute

NEWSPAPERS, JOURNALS:
Arctic: Journal of the Arctic Institute of North America
Athenaeum
Beaver
Edinburgh Review
British Parliamentary Papers on Exploration in the Canadian North
Calgary Associates Clinic Historical Bulletin
Canadian Geograpical Journal
Canadian Medical Association Journal
Geographical Journal
Household Words
Manitoba History
Medical History
New England Journal of Medicine
Orkney Herald
Polar Record
Scottish Geographical Magazine

Bibliography

The Times
The Times Literary Supplement

ARTICLES BY JOHN RAE:
American Geographical Society
Anthropological Institute
British Association for the Advancement of Science
Canadian Record of Science
Ethnological Society
Household Words
Linnean Society
Manitoba Historical and Scientific Society
Nature (over 40 letters)
Orkney Herald
Philosophical Magazine
Physical Society of London
Royal Geographical Society
Royal Institution
Scottish Geographical Magazine
Society of Arts
Volunteer Record and Shooting News

ACKNOWLEDGEMENTS

Arctic explorer John Rae captured my imagination in 1985, when I read about him in *Company of Adventurers* by Peter C. Newman, the first volume of his excellent three-volume history of the Hudson's Bay Company. Later, when I asked Newman which of the early explorers had impressed him most, he replied, "That's easy: John Rae." Still, I did not contemplate Rae as a possible book subject until the late 1990s, when Victor Ramraj, one of Canada's leading post-colonial scholars, encouraged me in my intuition to do so. Then, at the University of Cambridge (Wolfson College), Irish scholar and journalist John Naughton greeted the project with enthusiasm and helped me clarify it as a work of creative non-fiction.

Still in Cambridge, people at the Scott Polar Research Institute allowed me to peruse the unpublished autobiography of John Rae—an 821-page palimpsest—and also much relevant correspondence. They were wonderfully warm and welcoming, and on one occasion Bob Headland even let me ring the ship's bell for tea. In Orkney, I enjoyed the hospitality of Ian Heddle, who is leading a campaign to restore John Rae's ancestral home; the expert guidance-around-islands of the irrepressible Sandy Firth; the enthusiastic kindess of Ivan Craigie, an ex-Edmontonian who took me joy-riding, on a three-wheeled motor vehicle, over the moors and sheep fields that surround the Hall of Clestrain; and valuable assistance from historians Bryce Wilson and Jim Troup. In Edinburgh, at the National Museums of Scotland, ethnographer Dale Idiens made a special effort to supply me with obscure but significant correspondence from Kate Rae.

Back in Canada, antiquarian-adventurer Cameron Treleaven not only accompanied me to Rae Strait, but also involved the resourceful Inuit hunter Louie Kamookak in our undertaking and generously granted me access to his stunning collection of Arctic books, photos, papers, and artifacts. In Winnipeg, the staff at the Hudson's Bay Company Archives proved extremely helpful. In that city, too, author Barbara Huck (*The Fur Trade Routes of North America*) and political scientist Peter St. John, the Earl of Orkney, showed me extraordinary kindness.

My literary agent, Beverley Slopen, manifested superb judgement and savvy in placing *Fatal Passage* with HarperCollins Publishers, where I have enjoyed working with an outstanding team of book-trade professionals, among them Judy Brunsek, Nicole Langlois, Roy Nicol, and freelancers Stephanie Fysh and Dawn Huck. Editor Phyllis Bruce, above all, contributed hugely, demonstrating why she is widely recognized as one of the best in the business: "Perhaps, precisely here, you should shift from narrative summary to scene?" Two outside editors also added much: the insightful Ramraj, again, who perceived the book's natural structure before I did, and the rigorous and informed C. Stuart Houston, an Arctic aficionado best known for editing the journals of George Back, Robert Hood, and John Richardson. Sheena McGoogan, my wife, not only provided sound editorial advice but gave me the unflagging support of which writers dream.

I owe personal thanks, as well, for reasons various and sundry, to Margaret Atwood, James Delgado, Silvie Bernier, Ludvik Prevec, Richard Sanger, Don Denton, Shannon Oatway, George Vaitkunas, Charlie Cahill, and also to the sales staff at HarperCollins Canada, who showed early fervor. Finally, I wish to thank the Alberta Foundation for the Arts, which unstintingly supported the research and writing of *Fatal Passage*, and the Canada Council for the Arts, which provided a travel grant for my airfare to Cambridge. John Rae lives!

—KEN MCGOOGAN

PICTURE CREDITS

INDEX

UNKNOWN
IN
1859

120°

100°W

PR. PATRICK I.

BARRY

ARCHIPELAGO

Byam Martin Ch.

BATHURST
I.P.

Crozier Ch.

MELVILLE I.

Byam Martin I.

McCLURE

Dealy I.

Mercy B - STR

MELVILLE SOUND

C. Walker

Barrow STR

74°N.

BANKS I.P.

P. of Wales STR

McCLINTOCK CHANNEL

P. OF WALES
LAND

Gateshead I.

PEEL STR

Franklin STR

VICTORIA

LAND

C. Bathurst

70

Dolphin & Union STR

WOLLASTON
LAND

Cambridge
B.

Victoria STR

K.
WILLIAM
I.P.

Simpson
STR

Parker B.

68

Mackenzie R.

MAINLAND

Dease STR

Finlayson I's

Peel R.

OF

CANADA

ARCTIC CIRCLE

Gt
Bear
L.

Coppermine R.

Gt Fish R.

120°

100°W.

R.T.Gould 1939

THE NORTH-WEST PASSAGE REGION AS KNOWN IN